Praise for *The Gratitude Diaries*

"If you liked Sheryl Sandberg's *Lean In* . . . read Janice Kaplan's *The Gratitude Diaries*."
—*Time*

"Uplifting and entertaining, this book is sure to give readers a more positive perspective."
—*Booklist*

"Kaplan's plan to be more grateful is approachable for anyone. Her conversational tone is encouraging, like talking to a good friend who's having a great day and wants to share it with you. . . . Simple, effective procedures that can be easily incorporated into even the busiest lifestyle."
—*Kirkus Reviews*

"Kaplan's study is insightful and loaded with compelling research and solid techniques for positive thinking, and her own example provides the most convincing testament to her ideas."
—*Publishers Weekly*

"The subtitle says it all: *How a Year Looking on the Bright Side Can Transform Your Life.* Kaplan interweaves anecdotes from her year of living gratefully with interviews with doctors, psychologists, philosophers, artists, and A-list actors, teaching you that working at being happy pays off."
—*American Way*

"Janice Kaplan has written a warm, inspiring, wonderful book, showing each of us how gratitude and focusing on our blessings can transform our lives."
—Jane Green, *New York Times* bestselling author of *Jemima J* and *The Beach House*

"Can there really be such a thing as a hardheaded woman's practical guide to living in gratitude? There can and there is. After reading about Janice Kaplan's transformative year, I'm here to say I believe it!"
—Jacquelyn Mitchard, author of the #1 *New York Times* bestseller *The Deep End of the Ocean*

THE GRATITUDE DIARIES

How a Year
Looking on the Bright Side
Can Transform Your Life

JANICE KAPLAN

DUTTON

DUTTON

An imprint of Penguin Random House LLC
penguinrandomhouse.com

Previously published as a Dutton hardcover, 2015

First paperback printing, August 2016

DUTTON and the D colophon are registered trademarks of Penguin Random House LLC.
The Library of Congress has catalogued the hardcover edition of this book as follows:
Kaplan, Janice.
The gratitude diaries : how a year looking on the bright side can transform your life / Janice Kaplan.
pages cm
ISBN 9780525955061 (hardcover) 9781101984147 (paperback) 9780698404168 (eBook)
1. Gratitude. 2. Life. I. Title.
BF575.G68K37 2015
179'.9—dc23   2015007213

Printed in the United States of America

1st Printing

Dutton value trade paperback ISBN: 9780593184837

Warmest thanks to Barnaby Marsh for his wisdom, energy, and ideas. He started me thinking about gratitude in all new ways, and for that I am ever . . . grateful.

Contents

Preface   1

PART ONE

WINTER: MARRIAGE, LOVE, AND FAMILY

5

PART TWO

SPRING: MONEY, CAREER, AND THE STUFF WE OWN

91

PART THREE

SUMMER: GRATITUDE AND HEALTH

173

PART FOUR

AUTUMN: COPING, CARING, AND CONNECTING

231

Epilogue: New Year's Eve . . . Again   297

Acknowledgments   305

Reading Group Guide   311

A Conversation with the Author   313

The Seven-Day Gratitude Challenge   319

Preface

Given that I am working on a new project about gratitude, I should have woken up on this early April morning to sunny skies, singing birds, and friends gathered in my living room singing "Kumbaya."

Instead, everything that could go wrong did.

But somehow, I kept seeing rays of sunshine.

To start, my old Volvo wouldn't spark and jumper cables had no effect. The neighbor who came over to help saved the day by driving me to the train station, twenty minutes away. I got to the city and stepped onto the rainy, windy sidewalk just as a bus raced through a huge puddle and sent a thick stream of muddy water all over me.

"Yuuck!" I screamed, though my language might have been a bit more colorful.

A few passersby clucked in sympathy, but I didn't want to go to my important meeting looking like a survivor from a Tough Mudder race. My favorite J.Crew was just a few blocks away, so I dashed over, quickly bought a bold-print skirt, and changed in the fitting room.

I got to my meeting on time, but the CEO I had come to see had a fake tan and extremely overmoussed hair. He texted while I talked and managed to look up only at the end. "Hey, you look hot in that skirt," he said.

Since I was pitching a project, not cruising Match.com, I should have been furious. But instead, I laughed and told myself I'd been saved from working with a man who spent more on hair products than I did.

I went to have coffee with my best friend, Susan, whom I have known since we met in summer camp at age eight. She is intensely loyal, fiercely critical, and relentlessly blunt.

"You must be miserable," she said when I outlined my day.

"Not really. I'm trying to be positive."

"How can you be positive about a dead car?"

I took a deep breath. I could do this. "The car was fourteen years old and had 150,000 miles on it. I never expected it to last this long. More important was that I have a nice neighbor who came to help."

"Yeah, that was good," Susan admitted. "How about getting soaked on the sidewalk?"

"Look at the funny side. The idiot CEO complimented my skirt. And think how lucky I am that I could buy a new outfit without breaking the bank. "

Susan dumped two packets of Splenda into her coffee and

stirred furiously. For years she'd heard me gripe about needing more money, so this appreciating what I had was a switch.

"I'm your best friend. You can bitch and complain all you want."

"I don't feel like complaining," I said, surprising myself as much as her. "I can't change what happened, so it feels good to change how I think about it."

Susan took a long sip of coffee. She has an ambitious, hard-driving nature. Though inordinately successful at work, Susan is often stressed, pressed, and occasionally depressed. Like all of us, she gets so busy concentrating on what she wants that she forgets to be happy for what she has. I worried my good spirits might grate on her. But she just raised an eyebrow.

"If this is that gratitude stuff you've been working on, I think I need it. How do I sign up?"

It was time to share my secret. So on the top of a napkin, I wrote the heading *Three Reasons I'm Grateful Today*. Then I pushed the napkin across the table and handed Susan a pen.

"Fill it in," I said.

Susan stared at the napkin for so long that I finally took it back and crossed out *Three Reasons* and changed it to *One Reason*.

"We'll start easy," I said.

That was exactly what I had done a few months earlier. I now knew that writing down one thing every day that made me grateful could change my attitude about everything else. A glowing sunset. A good friend's hug. The first hint of spring.

One thing.

Who can't do that?

PART ONE

WINTER

MARRIAGE, LOVE, AND FAMILY

Let us be grateful to the people who make us
happy; they are the charming gardeners
who make our souls blossom.

—Marcel Proust

PART ONE

WINTER

MARRIAGE, LOVE, AND FAMILY

I Don't Want to Be the Ungrateful Lady

Grateful to be starting my year of living positively

Happy to learn that gratitude can lower stress, improve sleep, and make me happier

Lucky to have a pretty journal that I will fill with only good thoughts

My desire to live gratefully started on New Year's Eve, at a few minutes before midnight, when I stood at a party clutching a glass of champagne with a plastic smile pasted on my face. I knew I should be counting my blessings, but instead, I was counting the minutes until I could leave. My feet hurt from the excessively high-heeled shoes I was wearing and my head throbbed from the loud music that had been blaring all night. I had on a little black dress that was just a little too little, and I couldn't wait to get home and take off the Spanx.

A TV in a corner of the room blasted *New Year's Rockin' Eve*, and as I watched people carousing in California, whooping it up in Washington, and being boisterous in Boston, I wondered if everybody in the country was having a better time than I was. Or maybe they were just better at faking it.

In New York, the million or so revelers gathered in Times Square let out a huge roar as the ball began to drop. Since it was twenty degrees outside and they had been corralled in metal pens all day with no porta-potties nearby, I understood why they were eager for midnight. Ringing in the New Year would be a great relief, in every way.

The Waterford ball finished its descent and the LED lights flashed the new date amid much horn blowing and confetti flying.

"Happy New Year!"

My husband, Ron, gave me a brief smooch and we clinked glasses.

Now that the anticipation was over, nobody seemed quite sure what to do. The TV showed an instant replay of the ball dropping, as if it were a moon landing or the final touchdown at the Super Bowl. Standing near the bar, I saw a woman pouring herself another glass of champagne. Her mascara was smudged and tears were streaking down her cheeks.

"Are you okay?" I asked her.

"No," she said, rubbing her eyes. "I hate New Year's. Why pretend anything is going to be different just because a ball dropped? Midnight came without any glass slipper to turn me into a princess."

I decided not to discuss the subtler points of Cinderella at midnight (that's when she *dropped* the glass slipper and *stopped* being a princess, my friend) and hurried away. But her question lingered in the air. What *would* be different? We celebrate New Year's with high hopes and crazy expectations—which may be why a lot of us feel so uncomfortable. (The Spanx don't help either.) But she was right that life wasn't going to improve just because the calendar flipped.

Objectively, I knew my life was good—I had two terrific sons and a handsome husband, an interesting career and close friends. But like many people, I often focused on the negatives of life instead of the pleasures. The last twelve months had been perfectly okay, but nothing thrilling enough to make me want to put on a funny hat and dance in the street. I tried to picture myself back in this spot next year. What would make me feel happier the next time the ball dropped than I did right now? I supposed in the coming months I might win the lottery, move to a Hawaiian paradise, or write a bestseller. But would any of that really work? I could already hear myself grumble that I had to pay huge taxes on the winnings, the sun on Maui was too hot, and six weeks on the *New York Times* list wasn't enough.

If the coming year was like most, some good things would happen and some not so good. I had recently overseen a big national survey on gratitude and been on the *Today* show to talk about it. The survey had started me thinking and researching a lot about positive attitudes. So I knew that how I felt about the twelve months ahead would probably have less to do with what actually happened than with the mood, spirit, and attitude I brought to each day. It wasn't the circumstances that mattered but how I responded to them. I could passively wait for the wonderful to occur—and still find something wrong. Or I could accept whatever events did come my way and try to appreciate them a little more.

I went to collect my coat and saw the woman-who-wasn't-Cinderella getting hers, too.

"I hope it's a good year for you," I said.

"It won't be," she said.

"Maybe you can make it better. That's a really pretty coat, by the way," I said as she pulled on a brown shearling.

"It's old. I wish I had a new one. Yours is nicer."

I could have pointed out that mine was equally aged and had a stain on the sleeve, but I stopped myself. What had I just decided about having the right mood, attitude, and spirit? My coat was suddenly a symbol for my whole life—if I had it, I should appreciate it. I didn't want to be the Ungrateful Lady.

"It's warm and cozy," I said brightly, putting my hands into the pockets. Whoops, one finger slid into a hole. But neither holes nor stains nor ratty hem was going to stop me now. If I planned to be happier by next New Year's, I had to start working on my attitude right now.

The next morning, I woke up earlier than planned, the mild winter sunlight streaming in around the pleated shades in our Midtown Manhattan apartment. After many years living in the suburbs, we had moved to the city just a couple of years ago, and I loved our large windows and wide river views. (My grown-up sons joked that we'd found the one part of the city that felt like the suburbs.) Weather reports predicted blizzard conditions moving in, and it had already been a snowy and cold winter. But I made myself stop and enjoy the bit of sunshine breaking through the steel-gray skies.

Hearing a clattering in the kitchen, I threw on jeans and a T-shirt and skipped out to where Ron was making breakfast. It was just the two of us this morning, but he seemed to have enough ingredients spread across the counter to feed the cast and crew of a James Cameron epic. I gave him a little kiss and said good morning.

"Do you think I'm ungrateful?" I asked.

"You don't have to be grateful for French toast," he said, flipping a piece that was bubbling on the stove. "I like making it."

"I mean it bigger than breakfast. Do you think I appreciate . . . life?"

"Oh, life." He stared into the frying pan, willing it to cook up a little homespun wisdom. "You probably don't appreciate what you have as much as you should. You pay too much attention to what's wrong rather than what's right."

"I'm going to try to be more grateful from now on," I said. "It's my plan for the year. I think it will make me happier. Maybe make us both happier."

"Worth a try," he said.

And that was that. Resolution stated and we'd see what happened next.

Ron put the spatula down and bits of hot grease dripped onto the counter. I started to say something, then bit my tongue. If I wanted to begin appreciating rather than complaining, I'd better ignore the puddle of butter gathering on the granite and concentrate on the warm smells of cinnamon and vanilla wafting through the room. I closed my eyes and reminded myself how lucky I was to have a husband who got up early to beat the eggs, soak the bread, and fry 'em all up. Better keep it to myself that I'd much prefer plain oatmeal.

Later that afternoon, I headed over to the grocery store, and as I pushed a cart along, a familiar Joni Mitchell song, "Big Yellow Taxi," was playing. I started humming along with the lamenting lyrics about how it always seems that you don't know what you've got 'til it's gone. Music playing in the frozen-food aisle isn't usually life changing, but I took it as a sign that I was on the right course. Hundreds of musicians from Bob Dylan to Counting Crows have recorded Mitchell's song because in any musical style, the message hits a chord. It happens too often that you have something terrific right in front of you but don't realize it until the lover is gone, the moment is past, and the flowers are wilted.

Standing there holding a container of Häagen-Dazs chocolate gelato, I vowed that I wouldn't wait and mourn what was lost. I would appreciate what I had. I planned to spend the coming year seeing the sunshine instead of the clouds.

When I got home, I began making my plan for a year of living gratefully. I'd spent my career as a journalist, so I immediately thought of gratitude as a project to research and study. I would find one area to focus on each month—whether husband, family, friends, or work—and become my own social scientist. I wanted to see what happened when I developed an attitude of gratitude. Instead of doing this casually, I'd make a full commitment to get as much information as I could and report and record my findings. I'd get advice at every turn from experts and psychologists and consult books by philosophers and psychologists and theologians. The Roman philosopher Cicero famously said, *Gratitude is not only the greatest of virtues, but the parent of all others*. If that was true, would my year's project also make me more honest, courageous, and generous?

When I started telling people in the next few days about my

plan to appreciate my life more, they nodded knowingly. Many insisted that they, too, wanted to be more thankful and keep a better perspective. But I got the feeling most weren't doing such a good job at it.

"Sure your life is great, but how grateful were you feeling last Tuesday night when you left your office?" I asked several people. Each laughed uncomfortably, and one even asked, "How did you know about last Tuesday?" Since I'm not psychic, I knew she'd have the same memory if I mentioned Monday. When we think about the big picture, we can make ourselves be grateful. But on a daily basis, a client is irritating, a boss is rude, there's a lice outbreak at our kids' school—and we get lost in the vexing details.

I understood the conflict because the survey I had recently done, funded by the John Templeton Foundation, had shown that most of us suffer from a huge gratitude gap. We know we should be grateful, but something holds us back. In the survey, 94 percent of Americans thought people who are grateful are also more fulfilled and lead richer lives. But *less than half* the people surveyed said they expressed gratitude on any regular basis.

You don't need to be a math genius to figure out that those numbers don't add up. We understand that there is something that makes us more fulfilled—but we don't jump to try it? It's as if there were a magical happiness rock sitting in the middle of a field and half of us didn't even bother to go over and pick it up. I was one of the people running around that field and never getting near the magic stone. I knew it was there. I kept thinking about it. But something always got in the way.

I might never have focused on gratitude if Barnaby Marsh, a top executive at the John Templeton Foundation, hadn't raised the topic with me a couple of years earlier. We met by chance, sitting next to each other at a charity dinner, and a few months later, he took me out to a very elegant afternoon tea to discuss some of the Big Ideas the foundation funded. I had recently left a job at the top spot of a magazine, and I was feeling a little at odds with the world. But the moment he mentioned Gratitude (with a capital G), I looked up from my mint tea. Being grateful sounded like a great idea—a nice replacement for resentment, indignation, and pique. I said I wanted to find out more and suggested the survey. By the end of the tea, I had a whole new mind-set (and an appreciation for cucumber sandwiches).

As I threw myself into the survey and research, I quickly realized that gratitude wasn't the same as happiness—it has a much deeper resonance. Most of us feel cheered when something nice occurs—a friend sends flowers or we spend an afternoon in the park. But those moments can be fragile and fleeting, and what happens when they're over? Because it's not dependent on specific events, gratitude is long lasting and impervious to change or adversity. It requires an active emotional involvement—you can't be passively grateful, you actually have to stop and feel it, experience the emotion. So it creates an inner richness that's sustaining in difficult times as well as good ones.

Over the years, my career has gone in three directions, interweaving TV, magazines, and books. I've produced network TV shows and even created some popular specials, been the editor in chief of *Parade* (the largest-circulation magazine in America at the time), and written a dozen novels, a couple of them bestsellers. Good career on paper, but none of it made me stop and say—*I've arrived!* Success at work is all about moving forward.

Reach one goal and there's still another to achieve. Gratitude requires that you take a different approach—relishing the moment and not fretting about the next step.

Savoring what you have is never straightforward. It's easy to look at someone else and think how lucky they are and how wonderful it would be to have their life and success. But what any of us feel on the inside is rarely the same as what is perceived from the outside.

Until recently, philosophers talked about gratitude but psychologists didn't spend a lot of time researching it. But in the last dozen years or so, academics have jumped on the subject and made efforts at serious research. The results have been startling. One study after another has connected gratitude to higher levels of happiness and lower levels of depression and stress. An article in the *Journal of Social and Clinical Psychology* evaluating all the literature in the field concluded that gratitude may have the highest connection to mental health and happiness of any of the personality traits studied. The conclusion: "Around 18.5 per cent of individual differences in people's happiness could be predicted by the amount of gratitude they feel."

Now, that made me stop. Being 18.5 percent happier is a lot of happier.

Pulling a number out of the air, I figured my happiness right now at about 76 percent. So being more grateful would bring me to over 90, a solid A.

What was it going to take to raise my grade? One of the consistent findings in the research was the value of keeping a gratitude journal. Researchers have found that people who write down three things they're grateful for every night (or even a few times a week) improve their well-being and lower their risk of depression. The results have been repeated over and over. Keeping a gratitude journal can even dramatically improve your ability to get a good night's sleep.

One of the psychologists who has led this research, Dr. Robert Emmons of the University of California, Davis, jumped into the field early, and quickly became one of the world's leading scientific experts on gratitude (there weren't many others). One of his findings is that you don't need good events in your life in order to feel gratitude. Instead, grateful people *reframe* whatever happens to them. "They don't focus on what they're lacking; they make sure they see the good in what they have," he told me.

Reframing takes many forms. I'd recently spent a day with Michelle Pfeiffer, the Golden Globe–winning actress known throughout her career for her stunning beauty. (Remember her shiny black suit as Catwoman?) Since I was writing a cover story about her for a women's magazine, I dared to ask how she felt about getting older. Still extraordinarily beautiful in her mid-fifties (I'd trade with her in a moment), she admitted that it was easy to yearn for the days when she had flawless skin and a perfectly taut body. We looked together at a picture of her at age twenty-five, when she starred with Al Pacino in the blockbuster movie *Scarface*.

"My breasts were very perky then, weren't they?" she said, smiling wryly at the photo of herself in a revealing dress.

But she didn't look back at her younger self with envy. She remembered being terrified and insecure during every moment of that shoot and was glad to be so much more confident now. Different moments in life bring different reasons to be grateful. The gift was to capture what you have when you have it.

"I'm really happily married now. I have a wonderful family and a handful of really close friends. I love my work and that makes me very lucky and blessed. So I get up with a purpose in life—and try to stay away from mirrors," she said with a smile.

Hers was a lovely and instinctive reframing, an eagerness to focus only on the positive aspects of getting older. It occurred to me that like Michelle Pfeiffer, I could avoid the wrinkles in life by focusing on the joys.

But in both small events and big ones, seeing the good can be a challenge, because a general rule of life is that negative events overshadow positive ones. If ten great things and one lousy one happen in a day, most of us will spend dinner telling our spouse about the lousy one. Nobel Prize–winning psychologist Daniel Kahneman says ruminating on what went wrong makes evolutionary sense. Our ancestors survived by remembering the one poisonous berry they encountered and telling their friends about it. Describing the ten tasty ones didn't do much good at all. We have simply updated that approach, as evidenced by every parent who has ranted about the one C on a child's report card while barely noticing the four As.

Many researchers have contributed to the bad-is-stronger-than-good theory, often with colorful explanations. The psychologist Paul Rozin has pointed out that a cockroach can completely spoil a bowl of cherries, but one cherry does nothing to improve the appeal of a bowl of cockroaches. Social media has made the power of a single negative comment very evident. Check out the reviews on a site like Yelp—and then decide whether you'll have brunch at the new eatery where most people like the pancakes but one guy got sick from a bad egg (or so he claims). Or will you spend a night at a hotel where one reviewer ranted about being stuck in a room with a dirty toilet and a leaky bathtub, even if others liked the comfy bed and the ocean view?

Some psychologists who've looked into the question say it takes four positive statements to counterbalance one negative one, and others suggest five. The real ratio probably depends on the individual and the strength of the comments. But I've never seen anyone put it at less than three good equals one bad (something to remember when talking to a spouse).

All of which brings us back around to a gratitude diary—since that turns out to be an antidote to our brains' natural attraction to bad berries and bugs. At the end of the day (quite literally), thinking about what made you thankful forces you to think of the soft bed and the tasty fruit—the cherry, not the cockroach. I liked the concept and I could see how it worked to reframe a day's events. But it wouldn't come naturally.

I'd kept journals since I could hold a pen, and as a general rule, I wrote in them when I was irritable, angry, or pissed off. I still had my faux-leather diaries from elementary school with their tiny locks and carefully scrawled *Please Keep Out* on the covers. Later, I used drugstore-bought notebooks with lined pages and cardboard covers for my private rants, and some years ago, I found a dozen of them in the back of a closet. A treasure trove of memory! I immediately sat down and began flipping through, but instead of happy remembrances of my younger self, I was stunned to read page after grumbling page of self-centered despair. Events that got me furious, fuming, or in high dudgeon pushed out anything else. Where were all the wonderful experiences from those years? I'd had many joyous moments—I did, honestly!—but I hadn't bothered to record them.

As I read the journals, I dreaded the idea of anyone else doing the same. I didn't want my husband or children finding the notebooks and thinking this was my life. Heck, I didn't want *me* thinking this was my life. It wasn't that I planned to rewrite history—I had just written it wrong the first time. So I tossed the grouse-filled notebooks into a large garbage bag and sent those biodegradable pages to molder in a dump somewhere, never to be seen again. (Or so I hoped. Maybe I should have considered the fireplace?)

A gratitude journal would have a different vibe and never have to be relegated to the proverbial (or real) landfill of history. And if Dr. Emmons and his colleagues were right, it would, quite simply, make my life better. I liked the concept, but being a journalist, keeping a gratitude journal also struck me as a little—squishy. A notebook full of appreciative words about glowing sunsets and the smell of fresh-brewed coffee sounded like a Nicholas Sparks novel (not that there's anything wrong with those . . .).

I called my friend Shana, who has endless energy—she teaches Zumba classes for fun—and is positive and upbeat but definitely not squishy. At age thirty-five, she's a talented business-woman and serial entrepreneur—and has kept a gratitude journal for years.

"I love that you're doing this. Gratitude is completely my thing these days!" she said when I told her about my plan.

Shana and her husband had a new house in New Haven, but she had some meetings coming up in Manhattan, so we agreed to meet at a tapas restaurant near Grand Central Terminal. Shana bounced in, looking as cheerful as always, and after we caught up on important topics (the new tiles she was buying for her bathroom), she eagerly told me about her gratitude journal. Every single night, she wrote down one thing that had made her grateful. Just one! No matter how busy or tired she might be, she could handle writing down a couple of lines. And she'd found that knowing she had to write something down every night changed her perspective on the whole day.

As we talked, she picked up one of the tapas—country bread with orange honey and figs and a bit of cream—and took an appreciative bite.

"Mmmm, this is a good example," she said, licking some honey off her lip. "It's so delicious that I'm thinking it could be in my journal. Though today it's more likely that I'll write about seeing you."

"I can't compete with fig *montadito*," I said with a laugh. But I got the point. By focusing on reasons to be grateful, Shana saw everything through a different lens. Our natural evolutionary tendency might be to look out for problems and peril, but Shana had redirected her instincts. She was alert to what made her day positive. When she couldn't find something—because that happens, too—she had to find a way to reframe the day.

"I can be going through a bad patch and feel thankful for nothing," she admitted. "So maybe I'll write that I'm glad it didn't rain very hard or that I have two feet. Honestly, it came down to that once. I was glad I had two feet."

I told Shana about the journals I had tossed away, and she nodded vigorously. She, too, used to spill her guts in a diary, scrawling melodramatic entries about having the weight of the world on her shoulders. "You know, *The gray skies outside reflect the darkness in my soul*," she said, and we both laughed knowingly.

Did Shana's current gratitude journals reflect a more or less realistic view than the gloomy ones?

When I raised the question, Shana smiled and quoted the famous line from *Hamlet*: "There is nothing either good or bad but thinking makes it so."

You don't have to be a Shakespearean scholar to follow Hamlet's reasoning. When the melancholy prince meets his old pals Rosencrantz and Guildenstern in act 2 and tells them that Denmark is a prison, they're a little surprised—the palace looks pretty darn good to them. Hamlet gives a little shrug (at least he did when I saw Jude Law play him on Broadway) and makes the comment about goodness or badness being dependent on our perception. Kings get killed, ghosts appear, and moms get remarried, but what really makes those events painful or not is how we look at them. If somebody had told Hamlet to keep a gratitude journal, maybe he would have concentrated on how fortunate he was to be a prince and to have his beautiful girlfriend, Ophelia. Really, it wasn't such a bad life!

But for some reason, we trust misery more than happiness. We're fascinated to see Hamlet wander the stage in despair, trying to decide if life is worth living. "To be or not to be" seems more profound than "Gosh, I'm one lucky guy."

But what makes a great play isn't necessarily the poetic basis for a happy life.

"Okay, I'm going to start keeping a gratitude journal," I told Shana. "Any suggestions?"

"Buy a pretty one," she said as we hugged good-bye.

A few days later, I was at our country home in rural northwest Connecticut and drove over to a nearby town, looking for a diversion from the stormy winter weather. I would have preferred being in the Caribbean, but I made myself appreciate how pretty the snow looked gleaming in the icy fields. Red farmhouses dotted the landscape, as if from a painting. I went to an art gallery I liked, then stopped in a favorite store that sells tea and teapots and other creative gifts. Browsing, I noticed some colorful journals near the cash register.

I thought of Shana's advice. I had plenty of notebooks at home, but if I wanted to keep a gratitude journal, it needed to be something different, a purposeful purchase, not a leftover from a gift bag. I picked out one with a geometric green cover, fresh and bright. Too pretty to hold anything but positive thoughts.

Before I went to sleep that night, I took out the journal and opened to the first page. Feeling slightly awkward, I wrote, *So thankful for . . .* , and then paused.

I went over the day in my mind. Should I focus on big things or small ones? A travel reporter I knew once joked with me that the first radio segment he ever did was about Paris. Ten years of broadcasts later, he was about to record one on his favorite apple tart at a small bistro in the seventh arrondissement. In other words, it's always a good idea to focus.

So thankful for . . .

The chance to start my year of gratitude, with this journal, I wrote.

I started to add, *Even though I'm not sure it will work . . .*

But I stopped myself. In my gratitude journal, I didn't need balance or complaints or shades of gray. It was okay to look at only one side of the story. Nobody was keeping score.

I put the journal in a prominent spot on the side of my desk.

Experts used to claim that it took just twenty-one days to form a new habit, but a recent study out of University College London found most of us need more than two months and sometimes as many as six to make a real change in behavior. I hoped that at some point in this year, an attitude of gratitude would become completely natural to me. For now, I would embrace the process—and have a nightly rendezvous with my journal.

CHAPTER 2

Falling (Back) in Love with My Husband

Grateful to pursue positivity in my marriage—and get our "happy brains" in sync

Thankful to learn to say thank you to my kind and handsome husband

So grateful that a marriage can get better after many years

As I started to plot my year of living gratefully, I decided the number one topic that needed a more positive approach was my marriage.

Theoretically, I knew that I had many reasons to be grateful at home. My husband was handsome and smart and didn't mind doing the dishes. We had two wonderful children, Zach and Matt, and that pretty house in rural Connecticut. We were all healthy and loved one another. We laughed together, took hikes in the mountains, and admired sunsets on the beach. Viewed that way, my life could be videotaped for the Hallmark Channel.

But it was also the life I led every day, which made it hard to keep in perspective. Psychologists call it habituation. We get used to something—whether a husband, a house, or a shiny new car—and then forget why it seemed so special in the first place. Brain-scan images show that how we respond to something the tenth time we see it is very different from how we felt the first.

The French novelist Marcel Proust famously said that the real voyage of discovery "consists not in seeking new landscapes, but in having new eyes." I realized it was time to bring those fresh eyes to the man with whom I shared my bed, my jokes, and my joint checking account.

My first thought was to devote the next few journal entries to my marriage, writing at least one reason every night that I was grateful to have my husband. But if I planned to have any effect on our relationship, I had to express thanks to more than my journal. In the survey I'd done and discussed on the *Today* show, we'd asked men about their marriages, and the largest number (77 percent) said they'd be very grateful if their wives just showed love and affection. That beat everything else by a large margin, including making dinner, planning a vacation, or taking care of chores. I was better with roasting a chicken than with telling my husband I appreciated him. I wasn't the only one. Fewer than half the women in the survey regularly said "Thanks" to their husbands.

Call it common courtesy, but it's not always so common with the people we love the most. A few more numbers from that same survey tell an interesting story. Some 97 percent of respondents said they would express appreciation to a server in a nice restaurant and an admirable 58 percent were even okay saying thanks to the TSA guy at the airport. When it came to a spouse, the number plunged. Remember that less than half (48 percent) of women expressed gratitude to the person who was supposed to be closest to them.

It sounds counterintuitive, but I could see why it happens. If a waiter brings the bread basket and remembers who ordered the cheeseburger with extra bacon, we're satisfied and ready to say thanks. But our expectations for a partner are huge. Bringing the bacon is just the start. We expect our spouse to be our best friend, passionate lover, weekend playmate, equal-time parent, entertaining dinner date, jogging partner, constant supporter, professional adviser, and travel companion. Oh, and did I mention soul mate? We can't forget soul mate.

So just at the moment when you are grateful to your partner for something that he is doing, you are hit in the gut by something else that he's *not* providing. Maybe he's still your best friend, but passionate lover has gone out the window and you're a little . . . resentful. Or he's a great parent, but you can't help noticing that everyone else on your block seems to earn more money.

Popular sex and marriage adviser Esther Perel, author of *Mating in Captivity,* has provocatively asked, "Can we want what we already have? That's the million-dollar question." She worries that we pile contradictory demands on a spouse—we want security and comfort on the one hand and adventure and excitement on the other. We expect one person to fill all the needs that a whole village once did. In her view, we are always saying, "Give me comfort, give me edge; give me novelty, give me familiarity; give me predictability, give me surprise."

But the bottom line is always *Give me.* Marriage makes us entitled. Once we are married, we aren't supposed to be unhappy or lonely or suffering from your basic existential crisis. And when—inevitably—we aren't feeling on top of the world, it is clearly (clearly!) our spouse's fault.

When you expect everything, it's hard to be grateful for anything. So I decided that now was the time to put aside impossible expectations and start appreciating the husband I had, rather than the imaginary cross between Brad Pitt and Bill Gates who would always remember to remove his muddy boots at the door.

Good intentions can go out the window, so I wrote down my plan. For this entire month, I would find a reason at least twice a day to appreciate the man I married. Nothing fake or pretend, I would just put aside any complaints—as well as the clever improvements to his life that I was so good at suggesting—and admire him for who he was. Instead of letting my husband's many positive virtues become the background wallpaper of our life, I would see what happened when I let them move to center stage.

The next morning, I woke up at six A.M. and with one eye open saw my husband on the other side of the bedroom, getting dressed for work. He's a doctor with a busy practice, but on another morning I might have snappishly asked why he had to leave so early or closed my eyes for a few more minutes' sleep. Instead, I took a long look at him in his slim gray trousers, crisp white shirt, and silky blue tie.

"You look very handsome this morning," I said, my voice hoarse with sleep. "It's nice to wake up to a good-looking man in my room."

He looked up at me in surprise, then smiled and came over and gave me a kiss. "You don't have your contact lenses in yet. You can't see a thing," he joked.

"Even blurry you're good-looking," I said, putting my arms around him.

The whole exchange didn't last more than thirty seconds, and Ron probably forgot it the moment he left. But it gave me a boost for the rest of the day. Giving appreciation can be as good as getting it.

Every couple has its divisions of labor, and the next day, I started to thank Ron for the things he usually did without any particular mention—balancing the checkbook, repairing a leaky faucet, and getting us home safely after a late-night party.

"Thank you for driving in the snow," I said as we pulled into the garage.

"I always drive," he said, surprised.

"And I appreciate that you do. Especially when it's dark and we're both tired. I realize how lucky I am that you handle that for me."

We didn't talk about it further, but Ron seemed to pick up the vibe that something was changing in our relationship. The next night, he thanked me for making dinner—one of the activities that's always on my side of the ledger. I shrugged it off (how much credit could I take for frozen ravioli?), but the comment still made me feel good. Whatever we do, it's nice to be acknowledged.

For the first few days, I consciously made myself stop and appreciate my husband. But as one week passed and then another, the flood of good feeling started to come naturally, and being thankful to my husband made me feel more positive in general. What was going on? I called Dr. Brent Atkinson, professor emeritus of marriage and family therapy at Northern Illinois University, and a director at the Couples Clinic and Research Institute in Geneva, Illinois. He believes there is strong neurological evidence showing that circuits in the brain can be primed to create stronger feelings of connection. He developed a new approach to couples counseling based on rewiring our automatic responses and actually changing the structure of the brain. I asked him if my gratitude practice could be affecting my neural circuits. He responded with an ardent "Yes."

"We're learning that whatever the brain does a lot, it gets good at," he said. "If through gratitude, you create a positive mood, you reinforce the brain pathways that will then generate more positive feelings. You can think of gratitude as a form of mental exercise that primes the mind for positivity."

Dr. Atkinson assured me that studies have shown that "compassion meditation"—where people spend extended periods of time focusing on kind and loving feelings—actually changes the volume of the brain and the circuits involved in emotional reaction. He uses a similar technique in his office, advising clients to sit for five minutes a day and dwell on good feelings or happy times they've had with their spouse. "Studies suggest that these simple mental practices can strengthen the neural circuits that generate feelings of connection," he said.

The idea that being grateful to my husband could change my brain sounded a little dubious—until I heard about a study done by Harvard neurologist Alvaro Pascual-Leone. He invited people who had never played the piano to take his instruction and then practice a tune for two hours a day for five days. Brain imaging done at the end of the sessions showed that the portion of the cortex devoted to finger movements had expanded impressively. That made sense, since other studies have also shown that whatever part of our body we use regularly gets more cortical real estate. Then he had another group of volunteers mentally focus on the piano-practice movements for an equal amount of time—but never touch the keys. Ready for this? They had nearly identical changes in their motor cortices.

If thinking can change our brain circuits, I was happy to keep at it—and that's apparently what I needed to do. Dr. Atkinson compared it to working out with dumbbells. Do just a couple of reps and your muscles won't change. But continue steadily with those biceps curls and the cumulative effect is noticeable. Similarly, he found that the interventions he did with couples once a week in his office weren't enough. Couples might have a moment of revelation (*I get it! Washing the car is how you show you love me!*) and a rush of good feeling, but it often faded before the next week. He began suggesting that couples work on priming those positive neural circuits at home. Not everyone was willing. "We all know we love our partners, but to spend five minutes a day focused on them seems extravagant!" he told me with a laugh.

For those willing to give it a try, he suggested sending a daily sentence-completion e-mail to their partners with two sentences. The first sentence:

One thing you did lately that I appreciated was . . .

The second:

One moment when I felt extra positive about you was . . .

He made sure to do the exercise every morning for his own wife, Lisa, also a marriage counselor. When I asked, he didn't mind sharing what he had written to her that very morning, in part to show that daily thanks didn't have to be earth-shattering. Completing the first sentence, he appreciated that Lisa had rushed around doing errands the previous day. "Maybe that didn't make me feel all warm and fuzzy, but it was raining and she was busy and I could see that she took one for the team," he said.

Sentence-completion two expressed how extra positive he felt about Lisa the previous night when he heard her laughing uproariously with her stepdaughter. He admired her ease in navigating the relationship with his daughter, and that *did* make him feel all warm and fuzzy. Why hadn't he said something at the time? Well, he got involved with dinner and then his phone rang and then . . . "It's amazing how a simple expression of gratitude or appreciation can fall through the cracks. That's why the daily e-mails are so important," he said.

I told him about the night I'd thanked my husband for driving us home and how Ron had responded the next day by thanking me for cooking.

"Bravo!" he said. "When people share positive emotions with each other, scans show their brains sync up and show similar activity. You increase your natural capacity for love."

Dr. Atkinson urged me to keep going with what he described as the "relentless introduction of positivity." Continuing my positive comments would make my husband feel good—but it would make me feel even better. Many studies show that the main benefit accrues to the person *expressing* the gratitude. With gratitude, it really is better to give than to receive. Dr. Atkinson said that he often ran into clients in the supermarket years after they'd finished counseling, and even if they didn't remember anything else he told them, many announced that they still did the gratitude e-mail. Most reported that the price of the counseling was worth it just for that daily ritual.

As we said good-bye, I thanked him for all the good advice. In my case, the value of the counseling was worth much, much more than I'd paid.

———

Eager to further stimulate our pursuit of positivity, I suggested to Ron that we take a weekend away that would be devoted to reconnecting and appreciating each other. He's usually reluctant to leave his medical practice, so I was pleased when he said yes. That was already a big step. I was going to be in Los Angeles for work, so we agreed that he would fly out and meet me afterward.

Looking for a romantic spot a reasonable drive away, I settled on Ojai, California, an artsy community that director Frank Capra used in his classic film *Lost Horizon* to represent Shangri-La. An earthly paradise with mystical overtones seemed like a fine spot to practice gratitude. Plus there were good restaurants.

Even though it was mid-afternoon when we arrived at the elegant resort in Ojai, our room wasn't ready, so we strolled around the extensive grounds and had a snack. When we were finally escorted to our room, it was small and on the first floor overlooking the road.

"I asked for something quiet with a view," I said.

"This is what we have," the clerk said.

It was the off-season, and from what we'd seen in our long walk around the grounds (and through the parking lot), the large resort had very few guests. I hesitated. In a weekend of gratitude, I wanted to appreciate whatever came my way. But being grateful didn't mean being a sap.

I marched back to the front desk and politely said the room wasn't what we expected. My husband sat down with pinched lips. He doesn't like a fuss and is the master at making do. After another long wait, we ended up in a nicer room with a pretty view, but I worried that some of the goodwill had seeped out of the day.

When we went to bed that night, I thought about a vacation

we'd taken many years earlier, when I was very pregnant with our first child. It was to be our last getaway as a twosome before launching into the unknown world of strollers and diapers, and pushing to the edge of our budget, I picked what I hoped would be a picture-perfect French Caribbean island.

The weather was gray the day we arrived, but we went to the beach anyway. I wore a maternity bathing suit the size of a pup tent and huddled miserably on my blanket as gorgeous women strolled across the sand, tanned and topless. *Topless?* But of course—it was a French island. In their skimpy bikini bottoms, they looked like sleek dolphins swimming in the ocean, while I felt like a whale. Why had we come here? As we lay in bed that night, rain poured down on the metal roof of our hotel. Oh, great. Storms on an island paradise. What else could go wrong?

The next morning I found out. The sun shone brightly and we drove around the island, which was quite beautiful, after all. Heading to a late lunch, we saw a car speeding toward us, the very drunk driver careening fast and swerving out of control. With a steep cliff dropping off to our right, Ron pulled our little jeep over as far as he could—but suddenly there was the sickening sound of metal crushing and glass flying as the car smashed into us. Then the world seemed to stop. I looked over and saw my husband's face contorted in pain, his leg a mealy mass of blood, cut open to reveal cartilage and bone. Blood pulsed out of a deep gash in my forehead, dripping down my face and splashing on my lap.

"Are we going to die?" I asked as we sat there on the empty road, unable to move.

We lived. An ambulance brought us to the local hospital, where a pretty French doctor (who probably went topless on the beach) stitched us up with the thick thread usually used for cadavers. She assured me that our baby, better protected than we had been, would be just fine. (I later liked to think it explained Zach's resilience.) We stayed overnight in a room that had an outdoor path to the bathroom and was ringed with shelves of Catholic saints. Not my religion, but I'd had a feeling those saints were sending me a message.

You didn't know how to be grateful for that first day on this island? Okay, try a car crash instead. Now do you get it?

We flew back home the next day and spent the week recovering at my in-laws' house. I felt lucky to be alive and to have family to take care of us. And I'd learned my lesson: Appreciate the moment, because you never know when it will be smashed to bits.

Now in our room in Ojai, I turned on the dim bedside lamp and reached for my gratitude journal. Switching rooms was fine— but I needed to make sure that negative feeling didn't overwhelm the weekend. I wanted to let those saints know that I could appreciate what really mattered.

So grateful . . . that Ron came out here for this weekend and that we are trying to stay connected, which is all that really matters.

Over breakfast in town the next morning, we reminded each other about the point of the weekend. Be grateful. Appreciate each other. A waitress who overheard us talking smiled as she brought over my herbal iced tea.

"Are you here for the vortex?" she asked.

"I didn't even know about one," I said.

"You'll find it," she said with a wink.

We had once visited Sedona, Arizona, which is also said to have a vortex—a concentrated energy that gives the region an extra spiritual power. You supposedly feel it when you sit on the red rocks and meditate, or simply breathe deeply to increase calmness and a sense of well-being. Ron and I had been walking on a popular trail when a woman in shorts and high heels rushed up to us and in a thick New Jersey accent asked, "Do ya know where the vortex is? I've been lookin' all over." Ron explained that it wasn't a place but an experience you had to let in. "So ya mean ya don't know where it is," she said, wrinkling her nose disdainfully and rushing off.

Now in Ojai, we joked about looking for the vortex. Ron suggested we go on a hike and see if we could feel it or find it (and let the New Jersey lady know). Maybe simply *believing* in the extra power made it true. Ron is a strong hiker with a great sense of direction, so he briefly studied the map, then drove a short distance and parked at the trailhead. We took off, Ron striding ahead but setting an easy enough pace for me, following the trail as it wound high into the mountains. Every bend seemed to offer exhilarating views out to the valleys below. Ron asked a few times if I wanted to turn back, but it was too lovely to stop, and as we got higher, both of us were floating on mountain air and a feeling of being connected to the cosmos.

"I don't know if it's the vista or the vortex, but I feel very grateful to be here," I said as we stopped at one glorious outlook to drink in the scenery—and some water, too.

"We're very lucky," Ron agreed. He put an arm around me and we looked out, feeling the mystifying affinity with the universe that mountain trails can bring.

"When we get back home and life gets busy again, we have to stop and remember how we feel right at this moment," Ron said.

We turned around to head down again, and as we sauntered along the trail, we decided to amuse ourselves with a variant of the "geography game" we used to play when our children were little. Each person had to say a place that started with the last letter of the word that came before. Only this time we'd do it with the things we were grateful for.

"I'm grateful for our kids," Ron said, starting in the obvious spot.

"Sunsets."

"Sunday afternoons."

"Sundaes!"

"Can we be grateful for something that doesn't end in *s*?" Ron asked.

"Sweet moments with my husband. I'm grateful for those," I said ardently.

With our heads in the vortex, we somehow missed the turnoff for where we had begun the trail. Half an hour later, we had landed on a suburban street, and even mountain-man Ron, who never gets lost, had to admit that all trails didn't converge. He noticed a man a block away and dashed over to ask directions to where we had parked the car.

"Oh, it's pretty far and the streets are complicated," said the man, whose name was John. "I'm out for a walk anyway. I'll come with you." Very slim, he had delicate features, curly silver hair, and a spritely step that made him seem like a grown-up Peter Pan.

We immediately fell into conversation and discovered that John was a musician who had moved to Ojai to send his children to the Oak Grove School, started by the Indian philosopher Jiddu

Krishnamurti. John tried to explain the guru's teachings to me, which seemed to have to do with cooperation and self-understanding.

"He said that truth is a pathless land. We can't come to it through organized religion or dogma, but only by relationships and knowing our own mind," John said. Or something like that.

Krishnamurti had lived in Ojai on and off for sixty years—visited by stars like Charlie Chaplin and Greta Garbo—and the town remained a center for his followers. The guru himself said he'd had his first spiritual awakening while living there. (Perhaps the vortex?) His home was now a retreat where people came essentially to hit the *Pause* button and get in touch with themselves.

When we finally got to our car, we apologized profusely to John for taking him so far out of his way and offered to give him a ride back to his house. He agreed immediately and slipped into the front passenger seat. It was the fastest friendship we'd ever made.

"It was good to meet you and walk in a different direction," John said. "As Krishnamurti said, you sometimes need to stop your experiences completely and look at them anew, not keep on repeating them like machines. You then let fresh air into your mind."

Ron and I hadn't come to Ojai to meditate or visit a guru, but this weekend was, indeed, meant as a way to stop and get a new view. A grateful view. I could see how that was fresh air for the mind.

It was early evening when we got back to the hotel, and Ron and I went out to a patio to wait for Ojai's famous "pink moment." Because of how the mountains are set, reflections bounce off them, and as the sun goes down each night, the sky above the six-thousand-foot Topatopa Bluffs is supposed to turn a scintillating pink. A dozen or so other people were also gathered for the big event. The sun settled behind the hills. The sky got dark, not pink.

"It was a beautiful 'gray moment,'" Ron whispered to me, and I laughed. The other guests near us looked annoyed—either that the solar fireworks had fizzled or that we didn't seem to mind. Maybe both.

As we walked back to our room, it occurred to me that if not for my current gratitude mood, I might have seen the day as a dud. We got lost on the hike and the sunset was a flop. I wasn't wild about the resort, and the weekend hadn't turned into the romantic wonderland I'd hoped. And maybe that was the best lesson. I couldn't change the day and make it a perfect vacation, but I could be grateful for what I'd gotten instead. I'd liked meeting John, and my husband and I could still laugh together. By thinking about gratitude, we were feeling ever happier with each other. And that made any vortex worth visiting.

When we got back home, I went out for a late-afternoon coffee with my friend Meg. She had started her own business a few years earlier, and she strutted into the Starbucks looking chic in a cashmere wrap dress and high-heeled suede boots—but I could tell immediately that she wasn't happy. We'd known each other long enough that nothing was off-limits, and we often shared stories that we'd never tell anyone else. Meg immediately launched into a litany of complaints about her husband—they'd just had a big argument about money, he'd canceled their vacation to Florida, and she didn't think they'd ever have fun again. Fed up and frustrated, she didn't know how to turn the relationship around. "And I'm not even sure I want to bother," she whispered.

She looked up, waiting for me to respond with similar gripes, but for once, I didn't have any. I'd already learned from my research that specific events were rarely as important as the perspective you brought. (My husband climbing a high ladder to do a roof repair could seem wonderfully bold and beneficial when I was in a grateful mood and ridiculously dangerous when I wasn't.) Instead, I told her that gratitude had started working wonders for my marriage and maybe she should give it a try. Gratitude could actually increase positive neural circuits and make both partners feel happier.

"It's pretty simple—but also amazing," I told her exuberantly. I suggested three steps that had seemed to work for me so far. Find a reason at least once a day to say thank you. Focus on the positives instead of the problems. Tell your spouse why you appreciate him.

She looked at me like I was crazy. "My husband needs to appreciate me, not the other way around."

"It works both ways. If you start being grateful, he'll naturally return it," I promised.

"I'm not going to fawn over everything he does. He's arrogant enough. I need to keep some power in this relationship." She looked at me, eyes flashing in warning. "You might be making a big mistake."

Her reaction surprised me. Sure there's a balance of control in any relationship, but gratitude had turned me into neither geisha girl nor Stepford wife. Appreciating my husband didn't strip me of my feminist credentials. My husband had responded to gratitude with gratitude—the more he got, the more he gave. It didn't really matter who took the first step. Being grateful had immediate advantages to the person expressing the positive feelings. So I could start out completely self-centered—trying to make myself happier—and also improve our relationship.

But every marriage is different, and I wondered if, in other cases, Meg could be right. Might other men (less evolved than my husband) take advantage of a wife's gratitude and goodwill? *Yup, babe, you* are *lucky you have me. So I'll be out drinking at the pub tonight.* I understood the fear that gratitude could be read wrong.

I checked back in with Dr. Atkinson, who chuckled at the concern. "People in good relationships don't worry about the other person having a big head. You infuse the marriage with positivity, and then you kick a little ass if you have to."

He told me that he saw the best relationships as "alternating between thunderstorms and sunshine as opposed to a steady dull overcast." I liked that view of marriage. You can be strong and assertive. You can be grateful and loving. But if you water down either of them, you just end up with the mush in the middle.

Many marriages last a long time with both sides mucking through the mush. Researcher Bob Emmons had warned me that people sometimes avoided being grateful to a spouse because they didn't want to feel indebted. "In a long-term relationship, the fear of owing something can be uncomfortable," he said.

Keeping emotional spreadsheets never works in a marriage. Thanking your spouse because he stopped to buy milk on the way home doesn't mean that you now have to whip up a milk shake, but if you don't stop to appreciate the effort, it's less likely to happen again. Years ago, a Hollywood friend of mine told me that whenever her husband shopped for groceries (a chore she didn't like), she gushed thanks—and never tried to make suggestions. "It doesn't really matter if he got smooth peanut butter and I like chunky. I just put those jars in the back of the cabinet and be glad that groceries magically appeared in my house. Never criticize magic!"

It was great advice, because many of us in the midst of a marriage forget to focus on the magic. It's much easier to focus on what's wrong. Instead of being grateful for the spouse you have, you want to improve, change, or otherwise reshape him. Or maybe you look over his shoulder and fantasize about the guy across the street, who is no doubt better at buying peanut butter. You can be perfectly happy with your spouse and still think what life would have been like if you'd stayed with your college sweetheart or given a second chance to the long-ago admirer who posts funny messages for you on Facebook.

I once wrote a funny novel called *The Men I Didn't Marry,* and whenever I wore the pink logoed T-shirt that the publisher made to promote it, someone stopped me with a story. In physics, one concept of string theory holds that there are parallel universes where every possibility gets played out. Whether that turns out to be true or not, we all walk hand in hand through life with the self we might have been if we'd made a different decision. But all we can really know is the life we have right now.

I've always admired the novel *The Unbearable Lightness of Being,* by the Czech-French writer Milan Kundera. I picked it up now and found a passage underlined long ago in yellow. "Living only one life, we can neither compare it with our previous lives nor perfect it in our lives to come. . . . We live everything as it comes, without warning, like an actor going on cold." I couldn't do anything about the lives I hadn't chosen and wouldn't have, but I could try to make choices that would give weight and meaning and satisfaction to this one.

Staying positive and connected when we got back home from Ojai was slightly harder than being on vacation. With a thriving medical practice and a deep commitment to his patients, Ron didn't have a lot of time to loll around being appreciative. I admired him as a terrific internist—smart and caring, a great diagnostician, willing to talk endlessly to his patients and be insightful about their needs. His peers admired him and his patients loved him. But for years I'd griped that if I wanted to see him more, he should be my doctor instead of my husband. In the couple of weeks after we got back, he missed a theater date we'd planned because his patient schedule ran late, and he slipped out of a dinner party during the salad course and stood outside to take calls. Okay, I had to face that none of that would change. But I could use my new gratitude tools and try reframing. Sitting alone at the theater wasn't the worst thing in life—I still got to go to Broadway even if he (sadly) missed it. By flipping problems on their heads, I could create my own parallel universe right here and now.

More and more marriage therapists are starting to recommend a looking-for-the-good approach, whether to smooth the edges of mostly good marriages (like ours) or to give warring couples a way forward. I got some insight into the latter when Ron and I went out to dinner with friends of ours—I'll call them Liz and Dick—who had gone through a turbulent time in their marriage. They'd always seemed like a great couple—attractive, sexy, and full of fun. But Liz was so horrified when she discovered that Dick had strayed (and strayed and strayed) that she threw him out of the house. Quite literally. She put his clothes into a garbage bag and tossed it onto the front lawn. He insisted he loved her, and after a lot of tears and soul-searching, and a full year being separated, they were back together in one house and one king-size bed. We admired that their intense efforts and genuine love had paid off.

Ron told them about my gratitude project and joked that he was glad I had committed to only a year.

"It's been great for me, but I don't know how much more appreciation I deserve," he said with a laugh.

"Don't knock it," Dick told him fervently. "Every marriage needs it."

He and Liz now went for a twice-monthly tune-up to a therapist who started every session by talking about gratitude.

"Call her," Liz urged me.

So the next day, I talked with Sylvia Rosenfeld, a marriage and sex counselor who told me that couples who came to see her usually stormed in, ready to air frustrations and problems. Instead, she asked each of them to tell her something (anything!) that their partner had done that they appreciated. Making them look at the total picture usually changed the mood in the room. "There's always something to appreciate. Even if it's just that he made me coffee," she said.

Like Dr. Atkinson, she thought the appreciation moment should come with a tagline: "*Do* try this at home!" Couples get very good at criticizing. We know each other's weak points and are usually all too happy to point them out. But part of the secret to marriage is acceptance—"which doesn't mean not asking the other person to make changes. It's just accepting someone for who they are. If you're discussing difficult things, lead with appreciation," she suggested.

I got a chance to practice my new skills that very night. Ron was on call for his medical practice, and at midnight, just after we'd gone to sleep, his cell phone beeped and he went into another room to take the call. A few minutes later, he came back and started getting dressed by the light from the closet. He was probably hoping that I wouldn't wake up and get annoyed.

"What's going on?" I asked.

"I have a patient in the emergency room. I need to go see her."

I took a deep breath. Ron's long hours and frequent on-call nights as a doctor had been a source of tension between us for years. I normally would have ranted that it was crazy for him to rush to the ER at this hour and there must be somebody on the hospital staff who could handle the case. I would get angry and he would leave upset.

But, darn it, I couldn't fall into the usual pattern. *Flip it,* I told myself. *Find the reason to be grateful.* Yes, my husband was excessively dedicated and would put aside his own interests for a patient in need. But shouldn't I be grateful that my husband was kind and caring? To err on the side of giving wasn't the worst thing in the world.

I lay in bed for a moment and tried to think of the situation from another view. A patient was lying scared and sick on a hospital gurney, and my husband was going to take care of her. I imagined how relieved she would be when she saw him arrive. And I thought how lucky I was to be safe and healthy in my own bed with a husband who cared so deeply about helping people.

I got up and went to the closet where he was getting dressed. He looked anxious—he doesn't like confrontation—but I stroked his arm and gave him a kiss.

"I was just thinking about how lucky your patient is to have you. She must feel so much better knowing you're on the way. The world needs more doctors like you. Thank you for being so special."

Ron couldn't have looked more surprised if I'd done a strip-tease on the bedpost. But he recovered in time to say, "Thank you. That's very nice."

"I'm sorry you have to go out so late," I said.

"Me too," he admitted. "I'll try to be back soon."

And that was that. Not an earth-shattering moment, but a sweeter one than it might have been.

As I got back into bed, I thought about the Greek philosophers I'd been reading. Two thousand years ago, Epictetus built a philosophy on recognizing that we can't control every event in our lives. In his long treatise that became known as *The Discourses*, he explained that a key to living right is understanding that we have power only over ourselves and our own reactions. *People are disturbed not by events, but by the views which they take of them*, he said. A couple of millennia later, the logic still held. Ron getting called to the hospital was an event that I couldn't change (however much I'd tried). But instead of seeing it as a problem, I could filter it through the lens of gratitude and come out with a completely different response.

Cuddling under the quilt now, I wished Ron were next to me. But I could take a broader view and know that he'd be back. The grateful spirit that had helped tonight also seemed to be changing our marriage overall. I said thank you more. I focused on the positives instead of the problems. I told Ron why I appreciated him. It seemed so simple, but why had I never tried it before? He had instinctively responded in kind, and the warm feelings between us had become stronger than ever. It had been a good month, because gratitude was making us both a lot happier.

CHAPTER 3

Raising Grateful Kids

Grateful for my amazing sons Zach and Matt

Thankful to spend time with Matt Damon and learn his view of appreciative kids

Happy to discover why teens aren't always grateful—and what parents can do

Since bringing a dose of gratitude and a new perspective was starting to make a huge difference in my marriage, I decided to give it a whirl with the rest of my family. First on the agenda were my two sons.

Scientists studying the human genome haven't yet located a gratitude gene, but that's possibly because they haven't been looking. Parents who are happy and optimistic seem to pass those traits along to their children, who then adopt similar habits when they become parents. Whether it's learned or inherited, a sense of gratitude clearly runs in families. I thought I was okay in the gratitude-for-kids category—but I was ready to improve.

I got the chance to practice sooner than I thought because my younger son, Matt, called to say that he was coming home for a few days of school vacation. I was delighted, since nothing makes me happier than having one of my boys around. But I also realized that parents can get so busy giving advice and suggestions to our kids that we forget to just enjoy them. So when Matt walked in the door, I offered my usual big hug and held him an extra-long time. Then I stepped back and told him how great he looked. He's well over six feet tall, with broad shoulders and a winning smile, and I always melt at the constant twinkle in his eye.

He studied me closely, then gave that endearing smile and said, "You think my hair's too long, right?"

"I didn't say a word!" I protested.

"I saw your eyes drifting up and that expression on your face," he said.

"You got me," I said, laughing, and Matt joined in. He's empathetic and aware and must have an emotional intelligence score that's off the charts. And since that gives him an ability to read my every expression, any emotion I shared with him had to be genuine.

"Can't you look great and still need a haircut?" I asked. And, of course, that was the point. Appreciating my son didn't mean fake flattery or agreeing with his every choice. It did mean recognizing that he had a right to make those choices (and, hopefully, get a haircut).

My natural tendency as a mom has always been to jump in with a thousand ideas for what my children might want and how I can improve their lives.

Do you need new socks?

I can edit that essay for you.

Did you call the guy you worked with last summer?

Let me put more milk in your cereal.

It's all well-meaning and loving, but it turns out to be exhausting—for both me and them. So I decided this time would be different. For the next couple of days, I sat back and just appreciated the charming, funny, smart (and did I mention great-looking?) young man who was now hanging around my house. I counted my lucky stars rather than the dishes he piled up in front of the TV. Often the comments parents consider *helpful* are heard by kids (maybe not wrongly) as critical, so I tried hard to give up on that mode. As I did, Matt relaxed around me more and more. He's whip smart and we've always had a close relationship, but one day he shared a story about a former girlfriend and stopped in the middle to grin. "Am I supposed to be telling my mom all this?" he asked.

"I'm grateful that you do," I said. "I'm not going to give any advice, but I'm always on your side."

Matt finished his story, then leaned across the table. "Thanks for always being there for me, Mom. I'm pretty lucky to have you and Dad."

"We're the lucky ones," I said.

Appreciating your child for who he is should be both natural and obvious—but I'm surprised at how bad many of us are at doing it. Kids of every age want their parents' approval, and it's a great gift to let them have it. After Matt headed back to school, I had lunch with my friend Jess, a mom in her midforties who likes to describe herself as a "reformed lawyer." She had quit a big firm to raise her children and did more volunteer work than almost anyone I knew. I told her what a great visit I'd had with Matt, and she immediately launched into worries about her own daughter, a sophomore in college. Jess didn't like that she was majoring in art history ("hard to get a job") or involved with a guy from Spain ("what if she moves there?"). Jess was always trying to get her daughter to share information about her life, but the nineteen-year-old had turned sullen and rarely called anymore.

"I wouldn't call you either, if I knew you were going to criticize me," I said with a shrug.

"It's constructive criticism," Jess said defensively.

"You think you're constructing, but she thinks you're tearing down. Try being only positive."

Jess looked at me blankly for a moment and then seemed to get it. She'd been on board earlier when I'd told her about my year of living gratefully and had even started her own gratitude journal. But it hadn't occurred to her that the same technique could have an effect on her relationship with her daughter.

"What do you suggest?" she asked.

"Something cheerful, upbeat, and short," I said. "A text message that just lets her know you appreciate her."

"You do that with your sons?" Jess asked warily.

"I do," I admitted.

I told Jess that when she didn't hear from her daughter, she missed her and wanted to know what was happening in her life. But what started as love ended up sounding like anger. As I'd learned earlier, the real issue wasn't the event (the daughter not calling) but Jess's response to it. The real message Jess wanted to send was *You're the best gift ever! I'm so grateful to have you in my life!*

Jess handed me her iPhone. "You're the writer. What should I write?"

"This isn't 'Ode on a Grecian Urn,'" I said. "You don't have to be John Keats to let your kid know you're grateful for her. Just be honest."

I quickly typed, *"Hope you're having a great week. No headlines from here, I'm just thinking of you with hugs."*

I gave the phone back to Jess.

"Not bad," she said, reading it.

"Adapt however you like. But that's the idea."

Jess hit *Send* and then sat back and stared at the screen.

"Gratitude doesn't need an immediate reply," I said. "You do it for yourself as much as for her."

The next day, Jess told me her daughter had a job interview that afternoon and she was thinking about sending some advice on what to wear. I vetoed the sartorial suggestions—which seemed to me like just an excuse for getting in touch.

"The real point is that you want to let her know you're cheering for her," I said. Then dictating a possibility, I offered, *"Good luck with the summer job interview. I think you're the best—and I'm betting they will, too."*

Within five minutes, Jess delightedly reported that she'd gotten a reply. *"Thanks, Mom! I'll call you later and tell you how it goes."*

It was a small victory, but it seemed to prove the point. We instinctively want to be with someone who appreciates us and accepts us unconditionally.

"She even said thanks!" Jess added cheerfully.

Getting a thank-you from children of a certain age is a rare and wonderful thing, and most parents are right to savor it—and not expect it too often. In the gratitude survey I had done, young people ages eighteen to twenty-four (the youngest millennials) proved less grateful than anyone else. Barely one-third said they expressed gratitude on any regular basis (for those over thirty-five, it was more than half), and they were also more likely to think in terms of the personal benefits of expressing gratitude—saying thanks in the hope that it would encourage other people to be nicer to them.

Gratitude is an issue for slightly younger teens, too, as I discovered when I went to a party and met an energetic group of working moms. Most of them had teenage children, and when they heard about my yearlong quest for gratitude, they offered a lot of eye rolling and teeth gnashing.

"I can't wait to read your book, because I have the most ungrateful kid in the world!" one of them said. The other moms were eager to compete with her for title of parent of "most ungrateful child." One reported that when she sent her fifteen-year-old to an expensive computer camp the previous summer, she suggested he show his thanks by calling home a few times a week. He seemed puzzled by the suggestion. "What am I thanking you for, Mom? Isn't sending kids to camp what parents are supposed to do?"

The question elicited knowing groans. Another mom who regularly drove her hockey-playing daughter to tournaments in distant towns said she didn't mind the long trips, but she wanted her daughter to appreciate the effort. Prodded for thanks, the young goalie turned defensive. "I'm a kid. Since I can't drive, you have to take me," she said, pouting.

Part of the problem could be attributed to the chemistry of the brain. If it often seems that kids don't know how lucky they are, it's because—they don't. How would they know? That's not where their brains are focused. Neuroscientists have shown that different regions in the brain develop at different rates. The prefrontal cortex, which controls reasoning and executive control, is on the slow track. Children and teens, like all of us, are partly products of their neural circuits. Parents need to use our (supposedly) better-developed prefrontal cortices to provide some perspective.

For advice on how to do that, I called Christine Carter, a sociologist from Berkeley, California, who coaches families on how to be happier. (Yes, California has happiness coaches.) When families come in for consultations, she often helps them set gratitude rituals. For example, at dinner each night, everyone discusses what made them grateful. Or before bed, they share three good things about the day. "Finding silver linings gives kids at any age more resilience and helps them short-circuit anxiety," she told me.

Carter's family had recently expanded, and with four children and stepchildren ages eleven to fourteen, she had adapted the rituals that she herself had been using for years. "You don't want gratitude to feel like a grind," she said. If Christine had to travel or the children were away, she might have them text her three good things that had happened to them. A neighbor who had a very shy son decided it was too difficult to share grateful thoughts out loud, so everyone got slips of paper before dinner and wrote "gratitude fortunes," which they dropped in a box.

I asked Christine if her kids ever objected to her approach. "They've grown up with gratitude as part of their lives, so they don't have that entitled attitude I hear parents describe," she said. I immediately thought of the moms at the party, and Christine wasn't surprised to hear their complaints.

"Teens don't want to feel like they're pawns in someone else's game," she said. "The more controlling parents are and the more they structure the kids' lives around enrichment, achievement, and college, then the more kids lose touch with who they are and what they want."

Which brings us back to those ungrateful millennials from my survey. When I conducted focus groups about gratitude as part of that John Templeton Foundation study, most of the participants—including professionals, working parents, and stay-at-home moms—got excited by the subject. Some admitted that they hadn't thought much about gratitude before but just having the session made them want to add more to their lives. "This afternoon was a life-changing big deal!" one woman e-mailed me afterward.

The sessions with millennials were completely different. College-age kids (and those in their early twenties, just starting careers) were struggling so hard to define themselves that they couldn't look beyond their own shadows. Many seemed almost offended by the whole concept of gratitude.

"I hate that feeling of *I owe you something*," said Greg, a twenty-two-year-old living in Boulder, Colorado, who took part in one of the discussions. "I don't like receiving gifts or acts of kindness, because they just make me feel awkward."

The other millennials in Greg's group quickly agreed. And they made it very clear that the people they *really* didn't want to feel obligated to were their parents. One young woman literally wrinkled her nose when asked about being grateful to her family. "I can be grateful to the counter guy at the deli, maybe. But my parents are just doing what nature intended. Even chimps take care of their children."

Ah, yes. Parents as chimps. If we're just fulfilling our biological imperative, why would our children say thanks? Part of the kids' biological imperative was to develop independence, and gratitude somehow felt antithetical to that. The kids in the focus groups were still at an age where they needed parental help, but they wanted to pretend they didn't. Greg said that when he couldn't afford an apartment, his dad offered to pay the security deposit.

"I didn't like it because the whole point was to live on my own. I took the money, but only with spite," he said.

A young woman named Emma understood. She had just graduated from a college in western Massachusetts and her parents were helping pay the rent while she started a film internship. "How I feel is all twisted around. Any gratitude gets smothered with guilt and annoyance that I have to be reliant on them. I feel the guilt a lot more than the gratitude," she said.

From the stories, it seemed like they had model parents—generous and eager to give their grown kids a positive start. But instead of flooding their parents with thank-yous, they took what was offered while holding their noses. It struck me that they were secretly grateful for the help, but even more chagrined that they couldn't yet handle the world completely by themselves. Guilt over gratitude, as Emma said.

"It's about control. You want to achieve on your own and not think someone else helped," Greg said.

The conflict and confusion registered most clearly in the story that a slim, dark-haired eighteen-year-old named Akil told. He had been given a full scholarship to a small urban college, and in addition to tuition, "they gave me a place to live, they gave me a laptop, they gave me stipends and stuff like that."

Surely, a $50,000-a-year gift should hit the list of reasons to be grateful for even the most muddled millennial. But Akil didn't see it that way. He softly explained that his real dream had been to go to Duke, where he could have cool friends and watch big-deal basketball games. Though he had accepted the generous scholarship and knew he'd learn a lot at the small college, he spent every day second-guessing himself.

"I'm grateful that I was given the scholarship and all, but I also resent it because I wanted something else," he said sadly.

What can you say about a kid who resents having no college debt? A lot of giving and goodwill had been doled out to each of these young adults and they didn't seem to appreciate it. Were they a bunch of ingrates? I didn't think so. They seemed to be typical college-age kids who knew in their heart of hearts that they were lucky to have support—whether a security deposit, a scholarship, or a safety net—but were still having the toddler-like tantrums of *I want to do it myself!*

Expressing gratitude outright to their parents wasn't in the cards, but they clearly had the nagging sense that something was necessary to balance the deck. Emma announced that her way of showing gratitude to her parents was by being the best person she could be.

"My mother told me she was in labor with me for twenty-four hours and my parents paid for my college, so I will be a good child and do equally unpleasant things for them in return," she said airily.

What kind of things?

She thought about it for a moment.

"Oh, I know," she said triumphantly. "Sometimes I've sat and listened to my mother nattering for forty minutes about the animals chewing up her vegetable garden. I know that's small-scale, but trust me, it's not something I enjoy!"

So there it was. Emma thought chatting about chipmunks was a fair exchange—and a perfect way to show gratitude—for all her parents had done. It brought to mind the lovely poem by Billy Collins, the former US poet laureate, reflecting on the lanyard he made for his mother as a child at summer camp. "She gave me life and milk from her breasts, / and I gave her a lanyard . . ." he wrote, going on to marvel at his childish belief that the "worthless thing I wove out of boredom / would be enough to make us even."

The poem makes everyone smile, not because it's so far-fetched but because it's so understandably real. Yale president Peter Salovey quoted the full poem once when he gave a speech to graduating seniors and pointed out that "the need to express gratitude reminds us that we are not entirely in control; that we might be indebted or dependent; that our destiny is not entirely in our hands; indeed, that on occasion we are vulnerable."

Indebted, vulnerable, and out of control are not emotions that any young adult wants to feel. Yet President Salovey went on to say that true happiness in life "may not be possible without the capacity to reject the myth of total self-reliance. The good life may be out of reach unless we are able to cultivate an openness to accepting help from others and expressing gratitude for that help."

So what's the best way to cultivate that willingness to be grateful? How do we give kids a bigger view and get them to understand that attending computer camp or getting money for college isn't their essential right? That maybe (just maybe!) we are all inter-connected and they are luckier than they know?

I thought about conversations I had on the subject with actor Matt Damon when we did a couple of magazine articles together. Handsome and charming in person, Damon also came across as smart and thoughtful and very sincere. The first time we met, he told me that when he was growing up, his mom, an educator in the Boston area, had a magnet on the refrigerator with a quote from Gandhi that said, "No matter how insignificant what you do may seem, it is important that you do it."

"I was raised to believe in sharing what you have, and I want my children to understand that too," he said. When he was a kid, he got an allowance of five dollars a week, and after a while, he started sending most of it to various causes that his mom sup-ported.

"Be careful how you say that or I'll sound like too much of a goody-goody," he joked.

One afternoon, we sat in the Polo Lounge of the Beverly Hills Hotel, a place where people usually talk about movie deals, back-end points, and their latest and greatest screenplay. But Matt sipped a cappuccino and told me about his travels around the world to try to understand global poverty.

"I spent my twenties really focused on my career, which is okay," he said. "But now my career is in a solid place and I have a family and I want my kids to see that their dad has a bigger world than just photo shoots."

Making that world bigger—for himself and his children—was a challenge. He knew that a guy who pals around with George Clooney and has made a fortune in Hollywood blockbusters like

The Bourne Identity (and its sequels) wasn't always taken seriously. After visiting Africa once to raise awareness on the refugee problem, he was interviewed on the BBC, and the somewhat condescending reporter asked if a celebrity like him could really make a difference.

"We'd just spent fifteen minutes on the air talking about Zimbabwe," he told me with a laugh. "I said, 'Would you have discussed this topic at all if you weren't talking to me?'"

A few years earlier, Damon was in South Africa, shooting the Clint Eastwood–directed movie *Invictus*. Damon played a white rugby star who became a key player in Nelson Mandela's efforts to heal the wounds of postapartheid South Africa. His family had come on location, and Damon thought about taking his oldest daughter, Alexia, then only ten, to tour the impoverished townships of Johannesburg with him. He asked his costar Morgan Freeman (who was playing Mandela in the movie) what he should say to her to explain the misery and poverty. What reason could he give for why her life was so different from theirs?

"Morgan said to me, 'You don't have to tell her anything. Just let her see. That's all the education anyone needs.' And it was the best advice I could have gotten. She just looked and looked and took it in. Those kinds of experiences can be life changing."

His approach was just right. It turns out that empathy is fundamental to gratitude—and to what psychologists now describe as "emotional intelligence." Various studies in brain and behavior suggest that IQ accounts for only about 20 percent of a child's success in later life. A full 80 percent is determined by other factors that revolve around emotional style. When kids can step outside of themselves for a moment and imagine what it is to be someone else, they are better able to respond to other people's emotions—and to recognize their own. They also start to appreciate both what they have and what others have done for them.

You don't have to be a big star or travel to South Africa to encourage empathy. When my own son Matt was in high school, he volunteered at the South Street Seaport Museum, helping renovate the 1885 *Wavertree,* one of the last big ships made of wrought iron. Matt's job one day was to scrape rust off the hull, and after several hours of hard labor, he was sweaty, exhausted, and filthy, his hands covered with black iron, which had also streaked across his face. As he sunk into his seat on the train home, he noticed people looking at him dubiously and moving away.

At dinner that night, he turned reflective—and as appreciative of his life as a fifteen-year-old could be.

"When I was dirty and in work boots, people treated me like a different person," he told us. "I realized how lucky I am that I was working at the *Wavertree* for fun and not because I had to."

That perspective stuck with him. It made an impression that I couldn't have achieved by telling him a thousand times how lucky he was. Instead, like Matt Damon, I didn't need to say a word.

Teaching values like gratitude on a wider basis is one of the missions of the Jubilee Centre for Character and Virtues in England. I exchanged some e-mails with James Arthur, the director of the center, and though he's based at the University of Birmingham, he agreed to meet with me on his next trip to London.

With an excuse to fly to one of my favorite cities, I grabbed the cheapest possible overnight flight and arrived in London early in the morning, much too exhilarated to have any jet lag. I walked around Hyde Park, dipped into the British Museum, and lunched at Fortnum & Mason. (Gratitude, thy name is scones with clotted cream.) Early the next morning, I took a taxi from my hotel near Kensington Gardens to the eminent Athenaeum Club on Pall Mall, founded in 1824 as a gathering place for artists and intellectuals. James Arthur, a distinguished man with silver hair and a firm handshake, met me in the huge lobby and led me up the impressive grand staircase. We took a quick tour through several massive and elegant rooms, including a library with floor-to-ceiling wooden bookcases (and not a Kindle in sight). Then we sat down on the leather sofas of the morning room, where we had tea and discussed his interest in bringing gratitude and other moral values into the school system.

"Virtue education has the potential to transform the lives of young people," he said.

His team had looked at how moral character was encouraged in seven different schools, from Eton (founded by King Henry VI in 1440) to a local primary school in Birmingham that included many children with special needs. He hoped to take the best practices and expand them. "We are seeking new ways to teach character and give young people a view beyond themselves," he said.

As one way to encourage gratitude, the Jubilee Centre sponsored the Thank You Film Awards for kids under sixteen (divided by age). Entries came in from all over the country, and the center held premieres at real theaters so kids could see their shorts on a big screen. The range of people thanked was impressive—from leaders in civil and women's rights to doctors in the National Health Service. Videos from some of the youngest kids expressed gratitude to daddies, "lollipop ladies" (the local name for crossing guards), and bumblebees.

Really, something was going right when five-year-olds wanted to thank bumblebees.

James Arthur was optimistic that encouraging gratitude could have an effect on creating a more generous and welcoming world. As we moved on to our second cup of tea, I realized that he was a deeply religious man, but he pointed out that the center stuck to what he called "post-religious language." He felt strongly that in an increasingly secular society, character and virtue couldn't be abandoned. We just needed a new way to approach them. Gratitude wasn't just a religious notion, it was a human one. Education has always been about preparing the young for the future—and won't it be a more hopeful future if it is imbued with the kindness and compassion that gratitude can inspire?

I nodded and swallowed hard. For James Arthur and his colleagues, research into gratitude wasn't just cold social psychology. Understanding how to spread gratitude to the next generation became his way of creating a better world.

Back in New York, it struck me that my personal quest to live gratefully had a much bigger dimension. Gratitude wouldn't replace math and science in the schools (though some might like that), but it had started to gain traction. More schools now intervened in social arenas—like trying to stop bullying or helping to mainstream students with disabilities—and James Arthur was right that all of those efforts fell under the bigger rubric of teaching values. I read about a private elementary school in Colorado that tried to incorporate gratitude into the classroom. Younger students talked about what made them grateful, and fourth and fifth graders kept gratitude journals. The head of school said simply, "If you raise kids to be grateful, they will find success."

What schools aren't doing yet, parents can try. If we want kids to know how blessed they are, they need a basis for comparison—and that requires the gift of a wider worldview. Some of those moms who worried about their ungrateful teens could think about taking them to a soup kitchen on a Saturday morning instead of a mall. Not as much fun, maybe, but a better deal in the long run. Or they could try one of my favorites: collecting all the charitable appeals that come in the mail into a big basket and finding a night when the whole family can sit down together to go through them. Parents set the budget for giving and the kids decide how it's distributed. Or parents could simply set the model of gratitude in daily life. I don't usually hang out on Instagram, Twitter, or Pinterest, but heck, go where the kids are. Why not have everyone in the family post or text (or whatever you do) a picture each week of something that inspired appreciation—whether a friend, a snowflake, or a sunset. If kids live on social media, the shared experience might as well help everyone see the world differently.

Doing research on gratitude and kids, I came across some brand-new studies by a guy named Yarrow Dunham, who seemed to be at Princeton. But when I called him, I found he was now a full-time professor at Yale.

"My wife studies medieval music, French and Italian fourteenth century, and I'm a psychologist—and we both managed to get appointments at Yale. Talk about gratitude!" he said exuberantly.

I didn't know enough about his wife's field to ask a single question, but his studies definitely had wide appeal. He had done important research on how people divide into social groups—whether Yankee fans or Hindu castes—and headed something called the Social Cognitive Development Lab, which looked at how children naturally adhere to groups. (Randomly assign some children red T-shirts and others blue T-shirts, and they will immediately become fiercely loyal to the group that two minutes earlier didn't exist.) Now he was starting a side project analyzing the ingredients that encouraged gratitude in children. Like James Arthur, he was interested in how gratitude could lead to a bigger circle of virtue.

"Adults make a distinction between gratitude and obligation," he told me. "Obligation is a debt that you have to pay back. Gratitude is that feeling when something good happens and you are happy with the world. Instead of a sense of debt, there's a bigger feeling of wanting to pay it forward. Children don't necessarily go through the mental gymnastics necessary for those distinctions."

In one study done with his colleague Peter Blake at Boston University, he brought little kids (ages four to eight) into his lab and gave them a gift, like a sticker book or temporary tattoo. Some were told the gift was a thank-you for coming to the lab—what Dunham called "a straight exchange relationship." The others were told that another child had given them the gift and was sharing his favorite toy.

Next, the children played a game where they were given ten

Starburst candies, and they could take all of them or share some with another child.

And bingo. The kids who felt they'd received a gift from another child—as opposed to payment for coming to the lab—were more likely to share. Dunham was excited to see that even with very young children, a bit of gratitude made them want to do something for someone else.

Evolutionary biologists have studied reciprocity, which is what happens when you do something nice for me and I now do the same for you. Voilà, we become a cooperative species. Reciprocity is the simplest form of gratitude. Many studies have found it in animals—who are more likely to groom or share food with others who have helped them. I recently saw a touching video of animal gratitude in action. Primatologist Jane Goodall and a colleague had rescued a chimp named Wounda from near death, and after nursing her back to health, they were releasing her to freedom on a leafy island sanctuary. The gangly chimp lumbered out to head into the woods. But then she stopped, came back, and shimmied up to wrap her arms around Goodall. She held Goodall for a long time in the kind of loving embrace we'd all like. Thanks given, she climbed back down and headed off. You couldn't watch that without thinking—there goes one grateful chimp.

Dunham was pleased to point out that feelings of gratitude in children (real-life human ones, that is) inspire even greater sharing than simple reciprocity. The children who were grateful for their little gift shared their Starbursts with *other* children. It wasn't just payback or obligation. Maybe that bumps us up a little higher than chimps on that evolutionary chain?

"Gratitude goes beyond the you-scratch-my-back-and-I'll-scratch-yours dyad and creates a broad network of possibility," he said. Dropping his academic veneer, he added enthusiastically, "That's very cool!"

Dunham hoped to look next at how gratitude might create in kids and adults "a self-perpetuating cycle of virtuous deeds." A child who's grateful does something for the next kid, who does something for the next, who does something for the next . . . And eventually (theoretically, at least) it comes back to the first child. So-called pro-social behavior seems to be contagious.

On the less positive side, I was interested in Dunham's discovery that the children who thought they *deserved* the gift (they had earned it by coming to the lab) didn't feel gratitude at all. I asked if that attitude might explain some teenage behavior.

"Great question!" he said, flattering me with his spirited reply. "Teenagers have a sense of entitlement that fights gratitude. If they code it that parents or the community or the world is obligated to provision them with the things they want, then the parent is just living up to their obligations. That's not a mind-set that creates a grateful disposition."

I liked his work and promised to stay in touch. And when I hung up, it occurred to me that maybe the problem I'd seen with the "ungrateful" kids and teens and millennials was really a question of obligation versus gratitude. None of us wants to think that we send our kids to camp or buy them cashmere sweaters out of obligation. But if kids see it as an "exchange relationship," maybe the moms I'd met who wanted their teens to be grateful for rides to hockey games or summers at computer camp needed to take a step back. Growing up, did any of us really recognize how much our own parents did for us? My dad came from a very poor family and struggled to put himself through Boston University. He was proud to get an education but poignantly couldn't afford to attend his senior prom, so he got a job working the front desk that night, selling tickets to his wealthier classmates. Watching them glide past him to go to the dance was a misery he never forgot. Thirty years later, he still felt the sting. I was in college (and a week from my own prom) when my dad told me that story, and only then did it occur to me how grateful my siblings and I should feel that he had fully covered our college costs. Moved by what he had sacrificed, I nobly asked if we could work out a plan so I could return the tuition to him as soon as I could afford it.

"You can pay me back but not with money," said my gentle dad. "The best return would be to do the same thing for your own children."

I didn't really understand it at the time, but now I would ask the same thank-you of my boys. Don't pay it back—pay it forward. That's the greatest gratitude. And it goes far to meeting the virtuous goals of people like James Arthur and Yarrow Dunham, who see gratitude as a step to a kinder world.

Probably the best thing parents can do is to set an example of gratitude, finding a balance between planning for the future and savoring the present. But we're often lousy at that. My older son, Zachary, was always so competent growing up that sometimes the best parenting trick was just to step back and admire what he did. But when he was a junior in high school, Zach noticed that every adult he encountered asked where he would be applying for college.

"It's as if what I'm doing now doesn't matter," he complained at the time.

He got good at deflecting the queries—he's always been clever—but once he landed in college, the same people wanted to know about his career plans. Hey, what about classes, professors, and the really cool experiments he did in the physics lab? Somehow, Zach instinctively knew to be grateful for the moments along the way. His freshman year at Yale, he and three other guys shared a suite so small he had to climb over the bunk beds to get to his desk. But the room was in a dorm on the Old Campus, a classic quadrangle built in the late 1800s on the model of Oxford and Cambridge. When I visited one day, we stood outside his entryway as the chapel bells pealed and the sun glinted off the century-old buildings. I wondered to myself if an eighteen-year-old could appreciate the scene, but before I could say a word, Zach gestured to his surroundings and asked me to stand still for a moment.

"Every morning when I step outside, I make myself stop and look around and appreciate that I'm here. I'll never get to live in a place like this again. I don't want to take it for granted," he told me.

That he could overlook the cramped quarters and simply feel the magic of the place amazed me. As parents, we can be grateful and teach gratitude too. Helping kids reframe their experiences and exposing them to the greater world is a gift, and a little later, understanding the mind-set that keeps teens from expressing gratitude can help everyone get through bumpy times. I'd like to take credit for Zach's grateful perspective and report all I did to instill it in him. But the truth is that he figured it out himself. When I think about my children, I am endlessly grateful to have them. And grateful that I can learn from them, too. The bottom line might simply be this: To raise grateful kids, be grateful for your kids.

CHAPTER 4

The No-Complaining Zone

So grateful to . . . stop complaining!

Thankful to enjoy the weather, however cold it may be

Grateful to discover how being positive can change my mood

With gratitude helping me with husband and kids, I started thinking about what else it could do for my daily interactions. On a wintry day as I slipped and slid across an icy sidewalk, I thought wryly that the one thing gratitude couldn't fix was the weather.

Well, wait a minute. Why not?

Everybody I met on the street seemed to have turned into weatherman Al Roker, announcing that it was five degrees with a wind chill that made it feel like ten below. One morning, I had found myself exchanging complaints about the cold as I bought a bagel, stood at the bus stop, and got into an elevator. By the time I landed at the conference room where I was headed, I was exhausted from all the griping.

My gratitude journal didn't contain any magic spells to turn the cold into Caribbean sunshine. (I don't know if even Harry Potter could do that.) But there was one thing I could do about the incredibly cold winter that was paralyzing the East Coast and parts of the Midwest. Stop grousing about it. Finding the good in every day meant overlooking (as much as possible) quotidian problems. Gratitude shouldn't be reserved for special occasions. So my plan for this month took shape. I'd stop complaining about the weather and use that as a stepping-stone to become more grateful for ordinary, everyday life.

People whining about the weather know it doesn't help—they simply take solace in venting. The get-it-off-your-chest approach has many adherents, but what you say has an effect on how you feel. Announce too often that you're miserable, and you begin to believe you really are. I had the sense that friends, strangers, and casual acquaintances commiserating about the bad conditions just made everyone more unhappy. There had to be a better way of bonding than bellyaching about something we couldn't change.

So as I walked down the street and bundled a plaid scarf a little tighter around my neck, I thought about using my new technique of reframing as part of the daily business of . . . getting through the day. Surely I could find a positive side to storms. I remembered a line from the English artist and social thinker John Ruskin that there is no such thing as bad weather, only different kinds of good weather.

Just then, a man who was clearing snow from the sidewalk in front of his building tossed back a shovelful—and it landed smack on my shoulder.

"Ugh!" I shouted.

"Sorry," the man mumbled, turning to see what he'd done. He

was wearing a thick hat and heavy muffler and probably hadn't seen me coming up behind him.

"Be more careful!" I said, my face flushed as I brushed the snow off my coat.

I started to walk off in a huff and then stopped. My attitude of gratitude had to hold in all conditions. I took a deep breath and tried the trick of flipping from bad to good. Sure he'd hit me with a shovelful of snow, but I was lucky to live in a part of the city where people kept their sidewalks cleared in snowstorms. And I was definitely grateful that he was out shoveling instead of me.

I hesitated and then took a few steps back in his direction and waved my hand. He stopped, shovel midair. "What's wrong?"

"Nothing. I just wanted to thank you for shoveling."

"Oh." He nodded and went back to work. He must have wondered about the crazy lady who yelled at him and then thanked him, but I felt much better.

Back home, I pulled out a book I had recently found with the meditations of Marcus Aurelius, emperor of Rome in the second century. While he was overseeing military campaigns, fighting off the hordes, and protecting an empire, he also wrote notes to himself about self-awareness and understanding the essence of being human. A central theme was recognizing what is in your control and what isn't—and acting on the one and ignoring the other. It's a philosophy that has resonated over the centuries.

Reading through some of the meditations, I found a passage that seemed right for the day: *Whether you are shivering with cold*

or too hot, sleepy or wide awake . . . do not let it interfere with do-
ing what is right.

I read it and smiled.

Marcus Aurelius was part of a tradition of philosophy whose
adherents became known as the Stoics, and though we now use
the word to mean long-suffering and resigned, the Stoics simply
encouraged people to be rational. Going back to the third century
BC, the Stoic philosophers taught that we could handle problems
based on how we thought about them. Marcus Aurelius believed
we all have an inner power to clear away destructive emotions. He
realized you can never be happy if you waste time frustrated by
circumstances you can't change.

I put the book next to my bed and left it open to one of Marcus's meditations: *When you arise in the morning, think of what a*
precious privilege it is to be alive—to breathe, to think, to enjoy, to
love.

The next morning when I woke up, I reread that lovely line
even before I checked my iPhone messages. Inspired by Emperor
Marcus, I was ready to appreciate the day—and that meant putting my no-complaining policy to a further test.

Given the weather, I would have liked to stay inside huddled
near a fireplace, but I had a meeting at an ad agency across town.
I put on a cashmere dress and leather boots, and taking a tip from
a six-year-old I'd seen playing in the park, I pulled on snow pants
underneath. I topped it all off with Gore-Tex gloves and a dorky
earflap hat. I trudged through the cold and snow and arrived early
enough to slip into a ladies' room to remove the skiwear, dry my
tote bag with paper towels, and brush out my hat-head hair.

When I stepped into his office looking respectable again, the well-dressed executive I was meeting introduced himself and by way of greeting said, "Horrible weather, isn't it? How are you holding up?"

I thought of the old proverb that says, instead of complaining that the rosebush has thorns, be happy the thornbush has roses.

"We're lucky that we work inside. It's very cozy in here," I said cheerfully.

He paused for a moment, then smiled. "Definitely better than digging ditches."

Maybe not a gush of gratitude, but surely more upbeat than discussing the dangers of frostbitten toes. And it probably made us both feel a little warmer too.

For the rest of the week, I took it as a challenge to find a positive twist to every conversation. When people moaned about the weather, I sang the praises of Heattech tights and rubber insulated boots. Often people forgot their griping and asked where I got them (Uniqlo and L.L.Bean, by the way). I applauded the storekeepers who shoveled the snow off their sidewalks. I mentioned how lucky we were to have pashmina scarves sold on New York street corners—five bucks and they kept you warm! As a last resort, I declared the weather good preparation for the trip to Antarctica I hoped to take. Staying endlessly upbeat, I was surprised at how easily I could change the mood and get people agreeing with me.

"You're right," said a man who had started talking about the weather as we waited for our orders at a coffee shop. "In a few months, we'll be complaining about the heat and humidity."

"Meantime, we get to drink hot chocolate without any guilt," I said, taking my frothy cup from the counter.

"Oh, that looks good," he said.

"Reason to be grateful," I said, raising my plastic cup in a faux toast.

That night, I took out my pretty gratitude journal and wrote a few events from the day that made me feel good. Then I added: *So thankful . . . that by complaining less, I'm feeling happier and more appreciative.*

But then I paused and thought about that. Was giving life a constantly positive spin creating a reality that wasn't . . . real?

The evidence from a variety of fields seems to prove a lot about the power of our perceptions. It's hard to talk about "reality" when our neurotransmitters respond to subtleties that we may not even recognize. When we believe something, we virtually *make* it true.

For example, a large percentage of people who are given what they think is a well-known brand for a headache (like Advil or Bayer) versus a generic pill report more pain relief from the big-brand pill. Doctors and pharmacists go nuts when they hear that because—*it can't be!* Advil is the same as generic ibuprofen. Bayer is the same as aspirin. The molecular structures are identical and the active ingredients are the same. And don't look for an answer in the inactive ingredients (those shiny sugar coatings), because the experiments have also been done with absolutely identical pills that people are just told are different.

Wittingly or not, our own minds create chemicals more powerful than any pain reliever. If you think the big brand will work better, it actually does. I knew the evidence—but it happened to me all the time. While my husband the doctor had only generic drugs on his side of the medicine cabinet, I had shiny Advil. I knew I was wasting money on packaging and name-brand advertising, but when I used his ibuprofen, it just didn't work the same. You can say it's the placebo effect, but you can't dismiss it as not real. Because in all the studies (including my personal one), people's headaches respond differently to what they *think* they're taking.

Similarly, even the most sophisticated oenophiles can be influenced by the price and provenance (real or not) of a wine. An expert opening a bottle that he thinks is a hard-to-get $200 Domaine de Chevalier will almost always find it tastier than if the label says "House Wine." Professor Paul Bloom of Yale, who has analyzed the underpinnings of pleasure, reported on one study where experts were given wine bottles with the labels changed. Some of the connoisseurs who got the wine with a cheap label thought it was worth drinking—but three times as many approved when it had a fancy label. Apparently all the erudite opinions about oaky, earthy, silky, and structured are affected by labels as much as by taste buds.

Even more impressive was a study where people agreed to have their brains scanned in fMRI machines while they sipped wine through straws (anything for research). Screens set up in front of the volunteers purported to give information, including price, about what they were tasting, though actually each sip was the same. Professor Bloom says the pleasure centers of the volunteers' brains "lit up like Christmas trees" when they believed they were tasting an expensive or rare wine.

So it's not just that we *think* we like something more—we actually *experience* it in a more positive way. As with the big-brand pain reliever, individual neural circuits can create different experiences from the same product. At dinner one evening when friends cooed over a fancy Napa Valley Chablis that they admired as oaky, lemony, and with floral undertones, I cynically suggested that they were drinking the label rather than the liquid. To me, it tasted like . . . wine. They condescendingly countered that my unsophisticated tastes couldn't appreciate terroir subtleties. All of us were probably right. With different expectations, our pleasure centers fired different messages. While we all like to think we are the one having the truly authentic experience, it's possible that there's no such thing.

What works for wine and pain relievers can be expanded to a general view of life. Not complaining about the weather was my version of affixing a nice label to a cheap bottle of wine. It didn't change the day, but it did change how I experienced it. That made sense since I'd learned a similar lesson in my marriage, that late night when Ron headed off to see a patient in the hospital. The event wouldn't change, but my reaction could. And if a positive spin could light up my brain's pleasure centers, I didn't mind turning my brain into the neon signs of Times Square.

When we appreciate what we have, we are more likely to be satisfied and less likely to be unhappy. On a roll with philosophers, I turned to the Greek philosopher Epicurus, who was born about 340 BC and figured out the value of appreciation a long time ago. He advised, *Do not spoil what you have by desiring what you have not. Remember that what you now have was once among the things you only hoped for.*

In the third century, the philosopher Diogenes agreed with the sentiment, and on a wall in Turkey, he inscribed a line from Epicurus: *He who is not satisfied with a little is satisfied with nothing.*

Wise as those comments may be, I also wanted to be a little

careful. Philosophy and theology can be all about placating us to be happy, and appreciating what we have doesn't mean we can't strive for more. Gratitude may be the secret sauce for happiness, but the recipe works for a lot of us only if it still allows for ambition and resolve.

Given that something as simple as not complaining about the weather made me feel better each day, I wondered what would happen if I didn't complain about . . . anything at all. I could identify two kinds of complaining—one where you're just fussing and finding fault (as with the weather), and the other where you actually want something fixed. My no-complaining policy would cover just the first category. The second remained simply practical. I didn't have to abandon asking the dry cleaner for fair compensation when he ruined the ruching on my favorite dress (re-ruching is apparently not possible), and when the heel fell off my brand-new boots, I still sent them back for a replacement. Being grateful didn't get in the way of solving problems.

But whenever I could, I reminded myself of Epicurus's advice that you shouldn't spoil what you have by wanting something else. (Or as the 1970 Stephen Stills song put it, "Love the one you're with.") So instead of getting irritated when I stood in line at the grocery store, I stopped to be grateful I lived in a place where we could buy fresh food (strawberries in wintertime!). I didn't complain about an editor who didn't get back to me—his in-box was probably packed. When a friend took me to a concert that neither of us liked, I said (genuinely) that it didn't matter—we had fun being together anyway.

All the goodwill started to feel natural. What began as a big effort—I'd make myself find reasons to be grateful every day!—

started seeping into my general attitude. It continued at home, too. Even though my month of being grateful to Ron had (officially) ended, the *flip it* position of seeing the bright side when he rushed off to tend a patient or take a call had made a difference. Thanks and appreciation and a positive outlook had started to be the norm.

The one downside to the positivity was that I suddenly found myself excessively sensitive to people who *weren't* grateful. My friend Dana met me for drinks one evening, and the moment she sat down, she told me how *horrible* everything had been. The big corporation where she worked had moved its headquarters downtown, and she hated the new location. Her own office was smaller and had no view. No decent shopping nearby. And the elevator was soooo slow!

A few weeks earlier, I probably would have sympathized and eagerly tossed in my own tidbits to match her misery. But quitting complaining is like giving up greasy French fries. At first it's hard—but after a while, you feel so much better that you never want to go back. And you want everyone else to reform too.

"You like your job, you get paid well, and you're one of the few people who still has an office rather than a cubicle. That's a lot! You should be grateful," I told her.

"Oh, please. You have no idea how miserable it is."

"Miserable might be not having a job at all."

"I have to take the subway home at night, which I hate!"

"But you get a car service in the mornings, which you love! Focus on that part!"

With too many exclamation points exchanged, Dana and I glared at each other, each trying to understand why the other didn't understand. Across the table from me, she looked as perfectly put together as always—her hair freshly blown out, a nice manicure, generous diamond studs in her ears. I told her about my gratitude project and the difference it was making in my life, but Dana wasn't coming around. We parted with a distinct chill between us.

When I got home, I told Ron how frustrated I was talking to Dana.

"She's so *ungrateful*. She has so much good in her life, and all she can see is what's wrong."

"Maybe you can help her."

"I tried, but I don't think I got through."

But a week later, Dana called me about some topic that wasn't very important, and only at the end of the conversation did I realize that she had a different agenda.

"Do you remember last year when I had all that back pain and ended up in surgery?" she asked.

"Of course I do," I said.

"I was walking down the street yesterday and I realized I have no pain at all anymore. And I started to feel grateful for every step. Isn't that amazing? Every time I'm walking now, I'm going to think about how grateful I am not to have pain."

I wished we were in the same room because I wanted to give her a big hug. "Grateful for every step. That's a great first . . . step," I said. And she must have felt my grin through the phone.

The next day, I took a train down to Philadelphia to talk with Dr. Martin Seligman, the renowned professor of psychology at the

University of Pennsylvania who runs the Positive Psychology Center and is often referred to as the father of the field. If therapists have traditionally focused on fixing unhappy states, Seligman made it okay to think, instead, about encouraging positive ones. When he was the head of the American Psychological Association, he encouraged a major movement to change the goals of psychology from healing illness to improving well-being. "Curing the negatives does not produce the positives," he explained, noting that someone can be free of depression, anxiety, and anger but still not feel satisfied and fulfilled.

I'd first met Dr. Seligman a year earlier when I was starting to think about gratitude and he invited me to join him for dinner at a fancy restaurant in Philly. Over several courses that included caviar, lobster puffs, a delicately prepared sea bass, and a terrific chocolate mousse, he discussed how gratitude improves well-being. (The dinner improved it too.) When he created positive psychology, he set "happiness" as the gold standard for what was trying to be achieved. But now that he had seen some results, he was convinced that happiness wasn't enough, and to truly flourish, we needed advantages like engagement, meaning, purpose, and gratitude.

"Life satisfaction isn't just about a cheerful mood. We now are looking at a greater sense of well-being," he said, tasting the amuse-bouche that the very gracious waiter brought.

For our meeting this time, I grabbed a sandwich at a local deli and then went to Dr. Seligman's office. An entire academic discipline had grown around his ideas about positive psychology, and his team investigating affirmative approaches was large enough to take up a whole floor.

We sat down and I told him about my effort to live gratefully for the year. He nodded approvingly.

"Of all the positive strengths we've looked at, people who are highest in gratitude are also highest in well-being," he said.

The correlation was strong, but Seligman also raised the issue of causation versus causality. It was the old chicken-and-egg question: Does gratitude improve your well-being, or do people with a high level of well-being also feel more grateful? The answer seemed to be: Both. Grateful people typically have more friends and social interactions and a rosier view of life that helps them flourish. But if you don't come by that naturally, what Seligman called "gratitude interventions" can have a big effect.

"You get relatively ungrateful people like me and have them do gratitude journals and letters and visits and see if their well-being increases," he explained.

Several studies have shown that the interventions have an effect that lingers for days, weeks, or even months. I mentioned that my gratitude journal was already changing my attitude and helping me refocus on the positive.

"Very good," he said with a nod. "And here's another variant. As you go through the day, take photos of the things that you might write about in your journal that night. *Doing* something has a stronger effect than just thinking about it."

From what I'd already learned about bodies and brains, I could see how an action would help send the right message to (and through) the neurons. An action helps cement the neurological pathways we're trying to encourage. In his earlier research, Seligman had found that the intervention that caused the most noticeable improvement was the gratitude *visit*.

In his plan, you start by thinking of someone who changed your life for the better and sit down and write a letter of thanks. Make sure it's concrete and specific, about three hundred words, and describes what the person did and how you were affected. Then arrange to get together with the person, not saying why. When you arrive, slowly and meaningfully read the letter. No interruptions allowed.

"Interacting is the big phenomenon. There'll be a lot of crying and emotion and hugs, but that aside, what we've found is that the person who has written the letter will be less depressed and feel more positive about life in general for a full month afterwards," he said.

A full month seemed like a big effect from a small project. On the other hand, I was working on a *year* of gratitude. I needed the lift to linger even longer.

"You could run your own experiment," Seligman said with a smile. "I've never thought of doing more than one gratitude visit, but see what happens if you do three over the year. Or twelve."

On the train home, I thought about a gratitude letter I'd written years earlier that still made me feel good. At the time, I was editor in chief of the largest-circulation magazine in America, reaching some 72 million people every week. I'd done a cover story on President George Bush when he was in office, and when Barack Obama was elected president, I thought it would be a great coup to have him write a cover story for the weekend before his inauguration. I spoke to his communications guy, who pointed out, reasonably enough, that the president was saving all the good stuff for his inaugural address. What did I have in mind that would be worth writing and wouldn't conflict? I had about thirty seconds to come up with a persuasive idea.

"Maybe the article could be a letter to his daughters about what he hopes for them in the next four years," I suggested.

"Not bad. Let me check," he said.

Within an hour, I had the reply. Obama liked the idea and would start writing. But as the deadline for closing the issue approached, I still hadn't received it, so I called again.

"I'm anxious to see the president's story," I said.

"So are we. He's actually writing this one himself," said his communications chief.

The article arrived that afternoon, so beautifully written that I didn't change a word. (Trust me—that's unusual. Even in a piece from the president.) When the issue came out, the president's letter got a rapturous reception and international attention. A couple of years later, the president turned the letter to his daughters into a children's book.

All the excitement around the article and the praise I got for publishing it made me reflect that good ideas—even "original" ones—came from somewhere. The seed for mine occurred years earlier when a rabbi we knew talked about writing an "ethical will." Typical wills dealt with money and property, he said, but shouldn't we also leave our children a record of our values and hopes, our dreams for their future? He read aloud the letter he had written to his then toddler daughter, talking about morals and values and the kind of person he hoped she'd marry. Moved by both his sense and his sensibility, I went home and wrote my own ethical wills to Zach and Matt, then just four and two. Tears streaked down my cheeks as I tried to imagine not being with them as they grew, so I used this letter to tell them what I thought mattered, what I hoped they would find in life. I sealed the envelopes and put them in a safe.*

That powerful experience had been in the back of my mind when I suggested the president write a letter to his daughters. And when the article came out, I sat down and wrote another letter—this one to Rabbi Jeffrey Segelman. I told him how his words had resounded through the years, stayed in my heart, and sparked an article that millions of people had now read.

I am so grateful for the inspiration you gave me these many years ago and proud to share it, I wrote.

Recognizing how someone has contributed to your life makes you feel deeply just how interconnected we all are. The rabbi sent me a gracious thanks, but I was probably more moved by writing the letter than he was by receiving it. Marty Seligman was right—a very sincere expression of gratitude makes you happy. His studies found the glow could linger (and even fight depression) for several weeks. And here I was, several *years* later, still feeling good about a gratitude letter.

Following in Seligman's positive-psychology footsteps, a number of academics have started to do gratitude research—some of them setting up rubrics and definitions for what makes us feel grateful to another person. I'm not sure I agree with all of them. For example, one popular line of reasoning holds that we feel

---

*Fortunately, the ethical wills sat in the safe until each boy turned eighteen, at which point I gave them the missives on their birthdays. No harm at that age having a letter saying how much Mom loves you and what she hopes for your future.

more gratitude when something is costly—whether in time, effort, or money. So we thank the friend who drops us at the airport when he's going anyway, but we're much more grateful to the neighbor who goes out of her way to drive us. We also appreciate actions done voluntarily and altruistically—that is, the person didn't have to do it. One research survey I saw raised the question of how grateful you'd be to a person who jumped into a lake to rescue you if you were drowning. Very grateful, probably. But how about if he were a lifeguard? Would you be equally grateful to someone just doing his job?

Personally, once I've stopped coughing up water, I'm not going to be making a lot of distinctions about who dragged me to shore.

Sitting on that train, I thought that the best kind of gratitude is the one you feel in your heart, not your mind. The rabbi I wrote to had given his advice as part of his job, but I was grateful for the wisdom and power of his words. All the techniques that Marty Seligman recommended—journals and photos and letters and visits—were just ways of helping us get into the moment and see the beauty of the world and the people in it. Amtrak isn't known for inspiring epiphanies, but looking out the window, I felt a deep sense of bliss.

My new grateful attitude hadn't improved the weather this winter, but I'd started to bring my own bit of sunshine into every day. My efforts to live gratefully were starting to add up. The first month of my project, I'd made saying thanks to my husband into a daily game, but now it was completely natural—and made us both feel good. I was still writing regularly in my gratitude journal, though three times a week seemed like a better rhythm for me than every night. That way it remained exhilarating, rather than a chore.

Looking for the positive in every event had changed my attitude—and it was also fun. I felt liberated to understand that it wasn't events that made me happy but how I chose to frame them. Whatever happened in a day or week, with my husband and children, with passing incidents on the street, I had more control than I realized. I could decide to feel annoyance and torment—or I could decide to feel joy. It still required some conscious effort, but gratitude was helping me to feel the joy.

PART TWO

SPRING

MONEY, CAREER,

AND THE STUFF WE OWN

We can only be said to be alive in those moments
when our hearts are conscious of our treasures.

—Thornton Wilder

CHAPTER 5

How Diamond Rings Shrink and Memories Grow

Grateful . . . to learn that I don't need "stuff" to make me happy

So glad for experiences that I can remember

Lucky to jump off the wanting-more treadmill

Being grateful for the people in my life over the last few months was changing my experiences and my view of the world. As I looked around my house, I wondered if the next step should be appreciating all the *stuff* around me—like photographs and furniture, artwork and knickknacks, new TVs and old toys. I liked most of the things I already owned, but I didn't feel like thanking any of them. I wondered if it was *new* stuff that made us grateful.

So on a Saturday afternoon when Ron had office hours, I headed over to Bloomingdale's—in the name of research, of course. The fitting rooms were crowded in the clothes departments so I went for the quicker pleasures of housewares. Prettily patterned dishes were on sale, and even though I didn't need them, I happily bought half a dozen yellow cereal bowls. Very cheerful! And how about new velvety towels? Some pastel colors would brighten our bathroom and look lovely with the new pale-green sheets I also bought (no-iron to make my life easier). Drawn to a display of cooking tools, I snagged a ceramic paring knife with a bright teal handle for only nine dollars. Given the price, I could buy two. I left the store laden with big brown shopping bags. It had been fun to buy, but as I walked home, the bags felt very heavy.

By the next day, the purchases weighed even heavier.

I wanted to be grateful for my new stuff, but the zing I'd gotten from buying was already gone. Most of us do our part to keep the consumer economy thriving. We buy when we're happy and buy when we're bored. Walmart boasts that most Americans live just six miles from one of their stores, but suburban malls are closing down as online shopping makes our desire for instant gratification even more instant. Very late one night, I bought a decorative pillow from my favorite home-and-accessories site, One Kings Lane. No reason to wait for daylight to shop. The immediate rush from that *Buy* button was so satisfying that I bought another pillow two nights later. And that was just the start. The UPS delivery guy was at my door so often I felt like I should serve him coffee.

Online retailers have sales in the hundreds of billions and they're soaring to the stratosphere. But once we get all that stuff, what do we do with it? The editor at a women's magazine once told me that her best trick to increase newsstand sales was the cover line "Get Organized!" I went over to the drugstore to see if that wisdom still held, and sure enough, half a dozen magazines offered tips to declutter storage spaces, organize closets and cabinets, and enjoy a neater home. I bought the one that promised techniques to tame clutter—as if our belongings were wild animals that needed to be whipped into shape. It's not just magazine editors who know that our possessions start owning us, rather than the other way around. The Container Store, which exists solely to sell products that let us sort, store, and stow away stuff, is a $750-million-a-year success story.

Writing in my gratitude journal after my visit to Bloomingdale's, I tried to extol my purchases, but I couldn't work up much genuine feeling. The cereal bowls were fine for serving Rice Krispies, but I had the feeling that in the long run, they wouldn't add much snap, crackle, or pop to my life.

The next day, I got in touch with Tom Gilovich, a behavioral economist at Cornell who has done years of research on the connection between how we spend money and how happy we are. His big finding is that the objects we buy—cars, computers, and big-screen TVs—can seem exciting for a while, and you might be delighted the first time you watch *Avatar* at home in 3-D. But material possessions are never quite as satisfying as we think they'll be. His research found (over and over again) that people get more lasting joy from experiences than from objects. Taking a vacation at the beach, going to a concert at Carnegie Hall, or throwing a family barbecue in the backyard is likely to bring an enduring satisfaction that the TV (alas) does not.

The problem with stuff is that we get used to it. We want something and want it, but as soon as we have it, we stop noticing or stop caring. It's the same problem of habituation that I mentioned earlier. We're not ingrates—we're just creatures of our nerve cells, which respond vigorously to new stimuli. When those brain neurons see something new, they get all charged up, but when they recognize a familiar form, they fire less frequently. From a survival standpoint, that makes sense. You don't have to pay much attention when there's a steady state, because things that have been around for a while are less likely to cause danger. So the neurons can stay quiet. But a new arrival on the scene, whether person or possession, is reason for full alert, and our neurons respond appropriately. *Quick! Look up! Is that flying object a bird, a plane, or Superman?*

The stimulation of those nerve cells firing makes us feel excited and alive. It's a good feeling, so we constantly seek out the unexpected stimuli that will get them charged. The state of heightened attention that once worked to keep us safe from charging tigers now makes us eager to buy home accessories online at midnight. Smart marketers (like those at One Kings Lane) change their sites frequently so our brain cells never fall into adaptation mode. In other words, all the pretty pillows flooding into our house aren't really my fault. My neurons light up at what's new and tell me buying is the right thing to do.

Trying to battle our natural adaptation, we keep shopping and acquiring in what is clearly a game with no end. According to Gilovich, the possessions you accumulate just raise your expectations for more, and you're really no better off than when you started. I dubbed it the Porsche in the Garage Syndrome in honor of a guy I knew years ago who talked endlessly about wanting a Porsche 911 Carrera—the smooth handling, the sleek lines, the admiring glances from people driving Hondas! He finally splurged and was completely thrilled the first time he slipped into the soft leather seat and roared from zero to a hundred in ten seconds. (Forget the speed limit—it's a Porsche.) But after a few weeks of driving, he got as annoyed as always when traffic was heavy or he couldn't find a place to park. The magic chariot he had dreamed about was now just a car sitting in his garage that needed an oil change. And who fantasizes about that?

I first experienced a version of the syndrome when I was a little slip of a girl taking ballet classes—and the head teacher announced that I had mastered the pliés and pirouettes well enough to advance to a class *en pointe*. Toe shoes! I couldn't have been more thrilled if Baryshnikov himself swept in and carried me away in his arms.

But my mother objected, worried that toe shoes would ruin my feet. I cried that she was ruining my life. I begged. I pleaded. I tried to explain that if I had toe shoes, I would be forever happy and joy would reign in the universe. One day when I stayed home from school with a sore throat, I imagined that if I had toe shoes, I would tie them on to lie in bed and immediately feel better. In my mind, they acquired the powers of pixie dust.

My mother finally gave in, and the day we bought the first pair remains vividly in my mind. The pink satin ribbons felt like gossamer in my fingers, and I strapped them lovingly around my ankles.

The thrill lasted—at least an hour.

Though the pointe shoes remained silky smooth and sweetly pink, they lost their magic. If I'd loved ballet, it would have been different, but it was only the toe shoes I loved. (I always knew that when I grew up, I'd be more likely to write stories about a prima ballerina than become one.) As with most possessions, they had more power when I wanted them than when I had them.

So is there a way around the syndrome?

The obvious answer is to keep upping the ante. When you're

tired of the Porsche, get a Ferrari. When toe shoes lose their lus-
ter, try . . . tutus? The problem is that it doesn't work. Psychologists call it the "hedonic treadmill." You buy one thing you want,
and when it's not quite satisfying enough, you buy another. And
then another. Each may be fancier or more expensive, but the
cycle never stops. You can keep upping all you want, but each
time you set a new baseline, the urge for more starts all over
again. As Professor Gilovich explained, "You reach one target and
you want another."

My friend Lauren prepared for the follies of habituation when
she got engaged some years ago and her now husband gave her a
fabulous diamond to mark the occasion. The first time she flashed
her four carats at me, I gasped.

"Your ring is huge!" I said.

"Everyone tells me that it gets smaller as you wear it," she said
with a laugh.

Diamonds being one of the hardest minerals, you wouldn't
expect them to wash away like grains of sand. But our eyes adjust,
so Lauren knew to be ready for an ever-shrinking stone. I hadn't
seen her in a while when we had lunch again not long ago. Her
sparkling ring caught my eye and I told her that I'd almost forgotten how gorgeous it was. She looked surprised and held her hand
out in front of her, as if studying the stone for the first time.

"I never even notice it anymore," she admitted.

The not noticing anymore is why it's so hard to be grateful for
the things we own. I happened to walk by a shiny Apple store the
day the iPhone 6 was first released, and long lines of people
snaked around the corner, eager to replace the gizmo they had
with the gizmo they wanted. Apple sold ten million phones in the

first three days, and at least that many millions of people will probably line up when the next model is released. (They may be in line right now.) Whether it's Apples or cereal, you can get heartburn trying to keep up with the next new thing you hope will make you happy.

Gilovich had recently expanded his work to examine the connections between the stuff we buy and how grateful we feel. He did a variety of experiments to find out what purchases could inspire gratitude, and his conclusion was that stuff—however fancy, shiny, or expensive—just wasn't going to do it. Then he compared how people felt about money they'd put toward a material possession versus money they'd used for an important experience. Where did they get the most gratitude bang for the buck?

"By and large it's not an acquisition that leads to gratitude," he told me. "People report feeling more gratitude for their experiences than for their material possessions. If you think about meals you've had with family members, great concerts you've seen, vacations you've had, you are much more likely to feel grateful that it was money well spent."

I asked Gilovich why it is (beyond habituation) that acquisitions don't make us grateful. He pointed out that experiences define us in a way that objects really never do. You might like to think of yourself as a hiker, a skier, a dancer, or a concertgoer—and you can relish activities that support that image. But my friend Lauren would be horrified (and probably never talk to me again) if I referred to her as the woman with the big diamond ring, and a guy who tries to impress with his Porsche just comes across as sad. Enduring happiness—the kind that veers all the way to gratitude for life—needs something deeper and more substantive.

Psychologists talk about the "endowment effect"—which means that once you possess something, you start to attribute all sorts of advantages to it. People given an inexpensive trinket like a pen or mug during an experiment immediately think of it as theirs and don't want to trade. But even that only goes so far, because one big problem with trying to be grateful for stuff is that you're always comparing what you own to what someone else does. You may be excited when you buy a new laptop computer, but when a friend shows you that hers is faster and lighter and makes animated movies better than Pixar, yours no longer seems so perfect. Some of your pleasure goes out the window. You could have bought a better one!

The same kind of comparing doesn't happen with experiences. "The phenomenon of keeping up with the Joneses is much less pronounced with experiences than with material goods," said Professor Gilovich. Experiences are personal enough that you don't need to compare. If you liked the concert you went to at the Hollywood Bowl, you don't care that someone else had a good time at a nightclub. And if a friend stayed at a fancier hotel in Fort Lauderdale, you can shrug it off, content with your own memory of beach volleyball and romping in the waves.

It also turns out that it's much easier to romanticize an experience than a possession. If your car keeps breaking down, it's just frustrating and hard to find any positive spin. "Whereas you can have a miserable vacation and come back and say . . . yeah, it rained the whole time, but we stayed in and we played Scrabble and we bonded," said Professor Gilovich with a laugh. He told me about one experiment where people who were going to Disneyland were asked about how much they looked forward to the trip.

All of them were excited and talked about how great it was going to be. Interviewed at Disneyland, they were much less happy—the lines were endless, the weather was hot, and the food was expensive. Interviewed after they got back, they once again had a positive report—the family loved it and everyone had fun.

"You're grateful for how you remember an experience rather than what actually happened," Gilovich said.

Those positive memories are much more pronounced with experiences than with stuff. With big data important to research these days, Gilovich's team looked at reviews on websites like TripAdvisor, CNET, and Amazon, coding people's comments for expressions of gratitude. Many more grateful words spilled out when people recounted experiences like going to a restaurant or vacation spot than when describing purchases like clothes or electronic equipment.

Gilovich told me that while other researchers have looked into what it means to feel gratitude toward another person, he was more interested in "untargeted gratitude"—that sense of being connected to the cosmos and happy with the lottery of life. From the personal interviews, questionnaires, and reviews, he was convinced that experiences outranked purchases on just about everyone's gratitude scale. He was also planning to come up with experiments to determine whether he could induce a "virtuous cycle." That is, could enjoying an activity that made you grateful also make you less materialistic . . . which made you even more grateful? He admitted that he hoped his research would nudge people along that road.

"If you're trying to increase your gratitude, tilt toward experiential consumption," he said. "We don't always realize how materialistic we are and how much of our environment we've turned over to nonfulfilling enterprises like shopping malls." One advantage of experiences is that they connect you to other people in a way that material goods rarely do. Gilovich pointed out that you're probably not going to feel very grateful when you drive solo in your car to a big mall with a giant sea of asphalt around it. When you feel isolated, life doesn't seem as good. But when you've had a great experience with friends or family or out in nature, you feel grateful to the cosmos that provided it. Gratitude-inspiring events are very personal, but they almost always fall into the category of *experiences*. You can't buy cosmic gratitude in a mall.

Professor Gilovich's position that you should spend on experiences rather than stuff is gaining steam. After we spoke, I went online to buy a gift for a young couple I knew who were about to get married. Their wedding registry had the usual kitchen tools and wineglasses, but they also had a honeymoon registry for the trip they planned to Hawaii. I signed up to give them a day of scuba diving with a private instructor—figuring that would ultimately make them more grateful than a high-speed juicer. Professor Gilovich would approve of the increasingly common "experiential registries" where instead of requesting china and crystal, couples ask for a day of hot-air ballooning, a weekend at a B and B, or a champagne dinner. And it's a wonderful change. Silver place settings tarnish, but a memory keeps its polish and, with time, gleams more and more.

A gratitude-inducing, cosmos-connecting experience doesn't have to be artistic or high-minded. A tech guy I know has season tickets to the San Francisco 49ers and describes football-season Sundays as "the days I'm grateful to be alive." He is fine with working hard all week, but he is over the moon when he sits at the forty-yard line at Levi's Stadium (no dress code required) cheering his heart out. "I don't have a Rolex, but I'll always have my football games," he told me with a laugh.

But we have to be a little careful about commoditizing experiences and turning them into just one more object to acquire. A friend of mine recently got back from a week in Venice, where she stayed at the elegant Hotel Cipriani. She'd selected the spot after reading *1,000 Places to See Before You Die,* described on Amazon as "the world's bestselling travel book." When it was published in 2003, the book became a number one *New York Times* bestseller and has since given rise to a flood of similar titles that seem to create their own hedonic treadmills.

I expected my friend to tell me about romantic gondola rides, glorious churches, and fabulous food. Instead, she had a different approach.

"Venice was lovely, and I can check it off the list," she said. "We knocked off two other spots in Italy while we were there, too."

"Terrific," I said with a laugh. "If you live three hundred more years, you'll make it through the whole book."

Actually, it would take even longer, since a new edition has two hundred additional trips. How could my friend, or anyone else, expect to savor her joyous adventure in Venice when the taunting goal was just to get on to the next exploit in Vienna or Venezuela? We have to be careful about becoming experience junkies, where we are wanting more and appreciating less.

Behavioral economist and Nobel Prize winner Daniel Kahneman has said that it's hard to talk about what makes us happy because there are two different parts of ourselves to please—the experiencing self and the remembering self. The experiencing self lives in the present and takes in everything that happens in the 86,400 seconds in a day. The remembering self is a storyteller, weaving some small portion of those experiences into memories that become who we are.

The Roman philosopher Seneca said, *Things that were hard to bear are sweet to remember,* and we've all had experiences that seem miserable while we're going through them but make us grateful later.

A couple of summers ago, my husband and I went hiking in the Austrian Alps with our younger son, Matt. We trekked each day through verdant mountainsides where cows grazed lazily and wildflowers stretched in all directions, and at night we lodged at cozy inns where we devoured delicious dinners and snuggled down in comfort. The perfect trip—until day four. We spent the morning scrambling up a challenging mountain, which took us from alpine fields to rocky cliffs, and after lunch, inspired by the extraordinary scenery, we finally got to the top and could see in the far distance the pretty red hut where we would spend the night. Matt found the path to take down to the valley—and I saw his expression grow concerned. He searched for a few minutes to see if there might be an alternate trail. There wasn't.

"It's kind of steep, but I'm sure we'll be okay," Matt said, leading the way.

The narrow trail cut into a mountain with sheer rock on one side and a precipitous drop of several thousand feet on the other.

In other words, any misstep and I'd tumble off the mountain and never be seen again. Given that I can be clumsy, that seemed as likely as not. Some handholds and a cable had been cut into the rock, and I clung to them miserably, afraid to move. But I had no choice. Going back wasn't an option and the path was much too narrow and treacherous for anyone to hold my hand or help me. I could stay in place and burst into tears (my first choice) or figure out how to get through.

I concentrated, focusing on every footfall. Ron walked protectively behind me while Matt scampered ahead, and every couple of minutes he stopped and called out encouragement.

"Ten more minutes, Mom, and we're off this thing completely," he said at one point.

Looking ahead, I knew his timing was excessively optimistic, but I was grateful for the coaxing. Half an hour later, when the path grew wider and the sheer drop turned into a gentle incline, Matt raised his arms in victory.

"We did it," he called out.

Seeing me tired and tremulous, he took my backpack and slung it over his chest (his own was already on his back).

"You don't have to carry my pack!" I said.

"I like it. I'm balanced," he said cheerfully.

For the next few minutes, he walked next to me, telling charming stories, singing little songs, and whistling (quite literally) a happy tune. I felt like crying again, but for a different reason.

"Thank you for getting me through," I said.

If a researcher had called me during that descent, I would have had to admit that it was one of the most terrifying moments in my life. Happy? Grateful? Not in my vocabulary just then. But afterward, I was elated to think about what we'd done and filled with gratitude for my solicitous son. It didn't take long for the remembering self to kick in. When we all sat down on the terrace of the hut with our large lemonades, Matt said, "What a cool day of hiking!"

"Incredibly cool!" I agreed. With the descent behind me, I could appreciate how beautiful the hiking had been. And I'd done it!

In the mountain escapade, my experiencing self was miserable and my remembering self felt all the satisfaction—but it can work the other way, too. Say you have dinner at a new restaurant where the food is luscious, the service luxe, and you and your beloved canoodle over every bite. Your experiencing self gets two hours of sensual delights, and as you dip into the crème brûlée, you might feel very grateful for the rich pleasures. But for the final course, the waiter spills coffee all over your favorite silk blouse and when you go to leave, the checkroom has lost your computer bag. Was it a good evening? Kahneman would say those two hours of indulgence—each of the 120 moments—actually happened and can't be taken away. But your more powerful remembering self feels churlish. After going to the dry cleaner and trying to recover what was on the computer, you may give up crème brûlée altogether.

Professor Kahneman has found that the ending of an experience has an undue effect on our overall memory of it. So, for example, if you have a medical procedure that ends with a burst of pain, you'll remember the procedure as much worse than if that same pain occurred in the middle. And he found that the remembering self isn't affected by how long an event lasts. What matters is its intensity—its high points and low points. Those neurons that make anything new and different stay in our minds can work to your advantage. For example, taking several short trips in a year is likely to give you more peak experiences—and grateful memories—than one long but unremarkable vacation.

A couple of days after I learned about all this, I was walking outside with my friend David when we got caught in a sudden downpour.

"This is going to be funny later!" I said as we raced for cover, getting soaked. Once we were inside, I explained about the experiencing self versus the remembering one.

David nodded thoughtfully. "Okay, but which one should you try to please? Which makes you more grateful?"

An interesting question, because gratitude can flow from every part of our (different) selves. Expressing gratitude in the moment makes life more positive for the experiencing you. And if the remembering you manages to put a positive glow on something that happened in the past (hello, alpine hiking!), you get to be grateful all over again.

Thinking about Kahneman's research, it struck me that "stuff" improves our well-being only if it taps into the remembering self. The objects that we most cherish are probably connected to a memory, like the perfume bought on a trip to Paris or the outfit your baby wore on his first birthday. Sometimes the provenance of an object—the love with which it's given and the gratitude we feel—provides a sheen that lingers. But that's not an excuse for keeping a lot of clutter. Your remembering self can shimmer with gratitude for the joys of your wedding day even without the prompting of a slightly yellowing lace-and-pearl gown hanging in the attic. Even when we think we are grateful for what we possess, it's often the bygone experience that we want to have and hold.

Science and research can always win me over, so I thoroughly accepted the idea of spending on experiences rather than stuff. But something kept nagging at me. Ah, yes, the voice of my frugal and prudent mother. Ever practical, she had always believed in putting hard-earned dollars toward possessions that lasted. She considered vacations and parties and fancy evenings out to be fleeting frivolities that vanished with the wind. "Spend on things you'll see every day," she lectured me when I was younger, claiming that's what her mother had taught her, too. My mother rarely traveled, but she had great sofas.

I now understood that Mom was right about investing in things that endured—she was just wrong about what endures. Sofas get old and stained, and the problem with spending on objects you see every day is that you stop seeing them. Possessions recede into the background, but experiences stay vivid in our memories. Maybe the vacation you took to Miami extended only five days, but you can't really measure by clock or calendar. If it becomes part of your memory and part of who you are, it can make you grateful forever. Short-lived? Not at all. Poignantly, when my dad got very ill at the end of his life, I sat with him in the hospital, holding his hand and reminiscing about what had made him happy. He talked about his children and his wife and even described one of their very rare trips—a cruise to Alaska. He had glowing memories of glacial scenery and dinner under the stars. On the list of what made him grateful, he never mentioned the furniture.

Ron and I raised our children in the suburbs of New York, and once they had grown (sigh), we decided to make our move to the city. I had gotten tired of seeing the same walls and wanted something new. The house sold quickly, at which point I panicked and an odd *reverse* habituation set in. Now that they wouldn't be mine anymore, I looked with new eyes at the pretty wallpaper, the graceful fireplace, and the library-like bookshelves. How could I have grown tired of them? Our big basement and attic contained endless items saved from our children's childhoods—finger paintings Zach created in nursery school, homework Matt aced in first grade, at least twenty pairs of tiny blue Keds sneakers, and T-shirts from every season of Little League. I had trunks, file cabinets, chests, and boxes full of treasures.

"Why are we selling this house?" I moaned to my husband one night. "We raised our children here."

"Yes, but we're not selling our children," he reminded me.

I selected a few items to save (Zach's third-grade report on the Mayans made the cut) and took pictures of others (all those cute stuffed animals)—and then I got ruthless. I brought boxes of clothes to the Junior League resale shop and left huge bags full of blankets and quilts and cookware for the veterans' charity. I gave away hundreds of books and donated the boys' outgrown clothes and skates so others could use them. I finally understood that it wasn't the frayed baby blanket that made me grateful but the memory of the sweet baby who used it. The day we moved, I stood by as every single item I still owned was piled into a van. If you measured life by stuff acquired, mine had just driven away.

Once the house stood completely empty, Ron and I did a final walk-through—and felt strangely detached from the empty rooms.

"So it wasn't the house that made us happy—it was the people in it," I said as we closed the door for the last time. All the things I'd given away didn't matter, because I got to keep what did—the memories of birthday parties and laughter and family hugs. We decorated our new apartment in Manhattan with clean, minimalist lines, and people who visited marveled at the spare, open feel. One friend twirled around and said, "I feel like I can breathe in here!" I also liked being able to breathe.

In a study out of Baylor University, researchers in the Department of Psychology and Neuroscience found an inverse connection between stuff and gratitude. They concluded that "materialism has been consistently related to lower levels of life satisfaction." Instead of trying to fill the psychological holes of the soul with jewelry and clothes and cars, it's better to use gratitude to make the emptiness disappear altogether. As an extra bonus, people who are grateful are less likely to yearn for the stuff that ultimately won't add to overall well-being, anyway.

The idea that stuff, stuff, and more stuff won't make us happy seems to be catching on. According to *The Wall Street Journal*, a peak in clothes buying occurred in 2005, when Americans bought an average of sixty-nine garments per person. *Sixty-nine garments?* Even counting every pair of black tights I own (and I do own a lot of them) that seems stunning. By 2013, we were spending more but buying less—down to sixty-three garments. Instead of bragging about their endless purchases, fashion bloggers were now heralding the "minimalist closet" and Instagramming photos of half-empty shelves. The idea was to have less so you could appreciate more.

Though on board about the value of experiences over stuff, I realized that a few of my possessions *did* make me grateful. Ron and I both love art, and my terrific friend Margot Stein, an art dealer with an extraordinary eye, has found fabulous lithographs for us over the years that we could afford (only because she was so generous in pricing for us). Every morning when I walked into my living room, I stopped to look at my favorite prints, and they always made me smile.

I wondered if art might be an exception to Professor Gilovich's rule about experiences inspiring the most gratitude. But then it occurred to me that art *was* an experience. Whether I looked at interesting images on my wall or in a museum, I interacted with them. Surely other objects crossed that line to being experiences and so didn't fall prey to habituation or hedonic treadmills. I know a guy who collects classic guitars—material objects, maybe, but also instruments with a legacy that he shares every time he strums the strings. Comedian Jay Leno keeps 130 cars and 93 motorcycles in his garage (actually a hangar next to an airport), and each one has a key in the ignition because he drives them. "I never thought of it as a collection," Leno once said, explaining that he just kept the stuff that made him happy—whether it was a $1.2 million McLaren, a vintage Bugatti, or a Chevy.

Leno saw the cars as an experience in themselves, but possessions can also *create* experiences. When my terrific book editor Jill and her husband bought their first Volkswagen Jetta, they didn't care about heated seats or a turbocharged engine—only what the car let them do. Suddenly they could visit far-flung family on weekends or drive friends home from dinner parties at their apartment in Queens. ("We might feel bad asking them to come out here, otherwise," Jill explained.) For a vacation, they hopped in the Jetta and explored the countryside. The pleasure wasn't the car, but the adventures the car brought them.

My husband has a collection of vintage American postage stamps that he started as a kid and has expanded ever since. I walked in on him late one night as he studied a recently purchased 1858 five-cent Jefferson stamp under a magnifying lens, his eyes bright with excitement.

"You look like a man in the throes of passion," I said.

"I wouldn't trade my wife for a stamp—but this stamp does give me a lot of pleasure," he admitted.

So maybe we can experience the cosmic gratitude that Gilovich described through objects that inspire passion. We're grateful when we feel a real connection—whether to a person, an experience, or a postage stamp. I could be grateful for the few objects that crossed over to experiences (or allowed them), but otherwise, I needed to take the lesson I learned when we moved— I was likely to be better off with less stuff than with more.

So I found the receipts for my velvety towels, pale-green sheets, and yellow cereal bowls and headed back to Bloomingdale's. The salesperson was nice about accepting returns. I kept the ceramic paring knife because I didn't have to be grateful about everything I owned. Once in a while I just needed to be able to cut the cake.

CHAPTER 6

Money Matters—or Maybe It Doesn't

Grateful to get a new perspective on money

Thankful to discover how I can make myself luckier!

Grateful to stop measuring myself with money and just think of its practical value

When I told my husband that I was going to focus on money this month for my year of gratitude, his lips puckered as if he'd just bitten into a bitter lime.

"Talking about finances never puts you in a grateful mood," he said.

"That's why I'm going to work on it," I admitted.

My husband uses various apps and computer programs to organize our savings and investments and expenses, and every couple of months, I ask him to print out the statements so we can go over them together. It never ends well. As a general rule, I get a shocked look on my face and say, "Is that *all*?"

"What number were you hoping for?" he asked me last time.

I didn't really have one in mind. Just . . . more than that.

So my new springtime resolution was to be grateful for what I had in the bank rather than what I didn't. I decided to start by getting a little perspective on money—because it turns out that how grateful we are for what we earn is *all* a matter of perspective.

Standard economics says a dollar is a dollar and it doesn't matter how you get it or how many of them your neighbor has. But the newer breed of behavioral economists point out that how satisfied we are with our salaries depends a lot on what those around us are making. They've done studies and surveys and found that given a choice, most people would be happier earning $100,000 if their neighbors were taking in $75,000 than getting a raise to $110,000 if everyone else around earned $200,000. And asked to look at three years of salaries, most people would rather see the sum start modestly and go up every year, rather than start higher and go down. And they choose that even if the total over the three years was *less*. Apparently, when it comes to money, we may have dollars, but we don't always have sense.

A couple of years ago, a thirty-year-old bond trader named Sam Polk wrote an op-ed in *The New York Times* that many found infuriating. He explained that he had walked away from Wall Street after he got a $3.6 million bonus and was angry that it wasn't more. "My guess is that ninety percent of Wall Street feels like they're underpaid," he explained later. He admitted that instead of seeing his salary in the context of the world as a whole, he was comparing himself only to the guy at the next trading desk. It's pretty easy to decide that Mr. Polk was completely delusional. But behavioral economists say that we all have a similar response (though smaller bank accounts).

Bond trader Polk understood there was something wrong. He decided he had a money addiction and realized that he was on a treadmill that would never make him happy. When he got off, he told one reporter that instead of setting some bizarrely high goal, "my challenge is to accept with total gratitude the life I have already."

I discussed this with my husband, who glibly suggested that I didn't have Polk's problem—because if I were addicted to money, I'd probably have a lot more of it. But we agreed that before we sat down to go over our finances this month, I would try to figure out what number would make me content. My theory was that I didn't need a lot to feel grateful. I just needed enough money so I didn't have to think about money.

Trying to get a bigger view, I discovered that roughly one-third of the world's population lives on less than two dollars a day. Most of the poverty is in sub-Saharan Africa, so any of us living in a developed country should wake up every morning grateful for the good luck of where we were born. Back when I'd written those magazine articles with actor Matt Damon, I'd become interested in his charity, Water.org, and even spent time doing a project for them. Unlike many celebs, Damon wasn't just a figurehead—he had been truly shocked when he learned that some 760 million people on the planet lacked access to clean water. Changing that became an important mission for him (and the subject of our first article together). He regularly went on late-night talk shows from David Letterman to Jimmy Kimmel to explain the need for toilets and running water. But he knew people would rather hear about his latest red-carpet escapades.

"How many times can you repeat that a child dies every minute from a water-related illness?" he asked me wryly. On the one hand, he knew he couldn't say it enough. On the other, he realized we don't easily relate to the deprivations of extreme poverty. Accustomed to turning on a tap, we find it hard to imagine being in the sandals of someone who has to walk miles to a well.

Looking for comparisons that were slightly easier to grasp, I discovered that economists at the United Nations International Labour Organization had taken a shot at figuring out the world's average wage and came up with $1,480 a month, or just under $18,000 a year. That's a bit more in a range we can imagine. (The calculation came with endless caveats and complications and counted only people who got a salary.) When the number crunchers at Gallup took a shot at finding median household incomes all over the world, they spun out numbers from a low of $673 per year in Burundi to highs of more than $50,000 a year in Norway, Sweden, and Luxembourg. The United States and the UK came in somewhere around the $40,000 mark.

Putting those together, I figured that the average person living in the United States (or the UK) had a standard of living about twice the world's average. But as Garrison Keillor taught us in his stories from Lake Wobegon, we all expect to be above average. And like the guys on Wall Street, instead of comparing our standard of living to the whole world and feeling grateful, we compare ourselves to the person down the street and feel slightly bummed out. Unless you're Mexican businessman Carlos Slim, frequently number one on the billionaires list, there's someone better off than you. Think how poor Bill Gates and Warren Buffett feel in the years they slip to numbers two and three.*

---

*Bill Gates recently was back at number one, and with the grateful view his philanthropy has provided, he probably only cares how he can use that money for good.

I have a delightful friend I'll call Abby who is pretty and fun-loving with a sexy style that has always attracted men. Happily married now, she had stayed good friends with a guy she dated years ago. Through a combination of smarts (which he has) and extreme luck (that, too), he had become wildly successful. He picked Abby up one day to take her to lunch, and as they sat in the backseat of his limousine, he opened the latest issue of *Forbes* to point out his name on the list of the four hundred richest people in the world. She congratulated him, but he continued flipping the pages of the magazine—and a moment later, he exploded in indignation when he noticed one of his competitors listed twenty places ahead of him. "How could that jerk possibly beat me!" he exclaimed.

Since she had been his friend well before he became a master of the universe, she had a perspective on just how far he'd come. He obviously didn't. Having a global business, an adoring wife and children, and fabulous homes in various locations around the world wasn't enough—he wanted to be twenty places higher on the *Forbes* list.

Why do we sabotage ourselves that way?

It's easy to laugh at Abby's *Forbes* friend or be revolted by the Wall Street bond trader (before his reform), but on our own more modest levels, most of us are probably guilty of the same cutting comparisons. We feel a pang that the people next door can afford a bigger house or a fancier car or are remodeling the kitchen. You don't want a Viking stove so you can boil eggs faster, but you want it because it costs more, and darn it, you deserve it. (I've happily kept my GE Café stove, thank you.) A friend of mine says that the curse of living on the Upper East Side of Manhattan is that everyone she knows is richer than she is and eager to flaunt it. But no matter where you live, you can always find someone who has more money.

A lot of people have done research into money—how we make it, how we feel about it, how it makes us feel—and some of the most interesting research I came across had been done by Paul Piff, an engagingly bright social psychologist now at the University of California, Irvine. Piff recognized how readily we overlook the advantages we've been given. In one of my favorite experiments, he invited people to play Monopoly—and made it very clear that the game was rigged. One of the two players (chosen randomly) started with twice as much cash as the other, earned twice as much for passing Go, and rolled two dice instead of one to move around the board twice as fast. Piff noticed that the "rich" players quickly took on signs of dominance, smacking their pieces (they always got the Rolls-Royce) aggressively around the board and celebrating (smugly) each success. When asked to describe the game afterward, the winners pointed out how clever they had been to buy certain properties and earn their victory. "Almost nobody attributed their success to the initial flip of a coin that got them into their position of privilege," Piff told me with a laugh when we had a long and animated conversation about his work.

Even when there's no question that the world has been rigged in our favor, our instinct is to explain that we deserve what we got. Did the winning players appreciate that they had started with $2,000 instead of their opponent's $1,000, or that they received $200 rather than $100 for passing Go? Well, sure—but that was less important to the outcome than how brilliantly they had played (or so they claimed!). Piff said that our minds tend to make sense of positive experiences in terms of internal attribution. "That's antithetical to gratitude, which says I'm not necessarily entitled to the good things I have, but I'm lucky to have them."

An old Ray Charles song has the line "If it wasn't for bad luck . . . I wouldn't have no luck at all." Funny, but also profoundly true about how most of us mistakenly feel. There's no real answer to the question, "What am I worth?" so we take whatever we currently have as the baseline. From there, the only way to go is up, and if that doesn't happen, we bemoan our bad luck. But it never occurs to us that some of our good fortune is also at least partly luck—and we should be grateful for it. Instead of thinking it unfair when something goes wrong, shouldn't we just be grateful when something goes right?

Piff created the Monopoly game for its obvious real-world parallels to so many people—from offspring of privileged families to just about anybody who has been helped along the way to wealth and doesn't want to admit it. Piff told me that he remembered watching CNN sometime after the Wall Street bailouts and hearing interviews with guys cavorting with their colleagues in bars. They all explained that they had succeeded because of their own business acumen and know-how and that the bailouts had nothing to do with it. That the Treasury Department was spending up to $700 billion to save the situation that these guys had screwed up didn't seem to affect their reasoning.

"Wealth gives rise to an increased focus on oneself and a decreased focus on the external environment," Piff said. "There's a bias to construe the good things that happen in terms of what you did to deserve them." And to forget to thank the people who helped you succeed.

Fascinated by how money changed people, Piff did another study to compare the driving habits of people in expensive cars (like BMWs) versus economy models (like Toyotas). In California it's against the law not to stop at a crosswalk, but watching at one busy intersection, he found that 50 percent of the people driving the BMW equivalents didn't pause for pedestrians. Every one of those in modest cars followed the law and stopped.

Between the BMW drivers and the Monopoly players, it became pretty clear to him that money gave people an undue sense of entitlement. Appreciative of others? Not very much. Their increased self-focus and self-satisfaction got in the way of compassion and sometimes plain-old ethics. Told that a jar of candy was being saved for little children doing an experiment in another lab, most people didn't touch it, but wealthy folks took whatever they wanted. Yup, they would steal candy from kids. Other studies have shown that the rich donate a smaller percentage of their earnings to charity than those less well-off. Piff suggests that people who feel entitled to everything they have are less likely to share it.

Which is where gratitude comes in.

Piff said that a "gratitude intervention" worked to mitigate the sense of entitlement and help people "focus on what the world has done for them, rather than just what they've done for the world." Even simple reminders could have a significant effect. Having people think about assistance they'd received from others at some point in their lives might lead them to be more cooperative—and less likely to take candy from children.

I teased Piff that he had become the rock star of social psychology—a talk he gave on money and entitlement has been seen some 2.5 million times on YouTube.

"If I'm going to be a rock star, I have to do something about my hair," he said with a laugh. "But really I think so many people watching is a testament to how resonant this issue is."

He was the first to say that most wealthy people have probably done a lot to contribute to their own success. "But we've all also been helped by others—even if it was just a parent who changed your diaper. A sense of gratitude changes your orientation from an internal focus to an external one and reminds you that the world has been good to you."

Back during the 2012 campaign, now senator Elizabeth Warren said in a speech that "there is nobody in this country who got rich on his own." She urged gratitude for the advantages of doing business in America—the police and fire departments that protect our factories, the highways that let us move our goods. President Obama tried to make a similar point, but his slightly mangled version ("you didn't build that") became a Republican rallying cry. Once the politicking died down and the election was over, most people would probably agree that any businessperson living in America started with an advantage that many around the world would be happy to share. Beating your chest and announcing, "I built that!" could seem—unseemly.

But money remained a very touchy subject. I now mentioned my gratitude project to just about everyone I met, and the responses were almost always positive. The unlikeliest people (including a cabdriver) told me that they kept gratitude journals, and most others concurred with the idea of being more grateful for family, friends, and everyday life. When I tentatively brought up money, though, gratitude didn't come into the picture. People told me how hard they worked and that they'd earned every dime. I didn't doubt it, because I felt that way myself. But if we're all playing a rigged Monopoly game, shouldn't we be a little humbler, and more grateful to the people, the country, and the circumstances that gave us our advantage?

I went to discuss it with my friend Dr. Henry Jarecki, who is a generation older than me and one of the smartest people I know. He began his career as a psychiatrist, then moved into business, eventually starting many different companies and selling them for a fortune. He lives in an eighteen-thousand-square-foot town house in Manhattan, owns two islands in the British Virgin Islands, and has a private pilot to fly him to his other residences. His further riches include a wife he's been with forever, four devoted sons (three of them successful movie directors), and legions of friends.

Since he's deeply thoughtful and reflective, I wondered if he had avoided the trap that Piff perceived of "internal attribution"— that is, assuming you deserve everything good that has happened to you. So I plopped down on a chair in his office and asked him if he felt grateful for his truly wonderful life. I wasn't surprised that he took a moment to think about it.

"Who would I be grateful to?" he asked finally. "Don't you have to be grateful *to* someone?"

"You could be grateful to the cosmos for all the twists your life has taken," I suggested.

He didn't dismiss the idea. Instead, he talked about how much of life is random. In his view, we are all surrounded by thousands of moments of chance. You have to be prepared and attentive so you can grab opportunities when they come. And then you need to work hard and apply yourself, with what he referred to as "focused energy." But even with all that, serendipity plays a role in any success.

"I ask myself regularly whether I got here by luck or skill," he said with a slightly abashed smile.

Recognizing the role of luck can be uncomfortable for most of us, but Dr. Jarecki did it with great delight, rolling off story after story of the people he met by chance who helped him along the way. "Randomness plays a bigger role than any of us want to admit," he said. Using simple math, he explained that in much scientific research, an event is described as less likely than chance if its so-called P value is less than .05. "Each of us probably has a hundred or a thousand events that occur in a day or a week, so if you multiply that by .05, you see that the probabilities of the unexpected are very high." Those events could range from running into an old friend on a street corner (amazing that we're both here!) to finding a business opportunity that made you rich. Dr. Jarecki thought his attentiveness to detail (obsessiveness, actually) allowed him to see "lucky" possibilities that others might miss. But Piff would have been pleased that a guy who has a pilot on staff to fly his own private Falcon 7X was able to look outward as well as inward to explain his success.

Thinking about the connections between luck and gratitude, I read some books and articles by Richard Wiseman, a professor at the University of Hertfordshire who holds a chair in the study of the Public Understanding of Psychology, the only such chair in Britain, if not the world. He's also a magician, suggesting that it takes some wizardry to help the public understand psychology. Wiseman became fascinated by what makes people "lucky" or "unlucky," and he eventually decided he could help people change their luck. Part of luck, as Dr. Jarecki suggested, was simply pay-ing attention to your surroundings. Another part was believing you're lucky so that you're open to good things happening. In one experiment, Wiseman asked volunteers to look through a news-paper and count the photographs. The people who had described themselves as unlucky flipped carefully through every page, counting. The lucky ones finished in seconds—because they no-ticed the big ad on page two that said, "Stop counting. There are 43 photographs." Lucky people also noticed the ad in another experiment that said, "Tell the experimenter you have seen this and win 250 pounds"—which the unlucky missed.

We're likely to be grateful when good scenarios occur, but maybe we can also make them happen. Imagine, for example, that you're out of work and headed to a coffee shop to get advice from a former colleague. As you arrive, you notice a twenty-dollar bill on the ground, and since there's no way to identify the owner, you happily tuck it in your wallet. Well, that's nice. You start to feel a little lucky. Your friend hasn't arrived, so you sit down alone and chat with the man at the next table, who is also alone. He laughs at your stories about searching for a job and ultimately gives you his card and says to call if he can ever help. Turns out he's an executive at a company where you'd love to work. You wait for your friend a little longer, then leave happy that the world is on your side. You'll call him tomorrow.

The same day could happen a different way. Anxious to meet your contact, you rush into the coffee shop and never see the twenty-dollar bill. You're too tense to talk to your neighbor so never know that your dream job is just a hello away. When the person you were to meet doesn't show up, you slink away, embarrassed and dispirited. How can you be grateful to the world when good things never happen?

However we get it—luck, lottery, cleverness, or hard work— money has a complicated connection to gratitude. Numerous studies around the world have shown that beyond a basic level, more money doesn't increase well-being. In the United States, the cutoff is said to be about $75,000 (toss in a bit for inflation) and above that, whether you're earning $300,000 or $100,000 matters only marginally.

Okay, that's a nice fact to toss around at cocktail parties and to make us all feel better, but is it really true? I have yet to meet anyone who says, "I'd like to be happier—so I need less money." I heard one researcher explain that people with bigger and fancier homes were happier with where they lived than those in less lush dwellings, but he rushed to add that the mansion dwellers weren't happier *overall* than others. But what does that mean? If you're happier with your house and your higher-paying job and your ability to eat in nicer restaurants, aren't you . . . happier?

I doubted there was some grand conspiracy among psychologists to slant their findings and convince us that money doesn't matter. It seemed more likely that they were mixing up happiness and gratitude. The extra money did make people happier on a day-to-day basis. But it didn't affect how they scored on tests that measured a deeper sense of well-being.

So in that way, the psychologists were right. "Well-being," as I knew from Dr. Martin Seligman, is much deeper than superficial happiness. It's affected mostly by the experiences we have and the joy we feel, the people around us and the love we feel. Dr. Seligman had discovered that our well-being goes up when we feel more gratitude. And here's the tricky point—we don't feel more gratitude just because we're rich. In fact, gratitude is sometimes helped by scarcity. You wouldn't say a crust of bread makes you happy, but if you're starving, getting a few crumbs makes you very, very grateful.

A sociologist friend of mine at Columbia University says most people think their lives would improve if they had one more room in their houses and 10 percent more in their paychecks. He finds it amusing that we don't imagine forty-room mansions or million-dollar paychecks. A lack of imagination? More likely we figure we're fine, we're okay, and if we could just improve things around the edges, we'd be even better. But being grateful for the current situation is a much better road to happiness than looking for that extra room or additional 10 percent. The problem comes back to that earlier finding that we judge ourselves against our neighbors and friends. Gratitude—stopping to appreciate the goodness already in your life—can prevent a toxic bout of envy. And few emotions are *more* toxic than envy.

Some years ago, the company where I had then worked for several years was acquired in one of the disastrous mergers happening at the time. (Remember AOL Time Warner? This was similarly bad.) I received some options in the new company, and once it was legal to sell, they turned out to be worth about $30,000. Hooray—an unexpected bonus! But then I learned that the executive I reported to—who had put together the deal— cashed his options for $30 million.

"He doesn't deserve a hundred times more than everyone else!

This is an insult!" I said to Ron, leaning furiously over the banister in our house while he sat calmly in a chair below.

"It's not an insult—it's thirty thousand dollars," said my ever-reasonable husband.

"I'm not selling them for that price," I roared.

"It would be a very substantial amount of money to get," Ron said, trying one more time.

I insisted we hold on to the options until they went up, which might make the whole thing seem more fair. They didn't go up. They plummeted to the point where they were worth a big round zero. I learned several things from that experience. First, when the guy who makes the deal sells his options, you should, too. Second, never compare—just appreciate what you have. But most important, I learned to marvel at the attitude (mine, of course) that turned a windfall into nothing—first in my mind, then in my bank account. A different mind-set that included a dose of gratitude at that point, and I'd have an extra $30,000 right now (plus interest).

Looking back, I'm embarrassed that I had ever been so ungrateful. Median household income in America is just over $50,000 a year, and about a quarter of the households are getting by on less than $25,000 a year. Only about 4 percent earn $200,000 or more. What had I been thinking? Like Piff's Monopoly players, I'd been given a double bonus for passing Go and forgot to say thank you.

But it's not the amount that really matters. I'd feel the same way if the sum had been half as much or twice as much. Behavioral economists say that financial losses bother us more than equivalent gains make us happy, so I suppose that's one reason the lost money has haunted me. But far more important was how I'd let myself use money as a measuring stick and a way to value my worth. I didn't want to do that anymore. Being grateful for what I had required seeing dollars in a purely practical light.

"What would you do if you had more money?" I asked my husband.

He thought about it for a moment and then shrugged. "I can't really think of anything. I have everything I want."

"Wow, that's crazy. Really?"

"Yup. How about you?"

"There's no *stuff* I want," I said, having learned my lesson about possessions the previous month. "But for other things . . ." I hesitated. Needing more money and doing everything possible to get it had always seemed like a given. But if money stopped being a measuring stick and I didn't let it define me, then the mighty dollar lost its power. Like Ron, I had what I needed and I suddenly didn't know how a bigger bank account would make me more grateful.

I'd been learning a lot from reading the Greek philosophers, so I decided to check out which ones had something to say on this subject. I dipped back into the world of Epicurus, who believed that having enough, but not too much, was a source of pleasure. Wanting more just caused trouble. *Nothing is enough for the man to whom enough is too little*, he said. (Very few of his original works still exist, so most of his thinking was reported later by followers and fellow philosophers.) I wrote that quote on an index card and tacked it up over my desk to remind myself that enough really was enough.

Epicurus taught the simple concept that pleasure was good

and pain was bad. (Can't argue with that.) It's ironic that "epicurean" has come to mean hedonistic or sybaritic since he warned against overindulgence. His view held that being grateful that you had enough brought pleasure while always wanting more increased pain. It occurred to me that you could draw a pretty straight line from his philosophy to the bond trader who angrily quit his job and the billionaire who wanted to land higher on the *Forbes* list. They had so many reasons to be grateful—but had missed the point and so lost the pleasure. Excess was the wrong goal.

A couple of days after deciding to add Epicurus to my list of Greek heroes, I chatted with a guy who lived a few miles away from me in Connecticut and had recently retired as a state police sergeant. He had a generous pension, but he was still on the young side and so had started being extra careful about expenses. He told me about calling the phone company to get a better plan ("they never let you know about it until you ask!") and finding a cheaper electrical provider. He missed working and getting a regular paycheck, but he was also happy to be relaxing a bit and enjoying time with his wife and their four children. "It's not like we're eating cat food," he said. "We have enough."

Enough could be my new mantra. *Grateful to have enough*.

Feeling good about my new attitude, I headed out to do some errands and stopped at the nearby cash machine. Five twenty-dollar bills spewed out as "fast cash" and I stuffed them in my wallet and rushed off. But then I made myself think about the fact that I could get money whenever I wanted. Wasn't that amazing? If I planned to be grateful for what I had, I needed something that would make the money feel meaningful.

Walking by a pastry shop, I remembered reading *A Little Princess* as a child and being enraptured by Sara, a little girl who has been left a pauper. Cold and hungry, she stared into a bakery shop window, and though she could smell the buns and imagine the warmth, she didn't have a penny to buy one. Reading that as a child made me cry and inspired my first stirrings of empathy. *Take one of my nickels, Sara! It's not fair that you can't buy a bun!*

When I got home now, I went to the basement to find my well-worn copy and reread it, tearing up all over again at the ending, where Sara learns she really is a princess with a large fortune. She's warm and pampered again and has nice clothes, but she can't forget being poor. So she goes to the bun lady at the bakery and says that whenever hungry children are staring at the window, she should invite them in and give them something to eat—and send the bill to Sara.

I closed the book with a sigh. It occurred to me that if I'd paid more attention to Sara when I was eight years old, I would have had the whole money-and-gratitude question nipped in the bud. Because a couple of studies have shown that money used altruistically is money well spent. In an experiment at the University of British Columbia, people walking through campus were randomly handed an envelope with a small amount of cash inside (usually five dollars) and were instructed to spend it by the end of the day on either themselves or someone else. Michael Norton, a professor at Harvard Business School who helped lead the study, noted that those who spent on themselves barely noticed it. Those in the group spending on someone else had to stop and think about what do with the extra dollars—and had a different kind of experience. The money seemed special, and at the end of the day, they reported a slight happiness boost.

Norton wondered if the positive effect of spending for someone else would also hold when people were struggling for basic needs. So he repeated the experiment in Uganda—and reported the same results. Spending on others makes you more satisfied than spending on yourself.

It reminded me of a night a couple of months earlier when Ron and I were walking through Times Square and he noticed a crumpled twenty-dollar bill stuck in the edge of a grate (dropped money is apparently more common than I knew). With hundreds of people passing by, we had no chance of finding who had dropped it, so he held it in his hand as we walked on. On the next block, a couple of street musicians playing reggae music attracted a crowd. We stopped to listen and then exchanged a long glance. We instinctively felt the money wasn't ours and needed to be shared. When I gave a little nod of agreement, Ron dropped the twenty in the musicians' collecting hat.

I can't really explain why that made us both so happy. I suppose we could have used the twenty dollars to buy grande lattes for ourselves or "I Love New York" T-shirts on the next corner. But if we did, we would have forgotten about the experience by now, just like the people in Norton's experiment. Instead, it's a story that's (obviously) stuck in my mind.

Dr. Seligman told me a similar story. Back before "forever" stamps, he went to the post office to buy some one-cent stamps on a day that postage rates went up. He stood in a long line, getting more and more frustrated, and when he finally got to the front, he bought the few stamps he needed. Then he had an inspiration—and asked for an additional ten sheets of a hundred each.

"Who needs one-cent stamps? They're free!" he called to the people standing in line. Delighted, he handed them out to anybody who asked—and in minutes all the stamps were gone.

"Best ten dollars I ever spent in my life!" Dr. Seligman crowed when he told me that story.

Being grateful for the money I had this month didn't leave me any richer or poorer than I'd started, but it did change my attitude. After years of being upset about money and worrying that I didn't have enough, I was glad to have a broader perspective.

I caught up again with my longtime friend Susan, who had started her own real-estate company a few years earlier. Always successful, Susan had just completed a very big deal, and I was unconditionally delighted for her. She had spent her entire career in a macho world (why do you think men build tall buildings?) and we joked that part of the pleasure of her big score would be all the men who heard about it.

"This one makes me happy," Susan admitted. "How are you doing?"

I shrugged. I didn't have the financial success that Susan did, but my concern about reaching the next rung of the wealth ladder had started to slip away.

"I earn enough so that I'm fine. I appreciate what I have. What else do I really need?" I asked.

Susan looked at me as if I'd just offered to jump naked into the Erie Canal. How could the person she'd known for so long behave this way? Having listened to me worry for years about money, she seemed somewhere between surprised and alarmed at my new position.

"Are you still working hard?" she asked worriedly.

"Very," I promised. Then using the lingo from multiple-choice exams, I said, "Think of being grateful for the present and working hard for the future as true, true, and unrelated."

A few days later, at the end of the month, Ron and I sat down with our financial statements. He seemed prepared for my usual moaning. But before I looked at them, I took out a checkbook.

"What are you doing?" he asked.

"I'm writing five checks for one hundred dollars each. I think the best way to be grateful for the money I have is to be able to give some of it away."

"To who?" he asked.

"That's going to be the fun part. We'll figure it out together," I said, giving him a kiss.

Money usually pulls couples apart instead of drawing them closer. But that night, our financial statement looked a lot better to both of us. And we looked better to each other, too.

CHAPTER 7

The Career Game—or What I Learned from James Bond

So grateful . . . that my job this year is writing about gratitude!

Grateful to learn about joy from talking to James Bond

Lucky that gratitude can increase my ambition and not detract from it

This month, I wanted to see how gratitude could change my attitude toward work and my own career. My recent exploits in exchanging stuff for experiences and rethinking money had worked to the good, but taking a new view of my own career made me nervous. Gratitude required appreciating the present rather than fretting about the next step. If I didn't fret, would there even *be* a next step?

Ambitious people don't usually pause to enjoy what they've achieved because they're fully focused on where they want to go next. In almost any profession, an enterprising soul can think of a way to move up—more money or a nicer office, a fancier title or an increase in power, a bigger box-office take or more followers on Twitter. When I mentioned to several people that my goal this month was to be more grateful for my current career as a writer, they looked at me dubiously, obviously concerned that if I took more pleasure in what I'd already conquered, I might veer off track and turn so happy-sappy in my work that I'd achieve . . . nothing more.

But I didn't think it would happen that way. In fact, quite the opposite seemed to be occurring. With gratitude so much a part of my life lately, I found myself more eager to face every day. I had started waking up earlier on these spring mornings and felt unexpectedly more energized. Seeing the good in the world made me want to be a participant. I decided to check with gratitude guru Robert Emmons, figuring that after a decade of researching the subject, he'd already encountered the question of whether gratitude would undermine ambition. I was right.

"I've often heard the concern that being grateful will make you complacent and lazy and not motivated to improve your lot in life," he said. "But our research shows just the opposite. Grateful people are more successful at reaching their goals than others."

I hadn't expected that gratitude would make me *lazy,* but I was somewhat surprised to hear that instead of detracting from a need to achieve, it would actually contribute. But how exactly did that work?

Dr. Emmons said that people who are "consciously practicing gratitude" gain a sense of purpose and a desire to achieve. To prove it, he had asked participants in one simple study to write down six things they wanted to accomplish in the next ten weeks. Some of them were then randomly assigned to keep a gratitude journal once a week. (Once a week? Piece of cake!) At the end of the experiment, Dr. Emmons determined that the grateful group made 20 percent more progress toward their goals than the non-grateful group—and seemed to be striving harder.

His calculations seemed questionable—how can you get 20 percent closer to earning a raise? But I didn't challenge the concept because the overall findings fit with my own experience. Dr. Emmons found that grateful people felt inspired to take action, not sit back passively.

From the outside, it seemed obvious that some people should be grateful for their careers. Who wouldn't want to be a movie star, a company president, a tech entrepreneur? But feelings of gratitude can't get written into the job description—no matter how fabulous. I first understood that in one of those dreamy moments in my own career, sitting in a posh suite in the Dorchester Hotel in London, talking to the actor Daniel Craig for a magazine cover story. He had just finished shooting the James Bond movie *Casino Royale,* and as hard as it is to believe now, the early buzz on him had been bad. I was the first American reporter he was talking to about being Bond, and when I walked in, he looked wan and worried.

We chatted casually for a few minutes while he ordered breakfast—the Japanese special from room service. When it arrived, he fiddled with his chopsticks and then looked at me with his icy-blue eyes.

"I don't want to be the one who fucked up the Bond franchise," he said.

He was physically exhausted from the grueling schedule of long days on the set and long nights at the gym, building the lean, muscular physique he wanted for his 007. Hunched over his breakfast, he didn't exactly look like an action hero. But he promised me that he cleaned up nicely in the film and looked darn good in a tuxedo. (After seeing the movie, I agreed.)

"All I really want to do now that this is over is hide on a lounge chair by a beach somewhere," he said with a sigh.

Craig knew his life was about to change, but he didn't know exactly how. Worried both about making a great movie for the fans and maintaining the integrity of his own career, he couldn't enjoy the moment. I was surprised to realize then (and now) that even for an actor on the verge of being a worldwide icon, happiness wasn't a given.

I noticed a bracelet on Craig's wrist and leaned over to see it.

"'The more joy we have, the more nearly perfect we are,'" I said, reading the inscription on the band.

Craig gave a tight-lipped smile. "It's from Spinoza," he said, referring to the seventeenth-century philosopher. "I love the idea that joy is what makes you perfect. It's a good philosophy to get through life, isn't it?"

At the time when the weight of the movie world seemed to be landing on his ample shoulders, his Spinoza bracelet reminded him to appreciate life and find its joy.

"Joy and gratitude. I'm not feeling either of them right now. But I plan to," he said.

Craig understood that he couldn't count on finding joy on a movie set—he had to bring it with him. Feeling gratitude in the midst of a pressured situation can help you calm down and gain some perspective, and Craig knew that mattered. In person, he got high marks for being edgy, sexy, tough, and insightful. But gratitude didn't come naturally, so he was smart enough to try philosophizing himself to happiness. Later, when *Casino Royale* made more money than any Bond movie in history, I hoped Craig felt better. It occurred to me that we could all use Spinoza bracelets to snap against our wrists, because whether you're a movie star or a cabdriver, finding happiness at work comes from inside, not out.

My year of living gratefully had gotten me so excited that I started to think about how I could share my findings. I wanted to let others know that they could make their own lives better *right now*. I had recently met a literary agent I liked, and on a blusteringly windy day, I walked across town to her office and told her what I had been doing.

"I love it," Alice said, getting the concept immediately. Then lowering her voice as if sharing a secret, she said, "It's so great how you changed your attitude toward your husband. My husband is amazing enough that I should be drowning in gratitude, but I get distracted and never tell him!"

"It's easy and it works," I promised her.

"Then you need to write about it," she said firmly. And just like that, we agreed that my own personal gratitude diary could become the basis for *The Gratitude Diaries*. My yearlong hobby was now also my job.

I'd spent most of the last twenty years with jobs that brought me to an office or a production studio, and now that I was writing full-time again, I missed having colleagues around. I couldn't share with anyone that my goal this month was to be grateful for my work. But I figured I could tell myself—and also discuss it with my close friend Robert Masello, a terrific novelist who lived in Santa Monica, California. Wry, smart, and endlessly funny, he had been making me laugh since we first met as young writers in New York. Whenever I called so we could commiserate about making deadlines or being stuck at the computer, he always cheered me up. In the many years that I traveled to Los Angeles regularly to produce TV shows, we had frequent dinners together. And since I had expense accounts then, we could even order dessert. ("We don't even have to split one?" Robert exulted once. "You mean I can have my very own tiramisu?")

Now I called Robert and told him I had a plan. I would start every day thinking of three reasons to be grateful for my job—and wanted him to do it with me. Seven A.M. on the East Coast, when I got up, equaled four A.M. in California, when he usually went to sleep. (Robert had been an insomniac for as long as I'd known him.) So we could write our lists at the same time, then tweet them or text them to each other. A gratitude chain across the whole country!

"Give me an example," Robert said warily.

"Okay, I'm grateful to be a writer today because I get to interview interesting people. I'm being paid to look on the bright side. And my new book will help people."

"My new book will help people only if they *don't* read it," Robert joked.

I laughed but told him that self-deprecating (which he did endearingly well) was out. Positivity was in. Sharing our encouraging thoughts about writing would elicit good vibes and make a day's work seem a little brighter. Our version of Daniel Craig's Spinoza bracelet.

"Come on, try it," I prompted. "You can come up with three reasons why you're grateful to be a writer."

"Sure I can," Robert said, getting into the spirit. "First, I can work at my own crazy schedule and never wake up to an alarm clock. Second, the popular girls who wouldn't go out with me in high school finally rue the day. And third is a discovery I made one afternoon while I sat in the park and watched other people rushing to get to their offices—being a writer is like being rich, only without the money!"

"You can needlepoint that one," I said, laughing.

Turning serious for a moment, Robert told me that he'd had his own epiphany about gratitude and work when he first moved to Los Angeles and got several jobs writing for network TV shows. They were the kind of high-paying, prestigious positions that a lot of people would kill for, but as a Princeton-educated, East Coast intellectual (he reads Chaucer for fun), he never quite saw the charm of his actual job, being story editor on the popular supernatural drama *Charmed*. He got frustrated sitting in the writers' room for hours and hours, brainstorming plot details, and one day, after his team spent about ten hours (or at least it felt that way) discussing the characters' motivation, Robert wanted to cast a spell and vanish into thin air.

"We were writing a TV show about three pretty women who were witches. How much motivation did they need? I started feeling very sorry for myself. Like my life was being wasted," he said.

Tired and irritable, he went to the men's room to splash cold water on his face. As he stared across the marble sink, a janitor came in, whistling happily, and as he wiped down the counter, he marveled to Robert about the beautiful day and how lucky they were to live in LA.

"Uh, yuh," Robert agreed, dabbing at his face with paper towels.

Still whistling brightly, the janitor went off to clean the toilets, and Robert turned and glared at himself in the mirror.

"I thought, *You spoiled brat!* I was probably earning more in an hour than that nice guy would make in a week, but he appreciated his job and I hated mine. What sense did it make that he was happier than me?"

Robert realized that whether cleaning toilets or writing a TV show (and no jokes comparing them), the actual job mattered less than the attitude he brought to it. Most work had both pleasures and drudgery, and focusing on the positives could change an experience from misery to joy. Being bummed or charmed about writing for TV was really in his own control.

"It was the kind of breakthrough realization you never forget," Robert said. "And I probably went at least ten minutes without forgetting it. Then I was back at my desk and in a bad mood all over again. But at least I knew I shouldn't be! That's progress!"

A couple of days after I spoke to Robert, I was contacted through my college alumni network by a guy in his early twenties who wanted career advice. I agreed to get together (who could say no?). He had what sounded like a solid first job at a digital advertising agency, but as we sipped our cafés au lait (my treat), he complained that the position wasn't much fun and some days dragged.

"That's why it's called 'work,'" I said, trying to make a joke.

"Yes, but I deserve better," he said, not amused.

Robert's word "spoiled" flitted through my mind, but I pushed it aside. I had been enlisted for guidance, not moral judgment, so I talked about the exciting directions digital ads might go. Instead of picking up on my positive approach, he griped about his boss ("He thinks he's so much smarter than me!") and his many late nights at the office. By the time we got to his lack of an expense account ("I'm stuck at Chipotle every day!"), his sense of entitlement was too much for me.

"You should be grateful to have this job at all!" I snapped.

Even as I said it, I felt my hair turning gray and whiskers growing on my chin, since I had obviously turned into some long-forgotten Depression-era great-grandpa. Being grateful for a job had real resonance back then, when millions of people out of work lived on stale bread and tinned sardines. But gratitude for a job didn't have much significance for a newly minted college grad with a supportive family (thank goodness for those) who thought he deserved to have fun from nine A.M. to five P.M.

After I left, it occurred to me that maybe my comment wasn't as old-fashioned as I feared. Men and women of all social and economic classes currently struggling to find work would, indeed, be grateful for a position, even if it wasn't perfect. "I've had people with three PhDs sitting where you are, crying because they lost their job," an office clerk told a social worker I knew as she submitted her unemployment papers. The anxiety remains for many, even if sardines don't.

But for those lucky enough not to have faced breadlines or collected unemployment insurance, gratitude for a job could be hard to find. When we asked people in the survey I did how grateful they were for a variety of things, "your current job" finished dead last. Only 39 percent expressed gratitude for their present employment. The number went way up for those who earned $150,000 or more, but even in that elite group, close to 40 percent said—nope, not grateful for my job. That's a big enough number to suggest we need some global changes in how people are treated at work (and I'll get to that). But as always, the main thing we can change, as my friend Robert realized, is our own approach.

When my sons were growing up, they used to talk about "being like Jeremy." They'd never met the guy, but they'd heard me talk about him (even back then) as an example of how to succeed in business by staying upbeat and grateful. At the time, I was the senior producer at a syndicated TV show and Jeremy was one of many summer interns we hired. With the relentless pace of a daily show, nobody had time to coddle them. Reporters asked them to pitch in with vital but humdrum tasks (*Log in that tape! Grab me some research!*), and the interns spent a lot of time huddled together complaining.

All except Jeremy. He thanked us for letting him be at the show. He felt fortunate to be getting experience. When reporters rushed to cut tape and make air, Jeremy offered to help, even if it meant making a coffee run. One night when I stayed late on a story, he asked if he could hang around in the back of the edit room and watch.

"You don't have to," I told him.

"But I want to learn everything I can. I really appreciate the opportunity to be here," he said.

At the end of the summer, we barely knew most of the interns' names, but we asked Jeremy if he'd drop out of college and come work full-time. He wisely didn't, but after he graduated, his career in TV took off. His grateful style had enhanced, not undermined, his ambition. The unhappy interns might have had reason to grumble (getting coffee and logging tapes can be annoying), but what did they achieve? Jeremy flipped the experience to see the bright side and gained a whole career. It's been a long time since I've spoken to Jeremy, and for all I know, he might have left TV by now and taken up life as an organic farmer. But it wouldn't matter. Everyone would want to pick fresh blueberries with him.

Any job has its good points and bad, but focusing on the negatives promises only a sour experience. Making an effort to zero in on the pleasures (however hard to find) can make most jobs tolerably sweet. We all notice Jeremys when we meet them—whether it's the one cheerful clerk at the drugstore or the helpful bus driver who reminds you of your stop. A positive spirit makes it more likely they'll get promoted or find a better position—because being grateful and spreading good vibes makes others want to help.

For some people, being upbeat comes naturally, but a lot of us have to work really hard at it. And that's where gratitude techniques can help. I learned one of them from Emily Kirkpatrick, the vice president of a nonprofit called the National Center for Families Learning, a literacy organization that I admired. Based in Louisville, Kentucky, Emily has three baby boys under age four (including adorable twins) and a husband with a high position in the state Republican Party. Passionate about both her family and her work, she often found herself too stressed to appreciate either one. "Optimism is not in my DNA," she told me when we had coffee during one of her regular business trips.

Driving home from the office most evenings, Emily found herself mulling over everything that had gone wrong in the day. Remember the psychologists who described the poisoned-berry theory of survival and how we're genetically programmed to focus on whatever is bad or threatening? Emily had that ability to the max—she'd be a big winner in the primeval forest. But ruminating every night on the one bad event rather than the five positive ones left her tense. So enough. She decided to turn the twenty minutes in the car into a time to recount every *good* thing that had happened.

"I had to fight at first to keep the right things in my mind," she told me with a laugh. "But after a while it became more natural." Instead of arriving home stressed and worried (as happens when you've focused on problems), the gratitude drive allowed her to decompress and get a positive mind-set. "I come into the house happier and filled with energy now, which is so much better for my children and me," she said.

Emily had done extremely well in her organization, but she had questions about the future—uncertainty about when the older president might step down, how the board would react, which direction politics might go. Would she leave at some point? Who knew? But now she consciously decided that even as she kept one eye on the future, the other would remain focused on being grateful for right now. Her twenty-minute gratitude drive each night was a clever way to do it. (If more people tried this approach, it might cut down on road rage, too.)

Tom Gilovich, the psychology professor at Cornell, said, "We strive to have great things, and then once we get them they're not so joyous. That's the downside of habituation." The achievements that make you happy at one point quickly need to be replaced by bigger and better ones, and that's true no matter what your field. If you have a small sales territory, you want to expand it. If you're running the division, you want to be running the company. But the position you yearn for may not be quite so satisfying once it's yours. As far as I could tell, the only way to avoid what Gilovich called "the remarkable power of adaptation" was with a big dose of gratitude for the right now.

When I got home from talking to Emily, I noticed a photo on my bookshelf taken on a triumphant night when I was the executive producer of *The TV Guide Awards Show,* then a big two-hour special on the Fox network. (We even had advertising on the Super Bowl that first year.) In the picture, I'm posed on the red carpet, slim as a reed, wearing a $12,000 silver-beaded dress borrowed from the designer and sparkling diamonds lent by a fancy jeweler on Rodeo Drive in Beverly Hills. My husband, handsome and equally dapper in a well-fitting tuxedo, has his arm around me. I'm smiling and look happy. But studying it now, I wondered—did I know to be grateful that night? I definitely appreciated the publicist who had snared me the diamonds, but mostly, my mind stayed focused on my obligations to the show and whether the ratings would live up to expectations. If I'd been keeping a gratitude diary that night, maybe I could have appreciated the good events a bit more as they happened. It would be a shame if gratitude for our careers existed only in the rearview mirror.

So how do we learn to appreciate the jobs we have now? There's certainly no question that it's worth trying, and no question that it's hard. An executive recruiter told me that he has started to encourage his clients to appreciate the job they're currently in and have faith that the next one will appear.

"You can almost hear the bell ring when they move from grateful to entitled, and all that does is piss off everyone they work with," he said.

He told me about one young finance guy who was so pleased when the recruiter helped him land a position that he sent a bottle of scotch in thanks. But he didn't drink it too quickly, since the guy began calling him regularly and asking what he could get next that would feel bigger, better, richer.

"I've been around long enough that I wanted to say, 'Hey, appreciate the job you have now because it may not last.' But nobody believes that."

I'd been thinking about gratitude when I watched the Winter Olympics earlier, because sports should be one area where achievement is pretty clear—you win gold, silver, bronze, or nothing at all. But the athletes' reactions at the end of an event seemed to have less to do with how they finished than with how they *expected* to finish. Some of the bronze medalists beamed and waved on the medal stand, thrilled to be there. Many knew that another hundredth of a second or so and they would have missed medaling at all. But certain second-place finishers looked devastated. World figure-skating champion Yuna Kim of South Korea had expected gold, so the silver medal around her neck probably felt like a lump of coal. Whether in sports or life, our attitude is affected by what might have been.

Back in 1892, the great psychologist William James understood that we live by comparisons rather than absolutes. He wrote about "the paradox of a man shamed to death because he is only the second pugilist or the second oarsman in the world. That he is able to beat the whole population of the globe minus one is nothing." An athlete can choose to look up at what she missed (like the gold medal) and feel defeated, or look down at others who achieved less and feel victorious.

Flipping regret to gratitude can be a matter of changing your basis for comparison. I watched a Canadian freestyle skier named Alex Bilodeau take a near-perfect run—then rush over to hug his disabled brother, Frederic, who stood on the sidelines, cheering wildly. Alex later told reporters that he felt lucky to be healthy and able to go after his dreams, while Frederic, who could barely walk, didn't have that chance. Gratitude for what you have doesn't come more heart wrenching than that. Or as life coach Tony Robbins regularly says at his famed weekend immersion seminars (meant to "unleash the power within"), if you trade your expectations for appreciation, the world instantly changes.

Athletes and stars who show a genuinely grateful side are endlessly appealing, as I discovered the year the popular TV show *Seinfeld* ended its network run. With his fame reaching crazy heights, Jerry Seinfeld had decided to step back and not do many interviews. But I had a prime-time network special on the fifty best TV shows of all time to produce, and I chose *Seinfeld* as number one.

When I called to let him know, Jerry sounded humble and gracious, saying how honored he was for the tribute. He marveled that his show had beaten out classics like *The Honeymooners* and *I Love Lucy* that he had watched as a child. Jerry agreed to appear on the special.

The day of our interview, he arrived at the studio all alone, no publicist, no entourage.

"Hi," he said, walking in the door. "Am I in the right place?"

The guy coming in looked very familiar to me, but for a moment, I couldn't place him. Had we gone to high school together? Summer camp? Oh, wait, of course. I felt a shimmer of recognition. Jerry Seinfeld had arrived. I'd watched him on TV for so long that he felt like an old friend.

He gave me a terrific interview and seemed deeply moved and appreciative. The number one ranking had the imprimatur of *TV Guide* (still a big deal back then), and Jerry marveled that he'd grown up reading it, so the next day, I sent him a big basket filled with *TV Guide* paraphernalia—umbrellas, mugs, T-shirts, sweatshirts, and even a little clock. I included a note that I was giving him a lifetime subscription to the magazine. He had just refused $5 million an episode to continue *Seinfeld* for a tenth season (and would eventually earn $3 billion in syndication) and surely didn't need my free subscription. But later that afternoon, my phone rang, and when I picked it up, someone said, "Hey, it's Jerry. Thanks for all the stuff you sent." He wanted to give me his home address to receive the magazine subscription.

"Let me say again how much I appreciate your faith in me," he said in that familiar voice that made anything sound funny. "Your calling *Seinfeld* the best show of all time makes me very happy."

My friend Lynn happened to be in my office that afternoon, and when I hung up, she stared at me.

"Was that Jerry Seinfeld calling to give you his home address?" she asked.

"Actually, he called to say thank you."

"I can't believe he called!" she said.

I agreed it seemed a bit surreal to have Jerry Seinfeld being grateful to . . . me. It was probably the first time I understood that even someone as hugely successful as Jerry Seinfeld cared about being appreciated. With his willingness to say thanks, my admiration for him soared even higher.

Trying to be grateful for your job is almost as tricky as being grateful for your spouse—because we have excessively complicated expectations for both. Just as we want the person we marry to be our lover, best friend, social partner, personal adviser, and soul mate, we similarly overburden a job. We want it to provide a good salary, a sense of identity, a community of colleagues, an understanding boss, a chance to make a difference, and an affirmation that what we do matters. Oh, and an easy commute. That helps too.

We launch into marriage with at least the expectation of "forever," but we have no such myths around a job. We'll stay until something better (hopefully) comes along. But this month, I came to understand that being grateful for your current job doesn't make you less ambitious. It just makes you happier—and probably more productive—in the moment. You can be grateful for the *now* of your career—and still soar in the future.

Tweeting every day with my friend Robert about our careers had been a nice idea, but we hadn't followed through. (Not everything pans out.) Instead, I'd used my gratitude journal this month to write reasons why I felt grateful to be a writer. I had a lot of entries, and as the month neared its end, I wondered if I would run out of reasons before I ran out of days. But one morning, I went to my desk in our apartment and started working on my book proposal—and the next thing I knew, it was three in the afternoon. Positive psychologists refer to that as "flow"—the exhilarating feeling of getting so immersed in an activity that you don't notice anything else. It can happen when you're painting, sewing, solving a math problem, creating a computer program, running, reading, doing yoga . . . just about anything that gets you fully involved. That night's journal entry would be easy. The next day, writing felt a little bumpier. But by the afternoon, I had finished what I needed to, and I looked down and smiled. I took out my journal again.

So grateful I get to work all day in furry slippers and pajamas! I wrote.

Maybe it wasn't earth-shattering, but we all have more reasons than we realize to be grateful for what we do.

CHAPTER 8

Getting Thanks (and No Thanks) at Work

Grateful to talk to the CEO who wrote 30,000 thank-you notes

Grateful to have received a thank-you myself from Clint Eastwood

Lucky to meet the Wharton professor who says gratitude is a good business move

Now that I could think about having gratitude *for* my job, what about a little gratitude *from* the job? Good luck with that. Going back to my survey, I discovered that expressions of gratitude were as scarce around most workplaces as the proverbial hens' teeth. Only 7 percent of people regularly said thanks to their bosses and 10 percent to colleagues. "Thanks"—whether sent up, down, or sideways—was rarely heard.

When Daniel Kahneman and his colleagues at Princeton looked at the daily activities that put people in a lousy mood (or cause "negative affect," as the academics say), they found that spending time with a boss topped the list. I can understand it—because who would want to spend time with someone who never appreciates what they do? Bosses who avoid expressing gratitude at work are wrong on so many counts that I hardly know where to begin. But some more of those survey findings make the point:

- ✧ 81 percent of people said they would work harder for a more grateful boss.
- ✧ 70 percent would feel better about themselves if a boss expressed gratitude.

Being appreciated is one of the great motivators on the job—even better than money. Researchers at the London School of Economics analyzed more than fifty studies that looked at what gets people charged up at work, and they concluded that you'll give your best effort if the work gets you interested and excited, if you feel that it's providing meaning and purpose, and if others appreciate what you're doing. Financial incentives can actually have a *negative* impact. You need to start with a fair salary, but being given direct payoffs for performance can undermine the intrinsic and personal motivations that really make us want to give our all.

Some tough-minded executives withhold saying thanks to the people who work for them because they worry that gratitude makes them seem less powerful. My friend Beth Schermer, an executive coach and consultant in Phoenix, Arizona, told me that she tries to encourage managers to show gratitude all the time. "But the comment we hear is 'I say thank you to my employees every week. It's called a paycheck,'" she said.

Beth has handled major political projects and smaller corporate ones, and she's masterful at getting people to work together. An energetic redhead with an endearing smile, she has a genial style that is matched by her summa cum laude intelligence. But the "paycheck" comment is a nonstarter. As soon as someone tells her that, she knows she's in for a challenge. Beth often advises CEOs to start all difficult interactions with "thank you," because there must be *something* the person has done right. "It usually makes the conversation go better, even if you're firing them," she said.

Even if a boss thinks otherwise, gratitude usually turns out to be a smart career move. In our survey, 96 percent of people agreed that a grateful boss is most likely to be successful, since people will rally behind her. Execs who assume that saying thank you or appreciating someone's work lessens their power are missing the point. Nobody gets to the top on their own. If you help enough people and give them positive feedback, there's a good chance they'll turn around and help you out, too.

Adam Grant, a professor of management at the University of Pennsylvania's Wharton School, divides people into three categories—givers, takers, and matchers. Takers try to get other people to serve their needs, and matchers always play a corporate quid pro quo—they'll help someone if they think they'll get an advantage in return. Givers contribute to others without looking for a reward, and they'll offer help, advice, and knowledge, share valuable contacts, and make introductions. In a dog-eat-dog situation, that givingness sounds like it could hold someone back, and sometimes it does backfire. But Grant found that givers can also end up on top of the heap. Those who combine giving to others with an awareness of their own needs can be the most successful on all fronts. They benefit others and advance their own interests, too.

Grant is the perfect role model for how a grateful and giving soul can end up a big star. He graduated Phi Beta Kappa from Harvard, completed his PhD in three years, and became the youngest full professor at Wharton (he got the position in his twenties and is still in his early thirties). His list of consulting clients includes America's coolest companies—Google, Facebook, Apple, and Pixar—as well as the World Economic Forum (and many more). He's one of the most popular teachers at Wharton, and his office hours can stretch for three or four hours since he will tirelessly give advice, answer questions, provide contacts from his huge network, and write recommendations.

Known for his willingness to help people, Grant had an almost legendary reputation for promptly responding to the two hundred or three hundred e-mails he received every day, a large percentage from people he'd never met. Having heard about his giving attitude, people asked him for connections, recommendations, ideas, and jobs. But when I first tried to reach him, an automatic reply popped back, explaining that he now got *thousands* of requests a day and simply couldn't answer all of them. The instructive e-mail offered general advice and links to some of the articles he'd written. Apparently, becoming famous as the guy who helped everyone required some boundaries.

I called some friends at Wharton to get a more direct connection, but before I could try it, Grant had already replied to my original request. Yes, he'd be happy to talk about gratitude with me ("Your book sounds wonderful," he said graciously), and he offered three different times that he was available to connect. Did any of them work for me? After I picked one, he confirmed almost immediately.

Usually I approach interviews as just casual conversations, but with the hyperorganized and efficient Grant, I wanted to be as prepared as he was (probably impossible—I could never match his extraordinary memory). I worked myself into a mild frenzy rereading his research articles and his interesting book *Give and Take* and writing out my list of questions. But I didn't have to worry.

"I know it's ironic for me to thank you for writing on gratitude, but it's a big and neglected topic—so thank you. I'm so glad you're doing it," he said two minutes into the conversation.

Bingo! The Professor of Giving was quick to give thanks—and of course I believed him. It made us both feel good—and reflected the kind of comment Grant thinks could transform the business world. People want to feel valued as human beings and will respond with greater creativity, engagement, and persistence when they feel other people are grateful for their contributions.

"A sense of appreciation is the single most sustainable motivator at work," Grant told me. "Extrinsic motivators can stop having much meaning—your raise in pay feels like your just due, your bonus gets spent, your new title doesn't sound so important once you have it. But the sense that other people appreciate what you do sticks with you."

So if gratitude makes people work harder and gives bosses a successful edge, why aren't companies havens of happy thanksgiving? It comes down to the same "we pay them with a paycheck" attitude that my friend Beth tries to fight. Grant said it was part of the old Protestant work ethic (or whatever ethnicity currently takes credit/blame) that says our expected role is to get stuff done, so why bother thanking someone? And there remains the problem of credit-grabbing, I'm-in-control-here managers who don't want to look like they need anyone else. "The problem with this excuse is that it's simply false," Grant told me. "There's a difference between being dependent on someone else and valuing what others contribute and who they are."

Early in his career (not that he's yet close to late in his career, or even in the middle), Grant consulted for a college call center where students spent hours on the phone, trying to raise money. Most alumni have a simple answer when they're asked for a donation—they say no—and being regularly rejected was dispiriting for the callers. Trying to figure out what could keep them motivated, Grant asked a student who had received a scholarship through alumni donations to come in and talk with the callers. The results were remarkable. After getting face-to-face thanks and seeing that their work had genuine impact, the callers were reenergized. They upped their efforts—and the average money they brought in went from about $400 to more than $2,000. That's *five times* as much in donations. From a thank-you.

"It's one thing to think that your job has a purpose, and it's another to meet a specific person who cares, appreciates, and values what you do," Grant told me. "The call center people got a new sense of their worth—not only on the job but as individuals."

Intrigued by the power of gratitude, Grant and a colleague, Harvard professor Francesca Gino, designed another study, where they asked professionals to review the résumé cover letters of students applying for jobs. After receiving the suggestions, the students asked for help with another letter. Some 32 percent of the professionals agreed. But when students added a single line to their note about the first feedback—"Thank you so much! I am really grateful!"—a full 66 percent stepped up to give them that second round of help. A simple expression of gratitude *doubled* the response.

Then came an even bigger surprise. After a student had asked for help, Grant had a second student do the same. If the professional had received the "I am really grateful!" reply, the willingness to help the second student soared from 25 percent to 55 percent. In other words, after they had been appreciated (or "socially valued," as Grant put it), people's *general* willingness to help doubled as well. "I never would have guessed that receiving a tiny note of appreciation would then make you more likely to help a total stranger," Grant said. "Gratitude is more powerful than we realize."

When *The New York Times Magazine* wrote a cover story about Grant, he forwarded the reporter forty-one grateful e-mails that he had received the previous week, mostly from students thanking him for his help and saying how he had changed their lives. "Most people would be thrilled to receive one note like that in a lifetime," reporter Susan Dominus marveled. Grant said he got dozens every week.

When I brought that up now, Grant was slightly abashed and said he had sent the e-mails only to help her, in case she wanted to contact some students about him.

"You mean it's not typical?" I asked him.

"It's fairly common," he admitted. "To me those notes are a barometer of whether I'm making a difference. I should be able to do something that benefits a few dozen people every week."

I thought only God or Bill Gates helped that many people in a week, but college professor Grant took it as a matter of course.

The thanks of others, along with the realization that his contributions mattered, stood as one of his greatest motivators—with a few caveats. Thanks that came accompanied by a bunch of other asks made him wary. ("Then I wonder—is this person more of a taker than I realized?") And while he understood a prompt thank-you as obligatory politeness, he liked when someone followed up two or three months later to tell him that something he'd done had a lasting impact.

When I asked Grant how businesses could show more gratitude, he admitted that finding a formula was tricky. "I think it's hard because what's the ulterior motive? You can't thank people in a Machiavellian way. People see through that and separate genuine gratitude from manipulation." He told me that one of the people who got it right was Doug Conant, the former CEO of the Campbell Soup Company. A couple of days later, I tracked Conant down. Like Grant, he was smart, thoughtful, and happy to discuss gratitude. Talking to the two of them, I felt like Alice in Wonderland (MBA edition) falling through the rabbit hole into the land of the Good Guys in Business.

Conant came to a struggling Campbell's in 2001, and business savants credit him with turning the place around—not just in profits (which soared) but also in reversing what Conant himself called "a toxic culture." Unlike many corporate honchos, who pride themselves on their personal power, Conant believed success depended on the people who worked for him. "I couldn't be in every room making every decision, so all the people in the company represented me. I needed their heads and hearts in the game," he said.

Conant tried to move away from the standard business model

of focusing on problems. "It's usually the ten percent of things that go wrong that get ninety percent of the attention," he told me—and he preferred to celebrate the 90 percent (hopefully) that went right. Despite our usual instinct that makes the bad outweigh the good, Conant wanted to change the mentality and focus on the cherries in the bowl rather than the occasional cockroach. And though he was responsible for a $2 billion company with twenty thousand employees, he made it personal—writing thank-you notes to employees for work done well. Doug and a staff member watched for positive news around the company, and when he heard about something he admired, he sent his thanks. He figures he wrote ten to twenty handwritten thank-you notes every single day, six days a week, for the ten years he was CEO. "If you do the math, that will take you way north of thirty thousand thank-you notes that I wrote," he told me. Celebrating what went right became the new corporate culture.

Conant didn't write just to executives—his notes went to workers at every level of the company. Many would never expect the CEO to even know they existed. Conant might have ended up with writer's cramp, but his leadership style is now quoted in Harvard Business School case studies. His warmth was not weakness—he had financial targets and scorecards and replaced 300 of the top 350 corporate leaders when he first arrived to have people whose values were in harmony with his. Half of the replacements were promotions from within. "My message was that Campbell's will show we value you as an individual, and you'll help lift us up by performing at a high level," he said. He watched as managers across the company got the idea and modeled his example of leading with gratitude.

A poignant footnote to Conant's personal, gratitude-focused style occurred in 2009 when he had a near-fatal car crash on the New Jersey Turnpike. As he lay in the hospital trauma center, cards started coming in from employees around the world—New Jersey and Texas, California and Canada, Asia and Australia. Sitting at his bedside over the next several weeks, his wife read the cards and letters aloud to him. Most mentioned a thank-you note that Conant had written to them years earlier that made them feel a personal connection. Getting words of appreciation from the CEO had been incredibly meaningful, and some still kept his note on a bulletin board at home or displayed on the refrigerator. Whether someone was in sales or production or packing crates at a distribution facility, Conant had seen them as real people. Now they thought of him as a friend or member of the family, and their hearts and prayers were with him as he struggled through surgeries.

"What goes around comes around. Now I've lived it, and that's what gave me strength," Conant told me.

As we continued to talk, I mentioned the praise Campbell's had received under his leadership for its advances in diversity and as a place that cared about life-work balance. Conant brought it all back to the same central core.

"The notion of gratitude cuts across all generations, ethnicities, and social or economic boundaries. Gratitude is universal, and it's the one thing that can pull us together," he said.

After we said good-bye, I felt unexpectedly warmed and happy—like I'd just slurped down a big bowl of chicken noodle soup. People could debate about whether nice guys finished first or last, but I'd started to believe that grateful ones were always winners.

Conant joined a great line of leaders who understood the power of appreciating people. When I wrote my first article for *Cosmopolitan* magazine at age twenty-two, I got a handwritten note from Helen Gurley Brown, the magazine's legendary editor. In florid script on very nice stationery, she thanked me profusely and said how very lucky *Cosmo* readers were to have me. Awed that she even knew my name, I tucked the note in a drawer. I still have it.

Ms. Brown probably didn't match Doug Conant in her volume of thank-yous, but she sent them regularly to photographers, columnists, models, and actresses. Writing from her office with its pink silk walls and leopard-print carpet, she developed an unusually loyal following. Her flair for making people feel appreciated wasn't the only thing that led to her extraordinary success—cleavage-baring covers helped—but it played a role. When she died in 2012, the *New York Times* obituary said her style of "winning the right friends and influencing the right people was squarely in the tradition of Dale Carnegie, if less vertically inclined." (It also noted that she was ninety, "though parts of her were considerably younger.")

Dale Carnegie, of course, wrote the multimillion-selling book *How to Win Friends and Influence People,* which has stayed stubbornly on bestseller lists more than eighty years after it first came out. A CEO I worked with once had taken the Dale Carnegie course and had his certification framed in his office. Every week or two, on a Friday afternoon, I'd get an e-mail that said

Dear Janice,

Thank you!!!

Sometimes he elaborated to:

Thank you for all you do!!

One of the key principles taught at a Dale Carnegie course is to give honest and sincere appreciation, and while I realized that he didn't yet have the "honest" and "sincere" parts down, at least he was trying.

Any expression of gratitude (however awkward) is better than nothing. A young litigator I know at a Washington, DC, firm works long hours—arriving by eight A.M. most days and often not leaving until near midnight. She's paid well, enjoys the challenge, and loves feeling that she's at the center of important cases. But she also hankers for the Conant touch—some personal appreciation.

"My managing partner *never* says thank you. It would mean so much if he did," she whispered one day when we were sitting in her office.

She'd recently argued a big court case and hoped her win might inspire some grudging gratitude from her boss. But he never said a word—just telling her she'd be on his team for the next assignment. Craving some more extravagant pat on the back, she stopped by his office later and gently pressed about how she was doing. He coldly replied, "You should know I'm satisfied. If I weren't, you'd be gone."

"That shut me up," the young lawyer told me.

The law partner probably thought that withholding thanks showed his strength. I think it showed his insecurity. The too-tough-to-be-grateful pose is wrongheaded, as Adam Grant pointed out, and while executives can get away with different styles of managing, gratitude by default (*If I haven't fired you, you're doing okay*) doesn't help anyone.

Thinking about it now, I realized that one of the most gracious thank-yous I ever got at work came from Clint Eastwood—whose tough-guy credentials go unchallenged. Shortly before his movie *Flags of Our Fathers* premiered, we spent a whole afternoon talking in his bungalow on the Warner Bros. lot. At the start of the visit, I mistakenly pulled into his personal parking spot. In Hollywood, taking a star's parking space is practically a capital offense, but Clint was gracious. He came over to my car window and politely introduced himself (as if I might not know) and in a soothing voice said, "If you just pull up a little, there'll be room for both of us."

After that, we ambled into his bungalow together like old friends. Once we sat down, the conversation ranged in all directions, from heroism and bravery and the devastation of war (themes of the movie) to his continued need to challenge himself. At one point, as the sun streamed in the window over his craggy face, he stretched his long legs across the sofa and admitted that his fame still surprised him. "Deserve's got nothing to do with it," he said with a wink and a wry smile, quoting a line from his movie *Unforgiven*.

When I finally left, I sat down on a bench in the studio lot and called my husband.

"Gotta say, honey, much as I love you, he's the sexiest old guy I've ever met," I said.

"You've left his bungalow, haven't you?" he asked anxiously.

"Sadly, yes," I teased.

Clint had been far more charming than I could have imagined, kind and cavalier, and extremely genteel. His musings were thoughtful and even profound. But now came the tricky part. Instead of the usual celebrity profile, Clint and I had agreed that I would write an article in the first person, in his voice. I'd never ghostwritten before, and several writer friends promptly called me to tell me their own bad experiences. You get no credit. The star makes crazy changes. He pretends he's done the whole thing himself. You get blamed for anything that goes wrong.

But a deal's a deal, so I wrote the article and sent it off to Clint. A day later, it came back—with a single word changed. And late that afternoon, Clint called.

"Thank you for what you wrote. I liked talking to you, and you did a good job. You got my voice. In fact, you got me better than I get me," he said.

"I'm so glad," I said, blushing furiously and glad that nobody was around to see.

"Well, thanks. I appreciate what you did. Really, thank you," he said.

When I met up with Clint again a couple of years later, he seemed much older and some of the glow was gone. But to me, he would always be the big star who was willing to say thanks. He knew that gratitude can make your day.

The best stars and bosses are willing to give thanks—but like everyone else, they like to *get* thanked, too. Once when she was writing a cover story for me on actress Drew Barrymore, longtime Hollywood reporter Jeanne Wolf called from the photo shoot to say that Drew had been great—helpful, easy, and fun to work with. She'd also looked adorable in one of the dresses she'd modeled, and Jeanne wanted to let her keep it. Clothes for photo shoots are usually borrowed and then returned, so giving the dress to Drew meant paying the designer the full price.

"I'm not sure it's in my budget," I said, since I was running the magazine at the time.

"Well, it should be. A little thank-you gift goes very far," Jeanne said firmly.

Reluctantly, I told Jeanne to go ahead. She called me back a few minutes later to say that Drew was thrilled, sent profuse thanks, and offered to do whatever was necessary to promote the issue.

"I won't say 'I told you so,' but I'm glad you listened to me!" Jeanne said gleefully.

Jeanne had the right instincts. Stars are paid plenty, and Drew Barrymore could buy any dress she wanted. But it probably made her smile to know that being upbeat and sunny on the shoot had mattered. People had noticed and appreciated, and the cute dress was a simple way of saying thanks. The flashy gifts studio heads dole out—cars for the whole cast!—can come across as bribes or publicity moves, rather than genuine thanks. Jeanne's gifts were smaller but from the heart.

People at every level need to know they're appreciated, and it doesn't take a $400 dress to send the message. When my sister, Nancy, held a top position at a nonprofit consulting company in Washington, DC, she gave out Kudos bars at weekly staff meetings to thank people for their various efforts and successes. As a tastier equivalent of gold stars, the treats seemed to do their trick—until the owner and CEO of the company called her in to complain that she never gave one to him. It took Nancy a moment to realize that he wasn't joking. Though he owned the company and everyone at the staff meetings worked for him, he still wanted kudos—chocolate or otherwise.

Now I understood why my husband the doctor got such a kick out of the little gifts patients brought him—the homemade pizza from an Italian family, the fruit baskets at Christmas, the bottles of Harveys Bristol Cream that we'd never drink. Curious, I went to our basement and found half a dozen hand-knit blankets that Ron had stashed away, made by elderly patients wanting to reciprocate his kindness and caring. A shakily crocheted green-and-orange afghan had a note attached: *Made for you, because nobody is sweeter to me!* The note, signed *Mae,* had little pink hearts. I dragged it upstairs and asked Ron if she might have been flirting with him.

"She's ninety-three, so I wouldn't worry," he said.

"But you love to be loved," I teased.

"Don't we all?"

General internists aren't motivated just by money or they would have chosen a different specialty. Knowing that patients recognize his dedication has always kept Ron going. Thanks aren't a substitute for proper pay, but they reinforce each other. Even Daniel Craig needed more satisfaction than came with the $3 million he got for his first Bond movie (soaring to $20 million by the third). He cared about doing the right thing by both the fans and the franchise and wanted to be appreciated. In that way, my husband was a lot like him (a compliment to both of them).

My college friend and roommate Anna Ranieri, a psychologist and executive coach based out of Stanford, has found that even in hot tech companies, a bigger bonus didn't trump being appreciated. "A company known to value the people who work there will attract good talent, and giving those people extra thanks will keep them from leaving for the start-up down the road," she said. Anna figured the best way to sell gratitude to occasionally arrogant executives was to let them see the advantages to themselves. Since gratitude blossoms in all directions, the boss who extends the thanks feels better about himself, too.

In other words, even in Silicon Valley, gratitude could become the killer app.

A few smart companies are starting to make gratitude part of their bigger game plan. Google is widely considered a dream place to work, and not just because of the pool tables and free lunch (though they help). Recruiters for the company have a list of "Reasons to Work at Google," and the top five include:

    ✧ Life is beautiful
    ✧ Appreciation is the best motivation
    ✧ We love our employees, and we want them to know it

I can't code, program, or do much other than use Word on a computer, but if Google would have me, I'm pretty sure I'd do a great job for them. Because when someone says life is beautiful and they appreciate and love me, well then, gosh darn it, I want to do whatever I can to make them happy, too. Who wouldn't? Being in a conference room isn't all that different from being in a living room (or bedroom), which means that love works better than fear at the office, and when you're upbeat, people want to be around you.

Professor Grant told me that cool companies including Zappos and Southwest Airlines (as well as Google) have peer-recognition programs in which colleagues can nominate one another for having gone the extra mile. "It basically ends up being a gratitude note, which comes with a small bonus from the company," Grant said. "Empowering coworkers to appreciate each other is one way of making sure that gratitude doesn't get overlooked."

And sometimes if you want to say thanks, you have to *really* say thanks. Our dear friends Jacques and Karen came to visit for a weekend at our country house, and they arrived with amazing hostess gifts—rich-tasting olive oil and luscious honey that they had lugged back from a vacation in Greece. Having a wide circle of devoted friends (not just because of the great gifts they bring), they had stayed for part of their trip with a couple they knew from London who owned a summer home on the Greek island of Crete. The long-planned visit occurred at just about the time that their host, Mark Sebba, announced his retirement from the online luxury retailer Net-a-Porter.

"If you need an example of gratitude in the workplace, it doesn't get better than what happened to Mark," Jacques said as we all swirled spoons into the amazingly wonderful honey. (We planned to pour it over yogurt, but couldn't wait.)

Company founder Natalie Massenet, a former model and fashion journalist, appreciated all Sebba had done to help her turn her idea into an online powerhouse. Wanting to say a very public thanks, she'd planned a black-tie farewell dinner. But testimonials are standard fare in business, so Natalie orchestrated a more elaborate and memorable send-off.

"Mark thought he was just coming to work," Jacques said with a chuckle. "Since it was his last week, he might have expected a cake from Natalie—but nothing like this."

"This" was a cross between a carnival and a rock concert, as thousands of employees across three continents and various time zones gathered into a grand production to say thanks. As Sebba stepped off the escalator into the large open-space office, throngs of his London-based employees greeted him, some cheering and waving signs, others standing on their desks and dancing. A hip-hop singer in a flowing blue gospel gown called out, "Welcome to your world!" and with a bouncing chorus behind him belted out a music-video-quality pop serenade. Acrobats flipped, samba dancers shimmied, and a steel-drum band played in celebration. Lyrics of the popular Aloe Blacc song "The Man," revised for the occasion, included:

> It's time to say job well done!
> You're the best you're the greatest one!
> Go ahead and tell everybody . . .
> He's the man, he's the man, he's the man!

A large video screen flashed live to Hong Kong, Shanghai, and New York, where other employees at offices and distribution centers joined in the well-choreographed farewell, singing and waving their arms with all the spirit and feel-good appeal of a Coke commercial. When Sebba finally got to his desk, Natalie Massenet smiled and handed him a cup of black coffee.

While the celebration came with a high price tag, even more impressive was the time and effort the employees devoted to making it work. With the time difference, some of those in outlying offices arrived in the middle of the night. Massenet posted the six-and-a-half-minute video on YouTube with the title: "Amazing surprise for the world's most loved CEO." She sent it to all her employees, inviting them to share the link but not mention that it came from Net-a-Porter since she didn't want it to seem like a publicity stunt. The idea of a company head showing extravagant thanks was so appealing that the video soon had more than a million views.

Expressing gratitude with gospel choir and singing global workforce is as wonderful as it is rare. But maybe bosses, owners, and various executives are starting to get the message that at work, gratitude works.

PART THREE

SUMMER

GRATITUDE AND HEALTH

Nature always wears the colors of the spirit.

—Ralph Waldo Emerson

A sad soul can kill you quicker, far quicker,
than a germ.

—John Steinbeck

CHAPTER 9

The Powers of Vitamin G

Grateful to learn how gratitude can affect our immune system and improve general health

Happy to find that gratitude can lower stress levels

Amazed to find gratitude helping my headaches

After cold and rain through much of May (which I didn't complain about, of course), the first weekend of June was full of sunshine and warmth. At our house in Connecticut, the change was so dramatic that I suggested to Ron that we switch immediately from heat to air-conditioning. "Or we could leave on both," I joked to my husband, who generally preferred having on neither.

He headed out to the garage to start moving the stored outdoor furniture back to the deck, and I followed to help.

"It's really a one-man job," he said, lifting a table that looked like it needed more than one man to move.

"You don't need me?" I asked, trailing behind him and carrying nothing.

"I always need you," he said, panting slightly from the heavy weight. "For example, it would be helpful right now if you mentioned how grateful you are to have a strong husband."

"That's tonight's journal entry," I said cheerfully. "*Very grateful to have a manly man around.*"

When he put down the table, he came over and gave me a sweaty hug. Though he joked about my year of living gratefully, we were getting along better—and having more fun together—than we had in ages. My positive attitude had changed our general mood. Knowing I'd be looking for the good in whatever he did (and not to criticize), Ron had relaxed. Before the year started, our relationship had been fine but a little frayed. Like most long-married couples, we had stopped noticing each other. Now I was paying attention and so was he. We still had arguments now and then, but we got over them quickly. In the past, we often took three days to resolve a disagreement. Now with a deep reservoir of grateful goodwill, we took three minutes.

After I'd devoted the first month of my project to being grateful to my husband and saying thanks for what he did, Ron had joked, "This has been nice, but when do I get my wife back?" But now that appreciating him was the new normal, he didn't want that old wife back at all.

Ron had also started to use my living-gratefully approach with some of his patients. He tried it first with a basically healthy but grumpy older woman who came regularly to his office, full of complaints and worry. At the end of one visit, after prescribing what he should and helping how he could, he gently said, "Before you go, let's spend one minute on reasons you have to be grateful." She had been startled. But with a little more prodding, she got the idea—and managed to say she was grateful that she could still take walks (even though her feet hurt) and visit with her grandchildren (even though she couldn't lift them). "Those are both good things to remember," Ron said. With that little nudge, her mood improved, and she left feeling generally better. Ron is more insightful about patients' needs than any doctor I know, and I liked that he'd now slipped gratitude into his black bag of tricks.

With his approach in mind, it occurred to me since gratitude was now making me happier, maybe it could also make me healthier. Emotions always affect our physical state. We get simple proof of that every day—our hands tremble when we're nervous and we can feel our faces flush (or turn beet red) when we're embarrassed. And how about that pounding heart when you're scared? Numerous studies have looked at how negative emotions affect health, and anger and stress have been implicated in everything from diabetes (stress alters insulin needs) to asthma attacks (distressing emotions could trigger bronchial constriction).

But what about the other side? If negative emotions make us sick, could positive emotions like gratitude keep us healthy?

I'd already discovered from Dr. Martin Seligman that writing a gratitude letter (and delivering it in person) could lower levels of depression for as much as a month. Other researchers have found that keeping a gratitude journal can lower blood pressure and improve sleep patterns. Wanting to know more, I called Dr. Mark Liponis, the medical director of the famed Canyon Ranch health resorts and an expert in what he called "integrative medicine." His approach involved integrating every part of the body and mind and connecting a positive approach to a healthy life. We had a cheerful conversation and he invited me to come visit, so a few days later, I took a very pretty drive up to the Canyon Ranch in Lenox, Massachusetts.

After the guard at the gate showed me where to leave my car, I walked across the idyllic grounds toward the restored 1897 mansion that now includes a spa and health center. Other than a few chirping birds, the surrounding scene was completely quiet and serene. Two women in terry-cloth robes smiled as they strolled by a flowering garden, and for a moment, amid the rolling lawns and clear fresh air, I felt like I had stumbled into the sanatorium in Thomas Mann's *Magic Mountain* (minus the tuberculosis, of course).

I paused at an expansive patio that had chairs arranged for contemplating the peaceful vistas of distant peaks. (Mann's mountain?) The tranquil environment seemed designed to make even the crankiest overachiever relax and appreciate the view, both literal and metaphoric. I'd arrived in gratitude heaven, without the dying part.

I went inside the mansion, and peeking into the dining room, I felt healthier just reading the menu, with choices like marinated tofu, salads with garbanzo beans, and a burger made with veggies, gluten-free oats, and pumpkin seeds. Instead of prices, it listed calories. A staircase led up to the health center, which felt more like a gracious corporate suite than a doctor's office.

Dr. Liponis came out almost immediately to greet me. In his mid-fifties, he was fit and handsome, his sport jacket and open-necked shirt the right cross between casual and professional. He brought me back to his office, which had the same stunning view that I'd seen outside.

"I love that you're writing about gratitude," Dr. Liponis said, his eyes lighting up. "Keeping perspective is a big part of staying healthy. You can't be optimally healthy if you're not happy."

As the head of medicine at Canyon Ranch in Lenox as well as the locations in Tucson, Miami, Las Vegas, and soon in Southeast Asia, Dr. Liponis regularly treated the worried well—people who were healthy but would like to be healthier. He explained that they were often disturbed about something that occurred in the past, which made them depressed, or worried about something in the future, which produced anxiety.

"Thinking about the past or future are really the only two ways people can be upset by the world," Dr. Liponis told me.

So when people consulted with him, he asked them how they felt that moment, *right now.* And before they could launch into grudges, worries, or frustrations, he tried to give them some perspective.

"Let's start by making sure all the limbs are attached," he said, patting himself all over for an example. "Okay, I've got two arms and two legs. That's a good start. I can see out of two eyes, and I'm breathing and not in any pain. I ate today and I'm not starving. With all that—holy cow, I guess I feel pretty good!"

I laughed, but I liked the point. Instead of worrying about the past or fretting about the future, we could all do ourselves a favor by taking stock of the present. Two arms, two legs, and eyes that could see (with contact lenses for me). But what was the connection between that positive perspective and good health?

According to Dr. Liponis, many of the mysteries about our health revolve around the immune system. He told me that one of the biggest discoveries of the last decade was how pivotal a role inflammation plays in modern illness—including heart disease, cancer, diabetes, Alzheimer's, stroke, and many others. Inflammation was a stress response of the immune system, caused when the white blood cells rushed to handle what they perceived as a problem.

Throughout most of human history, infections were the biggest health problems we faced. The immune system developed to fight those, and it got a lot of practice, since not too long ago, the person who could get over typhus, tetanus, diphtheria, and dysentery would survive and pass on his genes. Others would not.

You can see the immune system in action when, for example, streptococcus bacteria get into your throat, causing the ever-common strep throat. You notice inflammation, redness, and swelling at the site as the white blood cells rush over to gobble up the bacteria. They call their buddies to help make antibodies and release the necessary chemicals, and blood flow to the area increases. The numbers can be staggering—as many as 150 *billion* white blood cells circulating under stressful circumstances, three times as many as normal. The chemical interactions lead to redness and swelling, and it's not just your throat that hurts. You may get a fever and feel achy all over, since when the immune system is revved up, there's a system-wide response as well as a local one.

The white blood cells fight the infection but leave inflammation in their wake—which scientists are now discovering can be dangerous in itself. Dr. Liponis pointed out that patients who have been hospitalized for pneumonia have double the risk of a heart attack in the next six weeks because of the inflammation from the infection. "There's a very different list of what's killing Americans now than there was eighty years ago. Now we're dying from the white blood cells attacking us instead of the germs," Dr. Liponis said.

But here's the really interesting part. It now turns out that the immune system may respond to *emotions*. Worry, anger, or fear send those same white blood cells out on patrol, and even though they don't have anything specific to attack, they leave a trail of dangerous inflammation. Feeling gratitude could actually counter that effect—and keep our immune systems from spiraling out of control.

"The hormones released when you feel gratitude, love, and compassion are very different from those released with worry, anxiety, or fear. Gratitude may be an antidote to many of those negative responses," Dr. Liponis said.

But how could my immune system know that I wrote in my gratitude journal or appreciated my husband? I had an image of these nice little white blood cells saying, "Oh, she's happy! No need to patrol!" My anthropomorphized chemicals made a lot of sense to me, but fortunately, scientists had looked for other explanations.

Dr. Liponis said that the string of physiological responses that unite health and emotion had been best described by a neuroscientist named Candace Pert. As a young graduate student at a lab in Johns Hopkins University, she discovered the first opiate receptor—a surface on certain brain cells to which only a specific molecule could attach. The huge breakthrough led to an understanding of endorphins—what she called "the body's own pain suppressors and ecstasy inducers." Her boss won the Lasker Award, which often leads to a Nobel Prize, for the discovery in 1978, and instead of being a good girl and standing quietly on the sidelines, she raised a fuss, pointing out that she deserved to be recognized too. She went on to numerous prestigious positions, including at the National Institute of Mental Health and Georgetown University. She was only sixty-seven when she died in 2013. I wish I could have met her.

Endorphins and other chemicals like dopamine, serotonin, and adrenaline are called neurotransmitters because they send messages of emotion across the brain. But Pert and her colleagues eventually realized that instead of being limited to the brain, receptors for messenger cells exist throughout the body. She described the proteins, or peptides, that flood our system as the "molecules of emotion." They circulate to share information. And here's what's startling: The white blood cells throughout the body have surface receptors, so they grab on to those circulating peptides. If you're upset, the white blood cells (essentially) figure it out because receptors on their surfaces get the message. Then they swing into action.

There used to be good reason for the immune system to be tuned in to our emotions. Worry or fear signaled that you felt at risk of being hurt, so when those worry hormones circulated, the immune system prepared to protect and defend. That early alarm to gear up would be a good and possibly lifesaving move if "hurt" means being attacked by a spear, but not so valuable if it's a result of being unfriended on Facebook. Most of our modern anxieties (*Will I get the raise? Will my son get into college?*) don't benefit from white blood cells rushing around on high alert. But the cells go on their mission anyway, leaving inflammation in their wake.

Gratitude's first role in keeping us healthy may simply be as a direct antidote to the negative molecules of emotion. When the gratitude, love, and compassion hormones circulate, the white blood cells get the message that the coast is clear and everything is okay. They can turn off their response. "The white blood cell numbers go down and the number of inflammatory molecules goes down and people feel better," Dr. Liponis said.

Gratitude keeps the immune system from going into unnecessary overdrive. But sending out those gratitude hormones once won't have a big effect—you've got to make it your steady state. Dr. Liponis had once referred to love as vitamin L, so I told him that I would now think of gratitude as vitamin G.

"Yes, vitamin G! Take it on a regular basis!" he said.

Though the shelves of CVS aren't yet stocked with vitamin G, Dr. Liponis tries to pop a (metaphoric) perspective pill every day. "I'll be feeling sorry for myself about one little thing, and I'll stop and remember that it's all relative. I remind myself all the time that I'm the luckiest guy on earth. The luckiest guy on the planet."

In case he forgets, he keeps an e-mail address at luckiestguyonearth .com.

Dr. Liponis realized that his perspective could change dramatically, depending on the people around him. When we met, he had just returned from a trip to Singapore, planning Canyon Ranch's foray into Southeast Asia. Spending his time with "a group of bajillionaire CEOs," as he described it, Mr. Luckiest Guy on Earth started to wonder why he worked so hard and would never have what they did. "It's so warped! You start thinking you deserve everything. Being in a group like that takes on a life of its own."

He quickly focused instead on a trip he and his pediatrician wife took a couple of months earlier to an impoverished village in

Laos. Bringing their own medical supplies, they set up a clinic in a barren cement room and worked from seven A.M. to seven P.M., treating the hundreds of people who lined up to see them every day. Parents carried babies for miles or even overnight to get care. Remembering the scenes now, Dr. Liponis shook his head and gave a wry smile. "The people in Laos we met had no clothes, no food, and they were drinking river water, and yet they found ways to make themselves happy. And here I am so lucky and have so much!"

His body probably suffered from less inflammation when he felt grateful and valuable in poorest Laos than when he traveled with the rich in Singapore, feeling stressed and (slightly) envious. "When I'm giving, helping, and not expecting anything, I get a level of contentment and satisfaction that's unmatched. There's something magical that happens when you're helping someone," he said.

I told Dr. Liponis how much I appreciated his help right now, even if we weren't in Laos. He had patients waiting, so he gave me a big hug as I left and promised to be available for anything else I needed. Outside again, I wandered through the grounds of Canyon Ranch, thinking about the connections between gratitude and the immune system and how my whole view of health had just been turned upside down. I had always considered illness as something palpably explained—a pathogen or bacteria attacks and makes you sick and that's that. But understanding that the white blood cells can respond to our emotions changed everything. A cold isn't just a cold if your immune system knows (or at least has been affected by) whether your current emotional state veers toward grateful and loving or angry and scared.

I wanted to know more about Candace Pert, so when I got home, I downloaded her book and watched some of the talks she had given on the molecules of emotions. I came across a PBS special in which she had appeared called *Healing and the Mind,* hosted by the respected and very serious journalist Bill Moyers. Animated and warm, Pert explained to Moyers that receptors of various types encrusted every cell in the body. Peptides were strings of amino acids, like pearls on a necklace, that tickled the receptors on the surface of the cells. Neuropeptides had first been discovered in the brain, but scientists had now mapped them on every cell in the body. "Everything in your body is run by messenger molecules," she explained.

Moyers carefully asked if it was correct that the mind talked to the body through the neuropeptides. She hesitated. As a way of simply explaining the science, he had it right, but she wouldn't let him get away with the wording. "Why are you making the mind outside of the body?" she asked. He finally gave a little smile and admitted that he'd always been taught to see the mind and body as separate. Pert suggested the time had come to end the turf war (started by Descartes and the Catholic Church, she said) between science in one realm and soul, mind, consciousness, and emotions in the other. They discussed it, and when Moyers asked another question, she responded, "The 'me' that you say is 'me,' you're still thinking it's your brain. The 'me' that's you is your whole body. It's the wisdom of the body. Intelligence is in every cell of your body. The mind is not confined to the space above the neck. The mind is throughout the brain and body."

Pert's elimination of any distinction between mind and body required a new kind of thinking. The words to consider them as one don't yet exist! She had spent years trying to prove from a neurochemical perspective what we could all intuitively see— that our bodies respond very quickly to our emotional states. When worried or tired or stressed, we all have our own vulnerabilities—some people get colds and others get backaches and many struggle with stomach problems as likely to be tied to anxiety as to gluten. I succumbed now and then to migraine headaches. I'd always tried to connect them to classic triggers like red wine, cheese, and chocolate, but none ever panned out for me. I'd tried adding caffeine (since I don't drink coffee) and cutting it out entirely (I still liked Diet Coke), but neither made a difference. Since my first full-blown migraine hit me ten years ago, on the very night that I had to speak at a big bookstore to promote a new novel, I always secretly suspected the headaches flared under stress. But even that theory didn't hold up. Big events came and went without the need for so much as an Advil. But I might be having a perfectly nice and unexceptional day when suddenly—*whomp.* My head ached and my eyes blurred and I could barely stand up.

Could gratitude cure a migraine? It sounded kind of woo-woo, but then, Mark Liponis was not the woo-woo type, nor (as far as I could tell) was Candace Pert, and both of them believed that positive emotions infiltrated every cell. I decided that the next time I had a blasting headache, I would close my eyes and summon feelings of gratitude—for my family, my health, and all that was good in my life. I was eager to try it out, but then I realized that my new generalized state of gratitude already seemed to be keeping the headaches at bay. It had been months since I'd gone to my medicine chest for one of the powerful prescription pills I kept there. Could it be that the gratitude hormones had taken the immune system off high alert generally and lowered the inflammation in my body? My personal experience didn't count as a rigorous medical study, but I was amazed to realize how much better I had been feeling. My most vulnerable stress point hadn't been activated in a while.

Excited by my new insights on mind and body, I got in touch with Linda Stone, a tech visionary I had met a couple of months earlier at the World Science Festival gala. The festival turns science into play on the streets of New York and was started by the acclaimed physicist Brian Greene and his wife Tracy Day, an award-winning TV producer. Between them, they brought power, glitz, and celebrity cachet to science. I had read Greene's best-selling book *The Elegant Universe* when my son Zach was a college physics major and then got his next book, too. I kept them both on my nightstand. But one night I picked up one when I had really been in the middle of the other and never noticed. Still, while you're reading, Greene makes you believe you can understand these complex theories. I was ever grateful to him for giving me enough insights into string theory (which apparently is not little violins floating in the universe) that I could talk to Zach at dinner.*

At the gala, Linda and I happened to be seated at the same table. (Dr. Marty Seligman, the professor of positive psychology

---

*I invited Brian to lunch at the Four Seasons restaurant when I ran a big magazine, and he arrived ten minutes late, sweaty and embarrassed, having gone to the Four Seasons Hotel by mistake. I tried to make a joke about the space-time continuum, but having raced seven blocks, he just wanted ice water. It didn't change my admiration for him.

from UPenn, joined us too. A good table.) The honoree that evening was geneticist Dr. Mary-Claire King, a rock star in the world of research scientists, the Bono of biologists. She discovered the BRCA1 gene that is connected to breast cancer and was responsible for the finding that humans and apes are 99 percent genetically identical. She led a project in Argentina to find children stolen under the military dictatorship and, using genomic sequencing, reunite them with their biological families.

Dr. King watched in delight as Broadway performers came onstage to celebrate her triumphs in song and dance. She admitted that a scientist rarely felt so appreciated, and in an interview, she explained why you had to grab the gratitude when you could. "I usually tell scientists that when a discovery turns out right, you can be happy for about twenty minutes. For a long time, everyone had been saying 'you're wrong, you're wrong, you're wrong' and by tomorrow they'll all be saying 'we knew it all along, we knew it all along.' So you have to enjoy the moment."

Being in a room with Brian Greene and Mary-Claire King felt like watching the finals at Wimbledon—you knew you could never be as good but you might get some ideas on how to up your own game. Both had used their scientific genius (no other word for it) for a bigger cause. With her strong humanitarian instincts, Dr. King had extended her genetic identification in Argentina to other countries and needs. Dr. Greene was bringing his love of science to everyone in earshot. Theirs were the ultimate expressions of gratitude—using their rare brilliance to give back, give more, and make the world better.

At the end of the evening, I shared my view with Linda, noting that I seemed to be seeing everything through the lens of gratitude these days.

"Gratitude? We have to talk," she said, grabbing my arm as we walked out of the stunning room in the Jazz at Lincoln Center building, where dinner had been served, into an equally stunning lobby for dessert.

We sat down together on an upholstered bench, and as we started talking about gratitude, something clicked. And clicked and clicked and clicked. When we finally left, ours were the last two coats in the checkroom.

Now when I called her, Linda told me that she was coming in from her home in Seattle to New York the following week, and we agreed to meet for lunch. I suggested a rooftop patio, but when we got there, Linda vetoed it as too hot. Sitting down at a cooler table inside, she calmly told the waiter about her very extensive food allergies. "Can you help me?" she asked pleasantly. She didn't get frazzled, so neither did he, and the lunch went smoothly.

In the relatively early years of high tech, Linda had been an executive at both Apple Computer and Microsoft, and became known for her pioneering work in multimedia and social media. She coined the phrase "continuous partial attention" to describe the always-on mode that occurs when we try to stay constantly connected. Afraid of missing something, we remain in the ever-alert state once reserved for crisis. (With our minds in overdrive, maybe the white blood cells are too?) Linda eventually began researching what happens to our bodies when we deal with technology. She talked about "e-mail apnea" to explain how we stop breathing when we sit hunched over a computer. (The solution—be aware of your posture and breathing and get up at least once an hour.)

Linda told me that after she left Microsoft, she suffered a series of setbacks. Her house in Seattle burned down and many of her possessions were destroyed. The apartment she moved into flooded when the sprinkler system short-circuited. Worst of all, she was struck by serious medical problems, including an extensive jaw infection that led to several painful surgeries.

"I reached a serious state of overwhelm," she said.

Wanting to turn the misfortune around, she started to keep a gratitude journal. But she described it as "gratitude through gritted teeth." Every night she'd write something down, but she didn't really feel it.

"Instead of gratitude from the mind, I needed it from the body, heart, and spirit," she said.

Dr. Liponis would have liked her approach, which involved staying in the present and noticing the good things around her. By being centered and calm, she tried to let her body feel appreciation and express it to others (as she did with our hardworking waiter at lunch). She referred to it as "embodied gratitude"—a phrase I immediately liked.

Given her medical issues, Linda began focusing on how to use technology to improve health and well-being. Giving a presentation to some high-level tech executives one day, she had an experimental device with her that measured heart-rate variability. It turned red when you were at a high stress level and flashed green when you calmed down. She started showing the breathing techniques that could lower stress. It should have been a simple demonstration, but even as she did one breathing exercise after another, the device stayed stubbornly red, red, and red.

Trying to figure out her next move, Linda looked around the audience and realized how many of the people sitting there were friends who had been helpful to her. She decided to take a moment from her talk to express her appreciation. She noticed one person in particular and, feeling a wave of gratitude, began to thank him profusely.

"I'd barely started when suddenly people in the audience started calling out 'It's green! It's green'" Linda told me, still slightly awed by the experience. "Expressing gratitude had changed my bodily responses more profoundly and rapidly than any breathing technique!"

Fascinated by what she'd found, Linda began trying it out on others. When a Microsoft executive complained about her stress levels and insisted breathing techniques didn't work for her, Linda explained that thinking about someone you loved or appreciated could also help lower stress. The woman's husband happened to be standing nearby, so Linda gave her the device and told her to try. The exec took it and focused. Nothing happened. But after a minute or so, it suddenly flashed green.

According to Linda, the woman turned to her husband with a big smile and said, "Sorry, honey. Thinking about you didn't work—but thinking about our cats did it!'"

Whether we take the time to appreciate cats, husbands, waiters, or the tech guy, our body responds with lowered stress and (potentially) improved health. The key is taking the time to fully experience the embodied gratitude. Even as she struggled with her pain and health issues, Linda particularly appreciated one doctor who regularly asked her, "What part of you is feeling good?" Looking for the positive kept her from feeling hopeless and despairing. She started noticing what worked in her body instead of what didn't. It made all the difference.

"The whole happiness movement drives me crazy because it's so binary. Are you happy or not?" Linda complained as we nibbled berries for dessert. "The real question should be—how can I appreciate this moment more? What feels good right now? There is always some positive in the moment that we can notice and appreciate."

When I left our lunch, I walked quickly down the street, feeling grateful for my own healthy body. I thought of Dr. Liponis's positive mantra: *I have two arms, two legs, I'm breathing. Life is good.* I repeated it to myself a few times and started to smile.

I turned up Madison Avenue and noticed a woman walking just ahead of me who was long legged, long haired, and model thin. I thought of a game I used to play when I was younger and spotted women like that (New York is full of them). If by some magic, I could trade bodies with her, would I do it? I'd still be me, but when I looked in the mirror, I'd be lanky and slim hipped instead of (slightly) pear-shaped. I could wear tight jeans with over-the-knee boots and have a voluptuous chest instead of my (slightly) flat one.

Kind of an obvious trade, right?

But this time, I hesitated to call my magic genie. According to the rules of my game, I got my doppelgänger's whole form, inside and out. My own body worked just fine. Would I risk the health I had for something unknown? I walked by the woman on Madison Avenue now and took a closer look. She sure looked darned healthy. She had glowing skin and a tiny butt and was standing in front of a designer store where she wouldn't have any trouble finding clothes that fit.

I smiled at her and she smiled back. Yes, she had been genetically blessed to be beautiful. It probably would have made my life easier, but I was grateful for what I had. My genie could stay in the bottle.

Two arms, two legs, I'm breathing.

As Dr. Liponis had pointed out, life was already good.

When I got home—still in my own body—I thought about how we know both so much about health and so little. It's wrongheaded to suggest that all illness is caused by a mind-set or that you can will yourself to be well. There are many positive people taken too young by serious disease. We can't control everything. But we can give ourselves the best advantage possible.

Back in the mid-nineteenth century, Louis Pasteur introduced the world to bacteria as a cause of sickness. More recently, the Human Genome Project allowed us to map every individual's genetic blueprint and identify the specific genes that cause many diseases. But illness or health isn't a mathematical equation. You can have a gene for a disease and not get the disease. You can be exposed to bacteria and viruses and stay well. The exact mechanisms are still unclear, but we can't overlook those molecules of emotion.

In one study begun back in the 1990s, Dr. Sheldon Cohen of Carnegie Mellon University did extensive interviews with volunteers to determine their levels of stress. He then injected them with a common cold virus.* The higher their stress, the more susceptible they were to developing the cold. That sounds like voodoo—but other scientists have praised it as one of the most elegant proofs yet done of the connection between emotion (in this case stress) and health.

Proving the connection was a great start. But figuring out *why* it happened was trickier. Dr. Cohen kept at it and not long ago came up with the actual physiological mechanism that he believed linked stress and disease. I got bleary-eyed reading a bunch of medical abstracts outlining his position, but the short explanation is that stress affects the body's ability to regulate inflammation— and that can lead to the development or progression of disease. (The longer story involves how stress alters the effectiveness of the hormone cortisol to regulate the inflammatory response. Immune cells become resistant to cortisol's regulation. But trust me, you don't need to know.)

I was back to what Dr. Liponis had told me—that gratitude keeps us well because it is an antidote to stress. When you are grateful, all the signposts of stress, like anger, anxiety, and worry, diminish. So the simple medical line goes this way: Gratitude lowers stress. Less stress means less inflammation. Less inflammation means you are not as susceptible to disease.

I thought again about my migraine headaches. My initial idea had been that when the next one struck, I would try writing in my gratitude journal or thinking grateful thoughts to make it dis-

---

*The first round was done at Britain's Common Cold Research Unit. A lovely name—but it no longer exists.

appear. But so far the migraines had (happily) refused to make a comeback. And maybe that was even more significant. Anecdotes aren't science and I wasn't going to report this to a medical journal. But I was convinced that being grateful these many months had changed my stress levels, hormones, physiology, and inflammation level sufficiently to scare off the headaches altogether. Maybe it wouldn't be forever. But I'd take it for now.

CHAPTER 10

Wonder Woman on the Appalachian Trail

Happy to discover the power of nature in increasing gratitude

Grateful to walk on a nature trail and see how it affects my body and mind

Lucky to discover that green makes us grateful

All the evidence about white blood cells and inflammation, about stress and the hormones of emotions, convinced me that living gratefully would make me healthier. But I got intrigued by the idea of turning the equation around. Might some physical action increase the gratitude I felt? This month, I wanted to find out if I could get a gratitude boost through exercise, meditation, or a walk in the woods.

Mind-body connections work in both directions, and sometimes your body gives the directive to your mind about whether to feel happy or sad or grateful. For example, researchers have uncovered a very simple (albeit temporary) way to cheer up, without any of the side effects of Prozac. If you're in a bad mood, take a pencil and put it horizontally between your teeth. Bite down gently and hold it for ten seconds. Feeling better? The pencil forces your facial muscles into the same position as a smile. In the constant interplay between mind and body, your brain gets the message that you're smiling, so voilà, you must be happy.

I wanted to think that my brain was clever enough to distinguish between real happiness and biting a pencil, but even geniuses like the ones I met at the World Science Festival can't outsmart their biofeedback loops. So how could I use those loops to improve my gratitude quotient? I kept a gratitude diary as a reminder to find the positives in life, and I regularly talked to myself (quietly, with nobody around) about seeing the bright side. But maybe the embodied gratitude I'd learned about needed to start from the bottom of my toes rather than the top of my head. If there came a day when my current mind-focused techniques didn't work, I could use a physical fallback—the gratitude equivalent of biting on a pencil.

I read everything I could find about mind-body connections, but nobody had yet described a physical trigger for gratitude. Okay, I'd figure one out for myself. I started with a fascinating study done by Amy Cuddy, a social psychologist and associate professor at Harvard Business School and an expert on body language. She knew that how we present ourselves affects how others see us and how we perceive ourselves. Humans and other animals express power through broad, expansive gestures— peacocks spread their tail feathers and chimpanzees puff their chests and if you watch business people at a conference table, the guy with his feet sprawled in front of him and his elbows spread wide is probably the boss (or wants to be). The person sitting with his legs tightly crossed and his arms at his sides, taking up as little space as possible, is signaling that he doesn't have much power (and isn't getting any).

But Cuddy also wondered about sending the biofeedback loop in the other direction. Could taking a high-powered pose actually *produce* power? If the body sent an "I'm powerful" message, maybe the mind would hear it. To find out, Cuddy and two colleagues invited a few dozen men and women into their lab and randomly assigned them a "high-power pose" (taking up lots of space) or a "low-power pose" (contracted, with limbs closed). Afterward, they tested for various hormones, including testosterone, which is closely associated with dominance. The results were stunning. When people spent two minutes in a high-power pose, their testosterone levels went up by 20 percent. And their levels of the stress-related hormone cortisol dropped some 25 percent.

Amazing! Your entire neuroendocrine system can change just by how you hold your arms! And that wasn't all. The high-power posers said they felt more powerful, and in a simple game (keep two dollars or gamble it on a double-or-nothing roll of the dice) they were dramatically more likely to take a risk.

Cuddy's personal story backed her theory that beyond "fake it until you make it," you could actually "fake it until you *become* it." As a nineteen-year-old college student, she was in a serious car accident and was told she'd never walk again. Now she strides—in high heels. She also suffered a brain injury in the accident, and even after she ended up as a graduate student at Princeton, she felt like an imposter, not worthy of being there.

Cuddy got encouragement to continue and eventually started urging others to find ways to believe in themselves too. She told women that before they went into an important meeting or interview, they should find a private place (the ladies' room always works) and take a "Wonder Woman" stance—feet apart, hands on hips. She talked about the value of "making yourself big" and the confidence that men could get from stretching their arms overhead. A talk she gave at the TED Global conference in 2012 was one of the most watched ever—seen by twenty million people who wanted to find out how the body could send a positive message to the mind.

I understood that power and gratitude differed in source and substance, but it intrigued me that if you put yourself in a certain place, pose, or position, your whole hormonal balance might change. Your body could send messages that altered how you felt and behaved. So I seemed to be on the right track in looking for a physical state that would also set up a gratitude loop.

If a gratitude hormone existed, I had the feeling that exercise would bring it out. I had started my career as a broadcaster for CBS Radio, and I reported on fitness and health for years after that. My first book, written the year I graduated college, was called *Women and Sports*, so maybe I had a built-in bias about the positive effects of activity. But I also knew that intense exercise releases a flood of endorphins (the naturally occurring opiates) into the bloodstream that changes our emotional state. Marathoners often describe the euphoria they feel as a "runner's high," and I had written many articles describing how exercise wards off depression and makes people more emotionally resilient.

New studies of the chemical causes and effects of emotion also show connections to exercise. A substance called kynurenine builds up in your bloodstream when you're stressed, and it can pass into the brain and cause the damaging inflammation that leads to depression. Researchers in Sweden recently found that when you exercise, your muscles create a large amount of a chemical that breaks down the kynurenine. (It's called PGC-1alpha1, but no quiz later.) So moving your muscles sets up a chemical cycle that can ward off feeling down.

Scientists have long suspected that the brain fires differently before and after a run, and new research using PET scans proves that runners' brains actually change after a run. The endorphins that increase in the blood during exercise do indeed cross into the brain. Other neurotransmitters like serotonin and dopamine also come into play when you exercise and perform their magic on your mind.

Excited by the idea that exercise might increase gratitude, I started going to the gym again. I used the elliptical machine one day, the exercise bike the next, and the treadmill after that. I even lifted a few weights. I felt vaguely virtuous, but the flood of gratitude I'd hoped for just didn't happen. Maybe I didn't exercise hard enough to get the endorphin flow, and the gym didn't exactly have a gratitude-inducing atmosphere, either. I have friends who manage to get to the gym daily and seem to love it. But for me, the emotional focus of gym exercise is all about the future—getting thinner or lowering your blood pressure or building your biceps. Appreciate the moments on a treadmill in the here and now? Not so much.

Dr. Liponis had told me that he did ten minutes of meditation every night before bed, which helped him be more centered and grateful. He pointed out that back in the 1960s, when the Beatles hung out with the maharishi, "transcendental meditation" became popular as a way to find nirvana. But in today's world, you meditated to control your mood and quiet the stressful voices in your head. It served as the one time in the day when you could focus on the present moment without being bombarded by thoughts about what you should do, could do, might have forgotten.

I'd never meditated, but I understood the value of being in the moment. It struck me that any activity that got you fully involved and focused could also get rid of the distracting voices in your head and set up ripples of positivity. Maybe that was the problem (for me) with going to the gym. Instead of getting rid of intrusive noise, the gym just added more, both figuratively and literally. With the TV blaring and music blasting as distractions to get people charged, exercise felt like a chore rather than a release.

So I thought again about physical situations where gratitude seemed to flow naturally and made a list. I quickly noticed that, for me, they all involved being outside and part of nature. I remembered a day when my husband and I, newly married, walked hand in hand along a mostly empty beach. With the soft sand underfoot and the warm sun on my back, I felt a surge of joy and an inexplicable connection not just to the man I loved but to the whole world. I stopped to gaze out at the horizon, and as the waves lapped at our feet, I had an epiphany.

"This is why people come to the beach—so they can contemplate the vastness of the universe!" I said, gesturing poetically.

Ron looked at me dubiously, a practical guy uncomfortable to think that he'd just married Sylvia Plath. "I'm guessing they come because they like sun and sand."

"But standing here, you feel the vastness of the universe, don't you?" I asked, not to be dissuaded.

"Mostly I feel like I'm getting a sunburn," Ron said.

Fortunately, poetry and prose can laugh together, and "the vastness of the universe" became our private joke.

Some of my rush of feeling that day could be attributed to having a hot (if slightly sunburned) husband, but the combination of sunshine and scenery and expansive ocean had also given me a rush of cosmic gratitude. I appreciated the whole world and felt connected to the universe in a new way. Maybe any walk in nature that let my mind float free would inspire that same surge of physical gratitude.

I decided to try it out. The next weekend, I drove two miles down the road from our house in Connecticut and parked at the edge of a trail that ran next to the Housatonic River. White blazes announced that it was officially part of the 2,200-mile Appalachian Trail, the rugged and mountainous footpath that goes from Georgia to Maine. This stretch happened to be flat and peaceful, so simple to navigate that my husband jokingly called it "Granny's AT." But coming to this beautiful and serene spot always made me feel good. It seemed a perfect place to test the connection between nature and gratitude.

I walked away from my car and stood by the river, touching my toes and stretching my muscles. I liked running outdoors but had never been very good at it. When I went to a jogging workshop in the Bahamas years ago and wrote about it for *The New York Times*, my dad called me up, very proud of the article but not so impressed by my athletic prowess. "Did you have to admit that your great triumph was a ten-minute mile?" he asked.

Now I ran even slower. But happy to be outside in shorts and sneakers, ready to move, I slipped on headphones to listen to a podcast I'd downloaded and started to warm up by jogging slowly along the road. But after just a few minutes, I realized I wanted to get *rid* of distracting voices, not add more. I tucked the headphones into my pocket. Now as I moved along, I could hear the chirps, whistles, and trills of birds all around me. I picked out the flutelike melody of the wood thrush, the only one I could identify, and the sound made me unaccountably happy. A line from author Joan Walsh Anglund popped into my head: "A bird doesn't sing because it has an answer, it sings because it has a song."[*]

Suddenly brimming with grateful energy, I picked up my pace and started to jog. I focused on how my body felt as I moved and felt lucky to have muscles that worked and feet (even slightly achy ones) that carried me along. The river sparkled alongside me and the green-leaved trees formed a luscious canopy overhead. Dipping through the sun-dappled shadows, I felt a burst of gratitude, and like that day on the beach, I had a sense of being connected to the sky and the earth and all around me.

I kept going for nearly an hour and got back to my starting point, flushed and happy. Catching my breath, I walked slowly by the river for a few minutes with my hands on my hips, thinking about why the experience had been so emotionally transporting (less geographically transporting, given my speed). I had been open to the experience, but I honestly didn't think it would be possible to run or walk on that trail and not feel gratitude for the glories of nature. On a physiological level, if the Amy Cuddy–described two minutes as Wonder Woman upped your testoster-

---

[*]This line has been misattributed to poet Maya Angelou and even appears now on a stamp with her portrait. But no, it was originally from Ms. Anglund. I had many of her sweet books as a child.

one level, who knew what sixty minutes of cruising through nature had done? Maybe the exercise released a brew of positive chemicals that made me appreciate every sound and sense. After his stay at Walden Pond, America's favorite naturalist, Henry David Thoreau, implicitly understood the healing powers of nature. Without knowing a thing about neurotransmitters or stress-related hormones, he concluded that "an early morning walk is a blessing for the whole day." My walk had been in the late afternoon, but it also felt like a blessing. A reason to be grateful.

Maybe the secret involved simply being outside. The next day, I went back to my research and found that famed Harvard biologist E.O. Wilson used the word "biophilia" to describe the intense connection we have to nature. He saw the attachment as biologically determined, an instinctive evolutionary bond that we feel with other living things. Wilson declared that we needed to affirm our affinity for the natural environment because "our spirit is woven from it, hope rises on its currents."

Less lyrically, studies have found that nature serves as a natural stress reliever and goes a long way toward keeping us well. Lots of evidence is gathering to show that being in a natural environment—the mountains, the woods, a flowering meadow—has a positive influence on our physical and emotional health. Japan has some fifty trails all over the country for what the Japanese call *shinrin-yoku*—or forest bathing. This "Forest Therapy" is supported by the government, which has plans to fund at least a hundred of these trails. City dwellers come to disconnect from technology and be immersed in nature—they listen to the birds, breathe the fresh air, smell the woodsy scents. Though the therapy is inspired by Buddhist and Shinto practices of letting nature into your life, there's no particular spiritual ritual involved. You can simply walk, listen to ducks quacking, rest by a rock, and enjoy the greenery. Scientists are using the trails for medical research, and the "bathing" has been found to lower blood pressure and ease depression. And it's not just the physical exercise, because one study found that an amble in the woods reduced the stress hormone cortisol significantly more than a similar stroll in an urban environment.

Countries including Finland and South Korea have set up their own Forest Therapy centers and are throwing millions of medical research dollars at them. What Henry David Thoreau implicitly understood about an early morning walk is getting serious research attention in this country, too. A study of veterans conducted at the University of Michigan found that being outdoors significantly boosted their well-being. (Admittedly it was funded by the Sierra Club, which seems unlikely to have concluded they'd be better off at their desks.) A well-known Texas study compared patients who'd undergone abdominal surgery and found that those whose windows overlooked trees needed less pain medication and got out of the hospital faster than patients facing a brick wall. That amazed me. Something about simply *seeing* green made people healthier and more resilient. Maybe the slightly wilted ficus trees that were a popular part of home decorating for a while had a real purpose. Being at one with nature made you feel calmer and more grateful for the world around you.

I gave a call to Marc Berman, a young professor at the University of Chicago who has been studying the neurological connections between nature, cognition, and emotion. His findings are so jaw-droppingly unexpected that if he didn't have huge credentials behind him (which he does), you'd wonder if he were making the whole thing up. In one study, he looked at how people did on memory tests after a fifty-minute walk in nature versus a walk of the same length through a city. (He even provided GPS watches to make sure nobody cheated.) At the end, those who had been on the nature walks showed a 20 percent improvement in their short-term memory performance.

"That's a crazy huge amount!" I said when he told me his results.

"Nature seems to change your brain physiology," he explained.

Being in a pretty environment also improved people's moods. When he tried the nature walks with people who were clinically depressed, they also got mood and memory benefits—though, interestingly, the two effects didn't correlate. That is, people weren't getting the memory benefit simply by being put in better moods. Something else was going on.

In a fascinating project that he undertook while working as a postdoctoral researcher in Toronto, Marc used satellite imagery to "quantify greenness" in the city. He then got regional health reports—including data on diabetes, heart disease, depression, and anxiety—and overlaid them with the environmental views.

"We were able to make direct connections and show that trees do have independent effects on improving health," he said.

Interacting with nature increases our sense of connectedness. Being surrounded by woods or strolling through a field of flowers is interesting and aesthetically pleasing. It provides sensory stimulation, but as opposed to something like watching TV, it's not harsh and all-consuming. The combination seems ideal for lowering stress and increasing feelings of gratitude.

The problem with walking in the city, Marc explained, was that it didn't allow the mind to similarly relax and make its own connection. Many people (including me) get great pleasure strolling through a city and marveling at the architecture or observing the store windows. Sometimes when I walk home through my favorite New York streets late at night, the lights in the buildings seem to twinkle as appealingly as stars. But the noise and crowds in an urban area demand some vigilance—or at least put you on hyperalert. Just crossing the street requires more attention. The extreme example might be Times Square, with its neon billboards and flashing marquees, not to mention strange characters dressed as Spider-Man or the Naked Cowboy. While navigating all that, it's hard for your brain to achieve the relaxed physiological state that would spin off into gratitude.

I told Marc that living in New York City, I walked a mile or two almost every day. It got me where I wanted to go, but as he suggested, it didn't seem to do much for my mood. But that hour in the woods over the weekend had been sheer bliss. Was it too big a stretch to think that nature could naturally inspire feelings of gratitude?

"It certainly could. Nature improves well-being, and gratitude is part of that," he said.

Well, that made me feel better. At least someone with a PhD thought I might be onto something.

The married couple Rachel and Stephen Kaplan (not related to me), two longtime professors at the University of Michigan whom Marc worked with in graduate school, began studying the restorative powers of nature decades ago. They set the stage by explaining that we feel stressed out when our "directed attention" is worn down. We're pulled in too many directions or concentrating so intently that we get depleted. In nature, our minds can wander and get revitalized. They described a natural environment as having "soft fascination," which allows us to relax and reflect without feeling overwhelmed. As Professor Stephen put it, "Clouds, sunsets, snow patterns, the motion of the leaves in the breeze—these readily hold the attention but in an undramatic fashion."

True enough, though it depends on what you consider "undramatic." Nature lowers stress and improves our ability to focus. New studies show it also increases creativity and may help children who have problems with attention and delayed gratification. Professor Rachel said the right environment could help people become more psychologically healthy by restoring a sense of balance and meaning. In an early study, she found that people who looked out to trees or other natural settings from their office windows were healthier, liked their jobs more, and reported greater life satisfaction than those with less inspiring views.

Various lab studies show that being in nature gives our prefrontal cortex (the area responsible for executive function) a rest. Being among those clouds, trees, and fragrant flowers produces a soothing rhythm that connects us to something bigger than ourselves. We feel grateful to be a part of this magical world.

The next weekend, I went out for another run on Granny's AT, and the scientific explanations I'd learned fit how I felt. I didn't have to think about anything—the positive feelings just came to me. Just as when I wrote in my gratitude diary, I felt connected to the cosmos and grateful to be alive.

I stopped at the edge of the river and stood for a very long time, mesmerized by the little eddies that formed at my feet and the green moss that covered the rocks like bits of velvet. Earlier in the week, I'd spoken to the marvelous filmmaker Louie Schwartzberg, who has had his cameras trained on nature 24/7 for the last thirty years. The resulting time-lapse films he created from years of steady work are breathtakingly glorious, showing flowers blossoming and mushrooms unfurling, butterflies emerging from cocoons and trees spiraling toward the sky.

"The images connect you to the outside world and you feel vibrations of gratitude deep in your heart for everyday wonders," he said. "The earth puts out magnetic vibrations, and what I capture and share with people freezes those vibrations. The feelings of gratitude occur on a visceral level before the cognitive brain even has a chance to kick in."

He created one film called *Wings of Life* (narrated by Meryl Streep), which intimately reveals bees interacting with flowers. "Pollination is a beautiful love story between the flower and the bee—a tiny event that occurs billions of times a day—and if it didn't, life on this planet would be radically different," he said. "That's the magic, this web of interrelated relationships in nature happening every moment, that makes us grateful."

His work mesmerized me as it unveiled nature's mysteries, too small or fast for the eye to otherwise see. "It's the little things that make us grateful," he said. "The moments people cherish are the small ones with children and family or Sunday breakfast with a cup of coffee. Those open your heart to gratitude."

Given all he had seen, I asked what images still made him pause with that heartfelt sense of wonder.

"I never get tired of watching flowers open, or slow-motion shots of hummingbirds or butterflies. I've seen some of my images several hundred times, and I don't get bored because I feel that visceral gratitude for what I'm repeatedly observing. Nature's beauty is a gift that cultivates gratitude."

The nineteenth-century naturalist John Muir once said that "the clearest way into the Universe is through a forest wilderness." Some emotion that I could only call gratitude emerged when I walked in a forest, stood on a mountaintop, or looked out to the ocean. Clearly both Muir and Schwartzberg know what it means to feel at one with the vastness of the universe.

When I got home, I found Ron sitting on an Adirondack chair on our large wraparound deck, staring off to the mountains. He had his iPad on his lap but didn't seem to be reading.

"What are you doing?" I asked.

"Just sitting here," said my usually hyperactive husband.

I plopped down in the chair next to him. "Then I'll sit here too," I said.

We sat very quietly, watching the sun settling behind the mountains as the sky lit up with streaks of brilliant orange. I told Ron about my run and my new theory about how being in nature inspired gratitude. We didn't have to consciously focus on how grateful we were to be here, to be alive, because nature announced its marvels, and we felt it deep in our bodies and souls.

"My soul can find no staircase to heaven save earth's loveliness," I said.

"Led Zeppelin?" he asked.

"It's from Michelangelo, actually. When he wasn't painting the Sistine Chapel, he wrote a few poems on the side."

"Nice." He picked up his iPad, and in a moment, the gentle strains of Zeppelin's classic song filled the air.

"Are you making fun of me?" I asked.

"Nope. It just struck me that you're right. Being part of nature is the real stairway to heaven."

He reached over and took my hand as dusk settled behind the trees. I thought of how many poems and songs have been written about love, and how many about the beauties of nature. When we are in the thrall of either, we feel a gratitude deep in our souls. Maybe it's oxytocin or endorphins or other chemicals that are released and connect us to the greater world. Maybe it is the joy we feel that makes us grateful. It is the stairway we mount to feel the beauty in the universe.

With gratitude improving all aspects of my life, I started to wonder what it could do for the one area that still bugged me—my weight. I've always been in reasonably good shape and have sometimes been very fit. But like many women, I currently weighed ten pounds more than I wanted. I'd lost and regained those same pounds many times over the years and spent too much time thinking about bulges, real or imagined.

My husband didn't understand my weight obsession. He always thought I looked great (bless him), and as a skinny guy who could stare down a chocolate cupcake and never flinch, he found it baffling that I moaned about my jeans being too tight and then ate a pint of rocky road ice cream. (The low-fat version, but nonetheless—a pint!) He tried to avoid conversations about my weight, but one morning, he happened to be in the room when I tried on a navy cotton knit dress and twisted around in front of the mirror.

"I can't wear this," I complained. "It makes my butt look the size of Rhode Island, don't you think?"

"Rhode Island is a very small state," he said.

I glared at him. "Are you joking? That comment is probably grounds for divorce in at least three states."

"I'm only being accurate. A big butt would metaphorically be the size of Texas, and you're definitely not that."

"Maybe Kansas? North Dakota? If we go by population, Massachusetts?" I asked, trying not to raise my voice.

"You look great to me," Ron said calmly, repeating his favorite refrain.

I sighed, knowing this was my issue, not his. Trying to be rational, I explained I felt bad about gaining weight because I had looked so good in this dress last year.

"How come I never heard you say that last year? In fact, I don't remember your ever appreciating how good you look," he said.

I started to disagree—but really couldn't. Maybe I'd learned to look on the bright side of life, but never of my own thighs. I could blame my mother, who had taken great pride in the twenty-one-inch waist she flaunted at her wedding and regularly chided my sister and me for not matching her measurements. But I was an adult now, and if I didn't mind the little bulge at my waist (not a muffin top—I like muffins), then fine. If I wanted to change, I needed to do something.

I'd been on board with Dr. Liponis's idea of having gratitude for a healthy body (*two arms, two legs, I'm breathing!*), and it struck me that the natural inclination when you appreciate something should be keeping it in good repair. From my years as a health and fitness writer, I knew plenty about nutrition and exercise (most of us do), so I didn't need more information to lose weight and get in shape—just the right mind-set. Maybe gratitude could give it to me. Over coffee one day, I mentioned to my friend Anthea that I wondered if I could use gratitude to lose ten pounds. A longtime executive with a quick mind and pragmatic, down-to-earth approach, she didn't seem to find that unusual at all.

"You have to meet my fitness trainer, because she starts every session with gratitude," Anthea said. "She thinks it's part of getting lean and strong."

Anthea seemed so unfazed that I wondered if I'd stumbled on a new trend. Had gratitude become the new gluten-free? I quickly made arrangements to find out and soon drove over to Litchfield, Connecticut, where slim, energetic Jen Abbott welcomed me into her fitness studio. Instead of the loud music and revved-up energy that courses through most gyms, Jen's space oozed calmness and serenity, with inspirational phrases (including *Be Grateful*) written in gold cursive script on the walls. I noticed a row of candles under a window, and Jen explained that before every workout, her clients lit candles and thought about their intentions. Taking a moment to breathe and "immerse themselves in mindfulness and gratitude" usually produced a much more effective workout.

Trained as a physical therapist, Jen had built a large business in Wellesley, Massachusetts, with numerous trainers working for her and hundreds and hundreds of clients. Always busy, she worked constantly while also going through a divorce (she was the family breadwinner) and taking care of her two little children. "I'd go to bed stressed and wake up feeling dreadful," she admitted.

She thought she was doing okay, though, until one day when she quite literally fell off the treadmill.

"Really, I was running on the treadmill and fell!" she told me, still marveling at the incident. "After that injury, I knew I was being driven by fear, rather than gratitude and love. I wrote two words on the ceiling above my bed: 'Trust' and 'Faith.' I needed trust that we'd be okay, and faith that I could find gratitude for what I had. That gave me the strength to move forward."

She moved with her boys back to the small Connecticut town where she grew up and opened her own fitness studio. Telling the story now, sitting on a big blue exercise ball instead of a chair, Jen looked as literally balanced as anyone could be. She had been amazed by the power of gratitude to pull her through and wanted to give that gift to her clients, too. She told me that she noticed how many came from what she called "a place of lack"—feeling bad if they weren't (in their view) thin enough or pretty enough or fit enough. Tough workouts and endless ab crunches wouldn't be enough to solve the problem.

"If we insult ourselves and see ourselves badly, we attract more bad feelings," Jen told me earnestly. "When you see yourself as fat and slow and tired, that's what you become. You have to catch yourself and flip it. Instead of feeling inadequate that the person next to you is running on the treadmill and you're walking, look for all the blessings. *I'm here at the gym and I had the motivation to get here! I have these strong legs to carry me and a heart and lungs that work! Thank you, thank you!*"

When she got her clients to flip to gratitude, she saw instantaneous results. Their pace on the treadmill would increase and they'd get a little swing in their step. Many reported that the next time they found themselves plopped on the couch wanting to eat chocolate, they decided to exercise instead. I told Jen that I'd recently learned how gratitude made people more motivated in work and careers, so it made sense that the same occurred with weight and fitness. But for some reason, gratitude for body hadn't yet kicked in for me—and I had an extra ten pounds to prove it.

"You can lose them easily. You've been that weight before, so you know you can do it," she said encouragingly.

"Actually, I don't know. I look at my skinny jeans and can't imagine wearing them again."

"Then that's your number one problem!" she said. "You have to believe it to do it!"

Jen suggested I write the words "Thank You!" on a card and put it next to my bed, so I saw it first thing every morning.

"Who am I thanking?" I asked dubiously.

"Yourself. *Thank you that I will eat right today. Thank you that I will become as lean as I want to be. Thank you that I will wear a sleeveless dress to my book signing and have great arms.*" She smiled. "Dedicate five minutes of your day to believing you can do this and being thankful you can."

She liked reminders everywhere and suggested I attach a "Thank You" to the refrigerator door to be grateful for the healthy celery and carrots and apples inside. (Better than the picture of a hippo I'd once put on the fridge.) A "Thank You" on my mirror to help eliminate negative self-talk.

"If all you're thinking about is that you need to lose weight, you're not remembering to be grateful that you're strong, grateful that you can buy healthy food, grateful that it's gorgeous weather and you can take a walk," Jen said.

Jen believed that a negative body image takes us out of gratitude. We feel overweight and worry that nobody will like us, so we stay home wearing sweatpants, then eat more out of loneliness and anxiety. It's a downward spiral—and the way back up is through gratitude.

"Love yourself from the inside out. Say positive things and be grateful for the way you choose to see yourself!" Jen said. "Put up the pair of jeans you want to fit into again and say thank you! *Believe it and be thankful for it!*"

Wow. I'd spent months focused on gratitude, but I'd never thought of thanking myself and being grateful to . . . me. I'd only intended to interview Jen, but after our stirring conversation, we agreed to meet for an actual training session.

A week later, I went back to Jen's studio, this time wearing sneakers and exercise clothes. She exhorted me to come up with a word that would inspire me—her version of a mantra—while I exercised. Knowing my goals, she suggested "lean" or "willpower." But I shook my head.

"I'd be more inspired by 'strong,'" I said. I wanted my body to be strong and my attitude to be a little tougher, too.

"Good!" Jen said enthusiastically. She sent me over to the candles at the window and urged me to close my eyes, breathe deeply, and visualize myself as strong. I tried, but all I felt was slightly awkward. As a journalist, I'm more comfortable observing experiences than actually having them, and I desperately wanted to reach for my notepad. But I batted down the urge and stayed in the moment. Jen pointed out that my arms were crossed tightly in front of my chest and suggested I relax my shoulders and open my hands.

"Visualize yourself as strong and lean and fitting into those jeans!" Jen said. "Then be grateful that you're strong. Let the gratitude flow in. *Thank you, I'm strong.*"

I squirmed like a middle schooler. My approach to gratitude all year had been fact based and scientific, and while I didn't mind Jen's more spiritual leanings, I didn't naturally respond. I really, really wanted my reporter's notebook.

Jen let me leave the window and get on the exercise bike to use up some energy. Then we spent the next forty-five minutes on a real workout—with exercise balls, functional training (the squats and lunges and balancing that you need for everyday activities), and some weights. I like to exercise, so that felt good.

At the end of the session, Jen had me lie on a mat while she stretched my arms and legs and talked about gratitude again. Finally, she took a note card and with red marker wrote *Strong* on one side and *Thank you, I'm Strong!* on the other.

"It's three simple steps," she reminded me as I left. "Think of your word—'strong'! Visualize yourself that way. And then say thank you!"

When I got home, I put the card on my kitchen counter. For the next few days, every time I walked by, it made me stop and smile and think. Maybe I wouldn't be Jen's best student, but her gratitude approach really felt empowering. I knew, though, that visualizing myself as strong was only the first step.

"Losing weight is really about what you eat even more than exercising," Jen had reminded me.

So I had an idea. I'd come up with the Gratitude Diet.

I walked around my kitchen and realized we had food everywhere—fruits, vegetables, yogurt, eggs, cheese, mustard, and olives in the refrigerator; cookies, crackers, cereal, flour, soup, tomato sauce, beans, lentils, and much more in the cabinet; a freezer packed with ice cream, chicken, pizzas, and various Tupperware containers I couldn't quite identify. Being grateful for food and plenty has been integral to cultures and religions throughout history, but I couldn't say I ever remembered to be grateful for a stocked pantry. When hungry, I just grabbed anything handy.

I thought about Jen wanting me to put "Thank you" on the refrigerator, and I decided it wouldn't be a bad idea. Driving home from my meeting with Dr. Liponis at Canyon Ranch, I'd stopped at the museum in Stockbridge, Massachusetts, dedicated to the artist and illustrator Norman Rockwell. You don't have to be a fan of nostalgic Americana (and I wasn't) to admire his iconic picture *Freedom from Want,* showing a family gathered around a table, delighting at the Thanksgiving turkey. And in the very poignant painting *Saying Grace,* an older woman and her grandson, cramped in a raucous restaurant, bow their heads before a meal. The original sold for $43 million in 2013, so apparently I wasn't the only one moved by its message of giving thanks, wherever you happened to be.

I'd heard recently about organic eaters who updated the notion of saying grace by taking a moment before a meal to think about the farmers who had grown the crops and the cycles of nature that produced them. One vegan friend told me she always paused to picture the land where the food grew. I couldn't see myself pondering rain falling gently on cornfields before I ate a taco, but I admired her ability to marvel.

There are pragmatic as well as spiritual reasons for appreciating the bounty in front of us. Mireille Guiliano, the former CEO of the company that makes Veuve Clicquot champagne and author of *French Women Don't Get Fat*, made the convincing argument that her fellow countrywomen stayed slim because they savored what they ate. Even rich foods like wine and cheese and pâté were fine when you had small portions that you took time to enjoy. It takes twenty minutes for our stomachs to tell our brains that we're sated, and gulping food at the counter American-style didn't allow that to happen.

Joining Norman Rockwell to Mireille Guiliano—perhaps the unlikeliest dieting team ever created—I decided that learning to *appreciate* the food I ate had the potential to make me happier and thinner. Doing that seemed simple enough—and made more sense than most of the diets I knew. Our notion of what's "healthy" changes—remember when bran muffins seemed the great panacea? Now it's kale and quinoa, and while I happened to like both of them, I had the sense that it was my approach to what I ate that would make the difference.

As usual, I went on a research binge (better than the ice cream equivalent), starting with the book *Mindless Eating*, by Cornell professor Brian Wansink, who heads the school's Food and Brand Lab. He's been on a quest to make people healthier by changing the external cues around food—apparently more effective than relying on our own desires and willpower. He quickly figured out that we judge how much to eat by the portion size we're given. If you use a smaller plate at home, you'll eat less. Take a tall narrow glass instead of a short fat one and you'll drink less, too.

Since we need some visual clue about when to stop eating, Dr. Wansink helped convince food companies to start selling snacks in hundred-calorie packs. (Enough people would pay more to get less that it turned out to be a good business plan, too.) In one memorable study, he gave moviegoers free popcorn, and those who received large buckets gulped down significantly more calories than those given medium ones. In a funny twist, the popcorn was stale and tasted like Styrofoam (one person asked for his money back, forgetting that it had been free), so nobody liked it. But they ate anyway—free popcorn!—and later claimed that the size of the bucket had no effect on how much they devoured. Dr. Wansink did variations on the experiment over and over, with M&M'S and Wheat Thins, trying different movies and theaters. But the results stayed consistent. Get more, eat more.

Another time, he invited students to lunch and served them tomato soup—not revealing that some of them had an invisibly refilling bowl. (An unseen pipe connected beneath the table did the trick.) If they judged by their stomachs, they would have stopped when full, regardless of the soup level in the bowl. Instead, those with the magic bowl ate 73 percent more than those given just a normal serving.

More recently, Dr. Wansink did several studies looking at whether our mood affects what we eat. He concluded—yup, it does. When you're feeling happy and at one with the world, you're probably not standing at the kitchen counter eating peanut butter from the jar. Feeling grumpy, grateful, or somewhere in between could make a big difference in your food choices. In fact, he found that being grateful could make you eat 77 percent healthier. That seemed like a whopping big number, so I gave him a call to talk about it.

"A lot has to do with the time horizon," he said, sounding like the kind of good-natured, cheerful guy who was (by his findings) more likely to eat broccoli than chocolate. "If you're in a negative mood, you want something that will make you feel better right now. When you're in a positive mood, you think more about how you'll feel in the long term."

Changing the mood can change your diet. In one study, he had some people write a story before they ate about the happiest day in their life and some about the worst day. It had a big impact—with the "happiest day" people choosing healthier food afterward.

Most of us aren't going to write a life-changing essay before ordering a cheeseburger and fries, so Dr. Wansink wondered about smaller changes. "I'm always trying to find the intervention that a real person can do in real life," he told me. He suspected that gratitude might be a simple way to move people from, as he put it, feeling "OK" to feeling "OK-plus." In a lunchtime study, he asked people to tell him one thing that had happened so far that day that made them grateful. "It was only lunchtime, so nobody said they had won the lottery or that their kid just got named class valedictorian," he said with a hearty laugh. "It might just be 'I'm grateful I got to work on time this morning.'"

Any grateful comment (however lame) had a big effect. The people who were prompted to be grateful ate about 10 percent fewer calories than others. Even more significantly, they switched *what* they ate—more salad, less dessert. "The ratio of fruit and vegetables to total calories accounted for that 77 percent healthier mark," he explained.

It wasn't lost on Dr. Wansink that offering a grateful comment before a meal would fit well into Norman Rockwell's world. It was the secular version of saying grace. "Making a grateful comment isn't a spiritual statement. It works for everyone," he promised. But you have to do it yourself and not rely on someone else. "When families say grace, it's the person who says the prayer who gets the benefit, not the others," he told me.

For his premeal gratitude interventions, Dr. Wansink tried different approaches—he had people write down a reason to be grateful, say it to someone else, or whisper it to themselves. It turned out that the personal whisper was as effective as the others.

"Could I just think a grateful thought?" I asked him, pushing the idea a little more.

"Much better if you make it tangible. You don't have to share your comment with anybody else, but at least say it out loud to yourself. The more muscles you move, the better."

A little whispering to myself before a meal might get me odd looks in a restaurant, but if it made me eat healthier, I wouldn't mind.

What about snacks? Could gratitude work its magic of cutting calories by 10 percent if I stopped to have a grateful moment on my way to eating a brownie?

"Better stick to meals," Dr. Wansink suggested.

Then practically, he suggested wrapping the brownie in aluminum foil and putting it in the freezer, out of sight. Gratitude couldn't do everything.

Still, losing weight through gratitude seemed a lot easier to me than counting calories. So after we hung up, I pondered the various research findings and started to outline my own eating plan. I came up with four rules for my Gratitude Diet. They were simple and straightforward, and I had the feeling they would work.

Since Dr. Wansink believed eating right was all about the environment and mind-set, I decided my diet needed an impressive name. So here it was:

The Amazing Gratitude Diet!

- ✧ Take a minute to appreciate any meal before I started.
- ✧ Sit down to eat—no matter what.
- ✧ Fill up on gratitude rather than food.
- ✧ Eat only food that made me grateful (in quantities that made me feel good).

It didn't seem like it should be that hard. And there was plenty of evidence that these simple steps would help me eat healthier. I started working out the details.

Rule #1: Take a Minute to Appreciate Any Meal Before I Started

How often did I really look at what I planned to eat and then savor its pleasures? When I had breakfast at home, I usually checked e-mail or read the latest news feed, and in a restaurant, I'd be talking to friends and barely pause when the plates were put down. Now I wanted to pay more attention. I set a sixty-second rule: I would take a full minute to appreciate the rosy redness of a just-picked apple, the fragrance of fresh basil, the shiny, smooth surface of a piece of salmon. If I paused to appreciate the texture and aroma of anything I ate, I probably would decide against greasy muffins and sugary sweets.

My friends who pulled out their iPhones in restaurants to snap photos of every course were actually on the right track. The maître d' might find it annoying, but taking a photo to post on Instagram or Yelp or Facebook made you look at food as something special. I didn't have to take a photo, but I would mentally register what I planned to eat and be grateful.

Rule #2: Sit Down to Eat—No Matter What

Norman Rockwell never made a painting of someone taking thirty seconds to scarf down a scone while she raced to pick up a kid at a soccer game. But I realized I consumed a lot of my calories while driving in the car or walking down the street. How could I be grateful for what I ate going forty-five miles per hour in an SUV? Since 20 percent of food in America is devoured in the car, a lot of real meals have been subverted for on-the-go consumption—like healthy yogurt becoming sugar-laden yogurt tubes, and cereal made more convenient (though how complicated was it to start?) with cereal bars. For me, food on the go was whatever I could grab with one hand. (Hello, energy bars!) If I made myself sit at a table for a snack, I'd be more likely to choose vegetables and salsa or pita bread with hummus—and appreciate it before it disappeared.

Rule #3: Fill Up on Gratitude Rather than Food

When I'd talked to Dr. Mark Liponis about losing weight, he'd pointed out that often we think we want food, but we're really hungry for friendship, love, compassion, and gratitude. Food smoothed over bad moods or lonely feelings. People who say they are addicted to chocolate (and there are a lot of them) are looking to feel calmed, soothed, more satisfied. Rather than stopping to consider what would really fill our needs, we let ourselves crunch, chew, and munch.

"Often the problems are loneliness and lack of fulfillment. If we had more connections and meaningful contacts, we wouldn't be reaching for food," he said. Women often told him that they lost weight without even trying when they started a relationship. "When the love is feeding you, then you don't have the hunger. I sometimes think if I could just find someone a boyfriend, that would solve the weight issue!" (The old "reach for your mate instead of your plate" had something to say for it.)

If I hadn't eaten since breakfast, hunger pangs around noon probably deserved some food to sate them. But sitting at my desk an hour later and frustrated that I couldn't get the sentence just right . . . well, maybe I needed to work on the sentence, not wander into the kitchen. Or if, as Dr. Liponis suggested, my hunger had a deeper cause, I could close my eyes and let myself think about all I had and fill up on my gratitude for the world. That would be longer lasting and lower calorie than a chocolate-chip cookie.

Rule #4: Eat Only Food That Made Me Grateful

Appreciating my body meant not filling it with versions of white flour and sugar that I ate simply because they were available—the boxed cookies left over from Christmas baskets and the Goldfish crackers long abandoned in the pantry. I didn't particularly like them, anyway, and they never made me feel good afterward.

Professor Wansink once watched people at a Chinese buffet restaurant, and he found that the slim ones scouted the buffet to see what they wanted before they started, while heavier people just grabbed a plate and began to fill it. "They didn't skip to the foods they really liked. Instead, they served themselves a bit of everything they didn't hate," he explained.

Only foods I *really liked* would make it into the Gratitude Diet. I appreciated the tart crunch of a Macoun apple when I got it just picked in early fall at the farm stand, but six months later, a grocery store variety that had lingered in cold storage tasted like a tennis ball. So "yes" to the apple, "no" to the tennis ball. Blueberries remained my favorite fruit, so starting my Gratitude Diet in the summer, when they were ripe and easily available, gave me a boost. Since they were healthy and low calorie, I decided I could eat as many as I wanted. My diet, my rules.

And that was part of the point. I picked the foods that made me grateful to eat. The healthy ones were the easiest and anybody could make their own list of fresh favorites. I eliminated processed foods because nobody could feel grateful after reading those labels. But what about the double chocolate cookies that I bought freshly made at a little bakery near our country house? They made me happy. I appreciated every bite. Since I was counting gratitude, not calories, they made the list. A cookie that I really loved—*one* cookie—was just fine.

And that was it. A Four-Step Gratitude Diet.

I didn't have to think about high protein or low fat, about Atkins or South Beach or Jenny Craig. Deciding simply to appreciate my food would change the choices I made. Instead of *what* I ate, I would focus on *how* I ate. And be grateful for every bite.

The next day, I came out of a meeting in Manhattan around lunchtime and stopped in a dive deli to grab a bagel and cheese.

But then I remembered Rule #2—I needed to sit down, not eat on the run. I headed to a more civilized spot a few blocks away and lined up at the copious salad bar. I tried to pick only foods that would make me grateful (Rule #4), and then I squeezed into one of the small tables jammed together in the back. I picked up my fork to dig in—but then I remembered Rule #1, being grateful for my food before I took a bite.

I put down the fork and gazed at the plate in front of me, appreciating the shiny glazed carrots, the black sesames on the tofu, and the many shades of green in the lettuce. I thought about how lucky I was to have such healthy variety available. I took the full sixty seconds to appreciate my plate. A minute lasts longer than you'd think, and the two men chowing down at the next table glanced at me nervously a couple of times.

"You okay?" one of them asked when he caught my eye.

"Oh, yes, of course," I said. To avoid freaking him out further, I didn't mention the delightful fragrance of my iced mint tea.

I ate slowly and felt surprisingly content when I finished. My first lunch on the Gratitude Diet, and I didn't even want a cupcake to top it off.

According to Dr. Wansink, 75 percent of dieters quit within a month and 39 percent never make it past the first week. But there was nothing to quit on the Gratitude Diet. By sitting down, looking at my food, making sure I was hungry, and eating only what I really liked, I could make meals (and snacks) a joyous part of my life. There was no deprivation or denial. I'd probably lose weight slower than on more extreme diets, but I wouldn't turn cranky either. Instead of being afraid of food because it might make me fat, every meal became a celebration. Dr. Wansink's research was pretty convincing that mindless eating made us fat. The Gratitude Diet encouraged *mindful* eating—which I hoped would make me thin.

Now three seasons into my year of living gratefully, I reflected that my grateful approach to the summer had made me feel healthier and more alive. With gratitude bringing stress levels down, I had been blissfully headache-free, and following Jen's ideas on positive body imagery, I still had that index card in my kitchen that said, "Thank you, I'm strong!" Instead of beating myself up about what my body couldn't do, I felt proud of what it could.

Sticking with the Gratitude Diet was making me feel surprisingly good, too. Being more appreciative of what I ate put me back in control—and I seemed to be consuming a lot less. I decided not to check the scale, because I wanted to focus on being grateful for my body and the food I put into it.

But off the record, I thought the jeans that had gotten so tight were fitting just a little bit better. And in another week or so, I might try on that navy cotton knit dress again.

PART FOUR

AUTUMN

COPING, CARING, AND CONNECTING

Unless you are utterly exploded, there is always something to be grateful for.

—Saul Bellow, *Herzog*

On the off-chance that you won't live forever, maybe you should try being happy now.

—*The Newsroom* (HBO)

CHAPTER 12

Making Bad Times Better

Glad to find that gratitude can bring comfort in even the worst of times

Grateful to get a new view of losing a job

Lucky that sad events can actually enhance our lives

My wonderful friend Rose had given me tickets to *Madama Butterfly* at the Metropolitan Opera, and the first act had been sheer bliss, with breathtaking staging and sublime singing. Rose, an entertainment lawyer who counts the Met among her clients, had provided seats in the seventh row of the orchestra, and for the first time ever at an opera, I actually could see (my nearsighted eyes again) and follow the story. The other times I'd been to the Met, we sat so far away it could have been another galaxy. Being up close put me in heaven.

At intermission, Ron and I walked up the red-carpeted staircase to the opera café, where the maître d' led us to an elegant table that was already set for us—chocolate mousse cake and cappuccino for me and tiramisu and tea for Ron. We sat down and tried not to giggle. It all seemed much more sophisticated than we deserved.

"Remind me how you know the fabulous Rose?" Ron asked, taking a spoonful of his dessert.

"She's a new friend," I said vaguely.

"Let her know we're . . . grateful." He grinned.

The next day, I sent Rose a little orchid as thanks (maybe I should have sent roses?) but I realized my gratitude went far beyond the night at the opera. Rose happened to be funny and smart, with a quirky style that made her thoroughly engaging and fun to be around. But beyond that for me, she served as proof that you never know the twists life takes. You might as well be grateful every day, because even seemingly bad events can have good outcomes.

The circuitous route that led to that glorious night at the opera started by my feeling completely miserable. I'd just left a big magazine job and the world felt unfair. What would I possibly do next? My older brother in California kindly stepped in and made some introductions that led to a project in the tech world unlike anything I'd done before. Very briefly an expert in apps, I got invited to speak at a conference and met a woman there who later invited me to a charity breakfast where I sat next to Rose, and we started working together on a business project and then became friends.

Got all that? The details don't really matter. The point is that when I first left that job, I couldn't think of any reason to be grateful at all, but you never really know where new opportunities will take you. Steve Jobs once gave a commencement speech at Stanford University where he said, "You can't connect the dots looking forward; you can only connect them looking backwards." He described being devastated at age thirty when he was fired from Apple, the company he had started. But it turned out to be the most creative period of his life and ultimately led to his meeting his wife, starting other successful companies like Pixar, and then triumphantly returning to Apple. "Sometimes life hits you in the head with a brick. Don't lose faith," he said.

For much of this year, I'd been seeing how gratitude could transform experiences from run-of-the-mill to truly satisfying. But gratitude could also be an antidote to life's troubles, helping put them in perspective and take away the sting. In the greater scheme of the world, I knew my misfortunes were small compared to what others faced, meaning I *should* be grateful. But a lot of research has shown that how we feel at any one moment has very little to do with externals. People with every advantage could still be cranky and unhappy, while those who faced huge obstacles sometimes radiated good feeling and bounced merrily along. The Benedictine monk Brother David Steindl-Rast, who had been teaching gratitude for years, had a simple explanation: "It is not happiness that makes us grateful. It's gratefulness that makes us happy."

In the midst of any struggle, we feel like our woes are the worst. But I had been learning this year that there is always another side to find, a different perspective to take. In his great epic *Paradise Lost*, the seventeenth-century poet John Milton wrote, "Long is the way and hard, that out of Hell leads up to light." This month, I wanted to see how gratitude helped us move from darkness to light.

I caught up over coffee with a former colleague named Lora whom I hadn't seen in a while and told her about my gratitude project. "You should come to an AA meeting with me. Gratitude plays a big part in meetings," she said.

She made the offer casually, so I tried to sound similarly off-hand in asking how long she'd been in Alcoholics Anonymous. It turned out she'd been sober for twenty years and had attended meetings at least once a week (and often more frequently) for all that time. I met Lora years ago when we worked together on the same TV show, and though technically her boss, I admired her as talented, funny, and very quick. Others admired her too, including an older on-air reporter who had a reputation as a drunkard and spent too much time taking her to bars.

"I always blamed him for getting you into drinking," I told Lora now. "You were just a kid in your first job."

"True, but my mom had also been an alcoholic, so I had a problem long before I met him," Lora said. "Not a lot of good role models."

Lora told me that when she found herself drinking seven or eight beers a day, she went on a final binge—and then showed up at her first AA meeting. She never stopped going to AA.

I didn't drink (I'd even given up Diet Coke for water), but one of the meetings Lora regularly attended allowed visitors on the last Monday of the month. We met for an early dinner that night, then went to an old church across the street. I didn't quite know what to expect—maybe something dark and degenerate, people with haggard faces and dull eyes, a grim scene out of *The Lost Weekend*. I anxiously followed Lora up a narrow staircase and into a small room set aside for the all-women's meeting. The moment I stepped in, all stereotypes of alcoholics went out the (open) window. Instead of haggard faces and dull eyes, many of the women perched on chairs in the center looked young and radiant, with long hair, slim bodies, and skinny jeans. A few well-dressed women who could have been business executives rushed in at the last minute, tucking away their cell phones.

The week's leader sat cozy and cross-legged in a big chair. Like Lora, she had been sober many years, but she described the "bone-deep, soul-piercing pain" she felt when drinking and added that back then, "I wanted to die on a daily basis." From the beginning of her sobriety, she kept a gratitude list, and she reminded herself that "I had been diligent with my drinking, so now I could be diligent with gratitude."

Those sitting in the circle then passed around an egg timer so anyone who wanted could talk for a couple of minutes. Several of the younger women thanked the leader for inspiring them. Others said how grateful they were to have the group to support them. One mentioned that she was "grateful for all the things not happening to me that used to"—like blackouts and waking up in a strange bed. She said she sometimes wished she could erase the past, but she could only move forward and "be grateful for the energy and joy I could bring to the future."

Gratitude wasn't the only theme, but it was sprinkled generously through many of the comments. Sitting outside the circle with me, Lora listened calmly and kept herself busy knitting a scarf. She nudged me when it was time to stand up, hold hands, and say the serenity prayer together.

Back on the street, Lora looked at me worriedly. "I tried to see this through your eyes and imagine being there for the first time," she said.

I told her I'd been moved by the women's warmth, kindness, and positivity and felt nourished to hear gratitude used as comfort, hope, and therapy. Having read the AA literature before I came, I knew one of the organization's principles was "an honest regret for harms done, a genuine gratitude for blessings received, and a willingness to try for better things tomorrow." That sounded like a reasonable plan for life in general.

"But help me out. I'm still not sure I understand how gratitude helps you stay sober," I admitted.

Lora nodded. "Okay, two parts. At the beginning, you keep a gratitude list as a reminder of all the positive trade-offs you've made by not drinking." For her, cutting eight beers from her daily diet meant she quickly dropped some extra pounds, so she wrote about being grateful to lose weight. And not buying booze gave her more money to spend elsewhere. "I had a lot of entries about buying new khaki pants," Lora joked.

Once sobriety became the norm, the playful reminders about pants and pounds didn't carry the same import. "Problems come when you've been sober for a while and it starts being the norm," Lora said. (Habituation, anyone?) "Then you keep the gratitude list as a reminder not to take the new state for granted. A grateful alcoholic doesn't drink." Or relapse.

Lora and her friends at AA couldn't change what had happened in the past, but as the Greek philosopher Epictetus taught, what really mattered was how they responded right now. External events may be out of our control or determined by the fates, but we can decide how to look at them. *If any be unhappy, let him remember that he is unhappy by reason of himself alone*, Epictetus said.

But what happens when those past events are so devastating that gratitude seems out of the question? I called my friend Jackie Hance to talk about gratitude—a favorite subject of hers, despite the fact that she had suffered an almost unimaginable tragedy. Her three adorable daughters, Emma, Alyson, and Katie, then ages eight, seven, and five, were killed in a shocking car accident on the Taconic State Parkway in New York in 2009. Even worse (if that's possible), her own sister-in-law had been driving the car and toxicology tests came back showing alcohol and drugs.

A full-time mom with a generous spirit and a fun-loving soul, Jackie plunged into the abyss. Her husband, equally shattered, couldn't help, and she wanted only to join her girls in heaven. A devout Catholic, she visited several priests to make sure God would understand. Her friends, determined to keep her on earth a little longer, stepped in with a different plan. They made a schedule so that at least one of them would be at her house and by her side 24/7. They cooked and cleaned, took her on morning jogs, brought her to therapists, enrolled her on a bowling team, and insisted she join them on shopping trips. In their fierce loyalty and devotion, Jackie found a crack of light in the impossible darkness.

The first time we met, about eighteen months after the accident, Jackie seemed so fragile that I feared she would break. Her eyes flashed constant pain and her voice came out as barely a whisper. But then we started talking about her friends, and her whole demeanor changed.

"I have the most amazing friends. I feel so incredibly lucky. I'm grateful to them every day," she said.

Awed that after all she had been through, she could describe herself as "lucky" and "grateful," I sensed Jackie had depths I hadn't begun to imagine. Under that vulnerable shell, she had a strong core fighting to be happy again (though worried that she no longer had the *right* to be happy). We went on to write a bestselling book together, a gratifying collaboration for both of us. She wanted to tell the girls' story, and I could share the message that life is random and horrible events occur, but even when the worst happens, you can still move on and find reasons for gratitude.

Jackie and I had stayed in touch, and twice now when I'd traveled abroad, I visited historic churches and lit three candles for the girls, my way of bringing them to places they hadn't had a chance to see. I'm neither religious nor Catholic, but I admired the courage Jackie showed every day just by getting out of bed. I liked to think about the spirit that kept her going and the gratitude that remained a key part of her life.

When I called her now to check in and talk about my year of gratitude, she jumped at the chance to add her view.

"I still try to find reasons every day that I'm grateful," she said. "I write a list in the morning and keep it with me all day."

Jackie told me that she typically got up very early to run with friends, and the six or so miles outside always improved her mood. Back home at six thirty A.M., she had a few minutes to herself. "That's when I let myself be sad. I take five minutes to cry because I miss my girls. And then I make myself write what I'm grateful for," she said.

I smiled at the distinctly Jackie pattern: run, cry, be grateful, and get on with life. The pain of losing her daughters would never go away, but once she decided that she wouldn't join them in heaven just yet, she fought not to be overwhelmed by anger, resentment, and despair. More than anyone else I knew, Jackie understood what it meant to appreciate every moment while you had it. "If I'm going to be here, I want to make it a great life," she said.

Jackie started thinking about gratitude after the accident when she heard a therapist on *Oprah* (she was a big fan) explain that in the moments you're feeling grateful, you can't also be sad. At that point, she had fallen so far into a black hole that she couldn't imagine ever crawling out. Psychiatrists had already prescribed antidepressants and sleep meds and tranquilizers, so keeping a gratitude list didn't seem like too much of an added burden. She realized very quickly that gratitude worked as well as anything else. She eventually gave up a lot of the drugs, but she never had to wean herself from the gratitude lists.

"Does being grateful come naturally to you now?" I asked.

"No!" she said with a laugh. "It's a decision to do it every day. Writing a gratitude list takes work for me, and I have to keep reminding myself not to skip it. But the feeling lasts, so it's worth it."

Jackie's thankfulness had, in many ways, saved her own life. Even in the haze of hopelessness that engulfed her after the accident, she was moved by the kindness of people (many of them complete strangers) sending notes, gifts, and donations. Appreciative of their time and concern, she determined to thank every one. At one point she announced that she still planned to kill herself—but she had twenty more thank-you notes to write first. "I might have been suicidal, but I wasn't rude," Jackie explained to me later.

Her thankfulness multiplied when she got pregnant again—something she never imagined could happen. She'd had a tubal ligation after Katie was born, and the in vitro fertilization she would need to conceive seemed prohibitively expensive. She abandoned the idea until a doctor named Zev Rosenwaks offered his medical help at no charge.

"How can I possibly thank him? A bottle of champagne just doesn't seem like enough," Jackie had said to me, only half joking, when she was pregnant.

She decided on the most heartfelt gift she could imagine and named her miracle baby Kasey Rose, the middle name in honor of Dr. Rosenwaks. (The name Kasey had a different significance since it used all the first letters of her lost sisters' names.)

Now Jackie joked that when she wrote her daily gratitude list, she knew it couldn't be only about Kasey.

"So what makes you grateful now?" I asked.

"Oh, I don't know. Sometimes it's little stuff like how good it feels when the sun is out and beaming on my face. Or the other day, I wrote about my legs. Who ever stops to be grateful for their legs? But they're such a strong tool for me, and I don't know what I'd do if I couldn't run."

Grateful people like Jackie create an aura of giving that immediately makes you want to reciprocate. Once when she heard Oprah (yes, again) exhorting viewers to stay away from people who projected "negative energy," she called her friend Jeannine to ask if she fit into that category.

"No, you've had a very bad time, but we still feel the positive person underneath," Jeannine told her.

Even with that assurance, Jackie promised that she would try to get rid of any negativity left. She wanted to be the person who brought energy into a room, not sucked it out. I marveled, because how many people in Jackie's situation would worry about being too negative? Everyone would have understood if she spent the rest of her life ranting and crying and being the saddest woman on earth. But Jackie wanted to live with gratitude, not grief.

Soon after we spoke, Jackie sent me a long letter that she wrote to her daughter Alyson on what would have been her thirteenth birthday. (She always sent the girls letters on birthdays and holidays. Sometimes gifts, too.) It was touchingly beautiful, telling Alyson how much her mom missed her and wanted to celebrate by her side. She wrote how hard it was for her or any parent to lose a child, and how sometimes her tears wouldn't stop. But then came the heart of the letter.

This year, my birthday gift to you is this list of what I have learned to be grateful for since you went to heaven.

She described her gratitude at knowing from her daughters what true love means, gratitude for her faith, gratitude for the little things people did: *A friend saying a prayer, sending a card, stopping by with coffee, or taking Kasey for an hour so she can have fun and I can be sad . . . these mean the world to me.* The list went on, eight reasons to be grateful.

I read the letter and tears filled my eyes. When so much had been lost, Jackie could still find a way to be grateful for what remained.

After spending time with Jackie and Lora, I started thinking about why gratitude was so closely connected with difficult situations. Jackie wasn't grateful for the life-shattering loss she had experienced—that would be beyond comprehension. But like Lora, she wanted some semblance of happiness again and achieved it through what I decided to dub *intentional gratitude*. They kept gratitude lists and consciously looked for reasons to appreciate the world around them.

I thought of a guy I knew in college named Jamie McEwan, a few years older than me and something of a legend. He had dropped out for a while to train for the Olympics and won third place in slalom canoeing, the first American in the sport ever to medal. Back on campus, he competed on the wrestling team, which I covered for the school newspaper. I liked watching him because he was handsome and strong and very smart, with an irreverent twinkle in his eye. He wrestled at 177 pounds, which I probably remember because he was solid muscle so had trouble cutting to the lower 167 weight class.

He married his classmate Sandra Boynton, who became famous for her clever children's books and greeting cards. (Her classic: "Hippo Birdie Two Ewe. Hippo Birdie Two Ewe." Say it out loud and you'll get it.) We stayed only intermittently in touch, but I knew they had a rambling house on many acres in Lakeville, Connecticut, where they raised four children and various dogs, and Jamie turned the nearby river into a kayaking slalom course.

The perfect life for the perfect couple.

So I had been shocked when we connected a few years ago and I learned that he had just been diagnosed with multiple myeloma, a cancer of the blood. We had a dinner with our spouses in the city and then Jamie and I talked a bit more regularly as he went through dramatic treatment therapies.

About a year ago, I drove up to his house in Lakeville. The ever-powerful Jamie looked thinner and had lost a few inches of height from the disease, but his playful spirit was untouched. He delightedly walked me through the real-life American diner that Sandra had built on their property, largely from items found on eBay. When we went out to lunch, he still had a sparkle in his eye and determination in his voice. He had been on various drug trials, but none had helped. We talked about gratitude, and he gave his appealingly lopsided grin.

"Gratitude? Heck, what else is there?" he asked.

He adored Sandy and his children and appreciated that he still went skiing with his kids and traveled all over. He used to compete in kayaking with his son Devin, but now when they went to races, Jamie held a stopwatch rather than his own paddle. But watching his son made him happy. When you can't do everything, you remind yourself to be grateful for what you *can* do.

I'm sure Jamie gave in to despair in his private moments (who wouldn't?), but his public face stayed optimistic and upbeat. He kept a blog online to track his medical progress, and after he had a stem cell transplant and spent two weeks in his hospital room, being alive seemed a great gift. "I was sprung from the hospital yesterday afternoon, walked outside to find May flowers in full power, and Mr. Tough Guy here had tears come to his eyes," he wrote.

Jamie and I made plans to meet again. "You should be a whole chapter in the book," I teased him. If he managed to stay grateful, none of us had an excuse to do otherwise. I wanted him to share his secrets—but he said it was simple. You just had to know that gratitude beat despair and live that way.

I didn't get to see Jamie again, and I was devastated when I heard he'd died. His positive spirit should have kept him alive forever, but cancer, life, God, and Darwin don't work that way. He flooded the world with his grin and stayed grateful for life, whatever it brought. We can't know how many days we'll have, so we can only make each one count. Jamie did that. I am grateful to have known him.

Thinking about Jamie, I arranged to have coffee with Jane Green, the bestselling novelist whom I first met when I asked her to interview the actor Hugh Grant for a cover of *Parade*. Sending a pretty Englishwoman to the notoriously reticent Grant had been a good call—they cooked dinner together and became fast friends. (And we got a great story.) I'd heard recently that she had been diagnosed with a malignant melanoma, but as soon as she sat down, she told me the surgery had been successful. Grateful to be cancer-free, she was still overwhelmed by the surge of gratitude she felt before the surgery—for husband, life, family, and friends.

"The time between the diagnosis and surgery should have been the worst—and yet it wasn't," she said, tossing back her thick, curly hair. "I plunged into a state of extraordinary gratitude. Everything felt brighter and more beautiful. I never would have expected it. Perhaps when you're shown that life may be finite, you appreciate what you have in abundance."

Shortly before the melanoma diagnosis, Jane had started getting daily texts from a friend whose life was falling apart. His wife had left him, he'd moved into an awful apartment, he had to fight to see his children, and he'd lost his job. But each day, he wrote a gratitude list and sent it to Jane. She was struck that despite how much he was suffering, he woke up every morning and made a conscious choice to be grateful.

"When you see gratitude working, you realize how transformative it can be," she said. Faced with her own bad situation, she decided to follow her friend's example. Despite the unknown of her diagnosis, Jane very intentionally worked to be positive. Every time she found herself spiraling into a place of fear before the surgery, she lifted herself up by thinking of three reasons to be grateful.

"I did it consciously because I don't think anybody stumbles upon gratitude," she said with a laugh. "But the more you do it, the more natural it becomes." Knowing she couldn't predict (or change) the outcome of her cancer, she tried for equal measures of acceptance and gratitude. "It's such a waste of mental energy to be furious that something isn't the way you want it to be. Fighting life is what causes problems. When you can accept life on life's terms, you pave the way for a measure of peace that you miss otherwise," she said.

Jane told me that she had prayed a lot before the surgery. "I didn't pray that I would be fine because I don't think prayer can change an outcome. But I prayed for the strength and grace to deal with whatever happened."

Jackie, Jamie, Lora, and Jane all faced tough situations, and instead of crumbling or giving in, they chose gratitude to get them through. They did it consciously, relying on gratitude lists or diaries as reminders—techniques all of us can try, no matter what the circumstance. Each made a concerted mental effort to flip from the darkness and find some cracks of light—and they didn't do it just once, but repeatedly. Every day. Over and over. You could almost see them working to be grateful, and the gratitude paying them back.

Browsing around to find other people who turned grateful in difficult times, I kept coming across . . . jailbirds. Not necessarily first-degree felons, but people convicted of crimes from assault to financial fraud. Many of them announced that prison was the best gosh-darned thing they could imagine. An athlete described being in jail as a "really good thing" and said he was "kind of thankful" to have been behind bars because it made him excited to be training again. A politician emerged from his prison sentence grateful to be a better person and father. A fashion designer expressed gratitude that his imprisonment on securities fraud had given him a new purpose and a new wife. And a reality TV star facing fifteen months in jail said her husband would get to bond with their four children while she was gone "and that is something I will be grateful for."*

Why were the former prisoners grateful for circumstances most of us would do anything to avoid? I doubted that going to jail could really be such a great experience. And curiously, unlike Jackie, Lora, and Jamie, they weren't grateful *despite* a bad situation but *because* of it. So in contrast to the *intentional gratitude* of my friends, I decided to dub this version *reactive gratitude*—an unconscious response that allows us to find redeeming value in

---

*The grateful prisoners here include UFC fighter Jeremy Stephens, footwear mogul Steve Madden, and Real Housewife of New Jersey Teresa Giudice, but there are many more.

the difficult event itself. Harvard psychologist Daniel Gilbert described a "psychological immune system" that kicks in when we can't change something. Like our physical immune system, which allows us to recover from illness, the psychological immune system provides the resiliency necessary to bounce back from emotional setbacks.

People respond to traumatic events in ways we wouldn't anticipate. So, for example, if you fight not to go to jail but that offshore tax deduction lands you in an orange jumpsuit anyway, your mind desperately tries to salvage the experience. Maybe you look good in orange or you're inspired to start a new line of designer jumpsuits. In the mid-1700s, the Enlightenment philosopher Voltaire wrote the picaresque novel *Candide,* about a young man wandering through life as one catastrophe after another befalls him. (Leonard Bernstein later turned it into a still-popular operetta.) But at each disaster, his optimistic tutor, Pangloss, reminds him that "all is for the best in the best of all possible worlds."

Voltaire meant his story as satire, but on some level, we are all Pangloss, grateful for this best of all possible worlds. Dr. Gilbert found that a significant percentage of people who survived major traumas claimed that their lives were *enhanced* by what had happened. "I know, I know. It sounds suspiciously like the title of a country song, but the fact is that most folks do pretty darn good when things go pretty darn bad," Gilbert wrote in his smart book *Stumbling on Happiness.*

While gratitude lists and AA meetings require conscious attention and a desire to find positive offshoots, reactive gratitude happens without our being fully aware of it. As Dr. Gilbert sees it, our minds "cook the facts" so the person living through a situation finds it much less dreadful than an outsider would anticipate. He gives the example of someone left at the altar by a cold-footed fiancé—what most of us would imagine as a terrible situation. But according to Dr. Gilbert, "once we've actually *been* heartbroken and humiliated in front of our family, friends, and florists, our brains begin shopping for a less dreadful view . . . and . . . the human brain is one smart shopper." It's easy to imagine the abandoned bride saying how grateful she is to find out now rather than later that Mr. Right is Mr. Wrong. Or the jilted groom being thankful that he gets to date the bridesmaid he really liked, anyway.

Because we don't realize how our minds will kick in to protect us, bad events are usually worse when we imagine them than when they actually occur. In several experiments, Dr. Gilbert asked people to estimate how they'd feel if they lost a job or a loved one, if they flunked an exam or flubbed an interview. Then he looked at people who had actually been through the experience. He found that people "consistently overestimate how awful they'll feel and how long they'll feel awful." In making the predictions, we don't realize that once the calamity occurs, that psychological immune system will work hard to make the awful seem more tolerable.

People who practice intentional gratitude—making their gratitude lists or planning pay-it-forward experiences—give themselves an extra round of immunity. When Martha Stewart went on trial for lying to investigators back in 2004, she was initially outraged and railed at the injustice of the system. But once the sentence came down and she couldn't avoid prison, her mind did the reactive gratitude play—*this won't be so bad*. At Thanksgiving (once her favorite holiday), she sent a message to her fans that she was safe, fit, and healthy. "Your good wishes and support mean the world to me—and I am eternally grateful," she said. To her enormous credit, she then went a step further. With a fifty-dollar budget to decorate the prison for the holidays, Martha gathered the other inmates and read aloud from the stacks of personal Christmas cards she had received. She wanted to be sure that those who didn't have anyone thinking of them could share her holiday cheer. She left prison saying how grateful she was to meet the women there and understand another side of life.

The philosopher Epictetus again: *We must make the best use that we can of the things which are in our power, and use the rest according to their nature.*

If you can change something that's making you unhappy, go ahead and change it. But if it's done, gone, or inevitable, what greater gift can you give yourself than gratitude for whatever life did bring?

Losing a job isn't in the same category as accidents, tragedy, jail, and illness, but it can feel pretty grim. Now that I understood how gratitude could help a bad situation, I allowed myself to think about leaving that job a few years earlier, the event that led (very circuitously) to meeting Rose and the night at the opera (and many other things, too). As editor of *Parade,* I had been on top of the world, with the magazine flying high and getting kudos from all corners. We had groundbreaking stories, major celebrities, and amazing writers. But then Walter Anderson, the man who had run the place for a couple of decades and risen to CEO, announced his retirement. We all expected the terrific company president to move to the corner office, but he didn't get the job and we were surprised by the outsider who did—a nice enough guy and a decent ad salesman, but not the powerhouse needed to lead a big enterprise. When he began firing talented people to bring in his own team, Walter called me with reassurances.

"You have absolutely nothing to worry about. He'd be crazy to lose you," Walter said.

So maybe he was crazy. Usually you know when a job is ending, but I didn't see this one coming and neither did anyone else. "You were like a general who's triumphantly winning the war— and then her stripes get ripped off," my best friend, Susan, said to me later. "It made no sense."

At the time, it all seemed random and unfair, and I railed that so much in business (and life) is arbitrary—your future determined by wrong timing, the wrong guy coming in, someone's arrogance rather than your achievement. When I saw Walter recently, we sat in the back of a theater after the performance of a play he'd written and talked about serendipity. We'd both moved happily on—him to plays, me to books—and liked our next stages. After the smart and talented president left and I did too, the magazine began to sink. The huge profits we'd been making suddenly became huge losses. In just a few years, it ended. The magazine got sold off.

"Your leaving was the best thing that could have happened, don't you think?" Walter asked. I looked at him in surprise, so he continued. "It didn't make you happy at the time, but you would have been miserable staying there while he went off in all the wrong directions."

Sometimes the simplest comment gives a new perspective. In

Walter's view, the new CEO had steered *Parade* into an iceberg, but I'd already landed in a lifeboat.

"I should be grateful to have escaped?" I asked Walter.

"Yes, gratitude is definitely called for," he said with a twinkle in his eye.

I left the theater pensively, reflecting that sometimes what seems like a push backward can actually be a leap forward. I couldn't be grateful for the sad fate of the magazine. It would have been better for everyone if the right person had gotten Walter's job and we continued strong. But you take what happens and go from there.

For some reason, a line from Shakespeare's *As You Like It* popped into my head. The banished duke has been thrown out of the court, but instead of being royally pissed off, he wanders through the forest finding "books in the running brooks, sermons in stones, and good in everything."

Gratitude was a way of finding good in everything.

Since leaving, I'd had interesting projects, met exciting people, enjoyed new experiences. I'd found books in running brooks. Gratitude is best done looking forward, but taking the Steve Jobs approach, now I wanted to connect the gratitude dots looking backward. When I got home, I pulled out a piece of paper and a big felt pen to write a gratitude list.

1. So grateful I had Susan

My best friend, Susan, had appeared at my office in what seemed like moments after I called her. She helped me pack boxes, had me write a farewell letter, and generally took control. She showed me she would always be there when I needed her.

2. Grateful that my brother put himself on the line
My older brother, Bob, and I had never crossed our professional lives before, but he sensed this time I needed the boost. He connected me to a high-tech media exec he knew in Silicon Valley, which led to a very cool consulting gig in the world of apps, and an entire new crowd of contacts and friends. The job was fun and came at exactly the right time. But most of all, I felt grateful to my brother because he cared.

3. Grateful to my husband for turning furious
A week after I left, the new CEO needed a favor (crazy, right?) and asked me to coffee. My kind, gentle, and nonviolent husband never curses, but now that his wife had been dissed, he suggested sending a hit man to the coffee or bringing a water gun to scare the (expletive) out of him. I was oddly touched by his fury. In any fight, I had a loyal partner who would never let me down.

4. Grateful to the colleagues who understood
A very well known media executive immediately e-mailed: "You r the best, they r nuts, come work 4 me." I didn't end up working for her, but the e-mail made me smile (and not just the spelling). Another colleague called to take me to lunch at Michael's, the restaurant where New York's media moguls hang out. I reminded her I'd left that circle and didn't want her embarrassed. "We're going!" she insisted. The eponymous owner gave us a prime table. "Everyone's been in your shoes—or will be," he whispered as we sat down. It is the only time I have ever been grateful for a Cobb salad.

Now I looked at my list and knew it could go on for many more pages. I wish I'd made the list years earlier—it would have helped. Fortunately, I'd had some instincts about gratitude early on. Walking home the day I left that job, I found myself musing how my life had changed. Then I stopped—quite literally—in the middle of Forty-Eighth Street and Third Avenue to talk to myself and reframe the day. Maybe my psychological immune system kicked in. "Your life didn't change. You still have your husband and children and you're healthy. All you lost was a job." I might also have lost my marbles, given the glances of people swerving to walk around me.

A famous saying holds that when one door closes, another door opens. I've seen the phrase attributed to Alexander Graham Bell, Helen Keller, and the Bible—though it's definitely *not* in the Bible. The second part of it says that "we often look so long and regretfully upon the closed door that we do not see the ones which open for us." I'd had many new doors and windows fling open. I finally felt grateful for the fresh air.

While doing my research on gratitude and adversity, I kept coming across a story about the violinist Itzhak Perlman and a concert he gave in New York. Appearing onstage to great applause, he hobbled slowly to his chair with braces and crutches, a result of his childhood polio. He finally sat down, lifted his violin, and started to play—and after just a few bars, everyone heard a loud snap as one of his strings broke. He closed his eyes and, instead of asking for a new violin, signaled the conductor to begin again.

According to a report that appeared in the *Houston Chronicle* in 2001, it is nearly impossible to play a symphonic work with just three strings. But that night, Perlman did it. "You could see him modulating, changing, recomposing the piece in his head," the story said. When he finished, there was wild cheering and Perlman smiled, wiped the sweat from his brow, and raised his bow. Then in a pensive tone he said, "Sometimes it is the artist's task to find out how much music you can still make with what you have left."

It is a lovely story. A broken body and a broken string. An artist grateful to make music with what he has left. The only problem is that I don't think it ever happened. No music critic at the time reported on the incident, and the *Houston Chronicle* article appeared to be more urban legend than serious news.

But however the story started, it probably lingered because it (ahem) hit a chord. We all understand that life can be a struggle. Bodies get damaged and strings are broken, children are tragically lost and jobs unfairly stolen away. A lot doesn't make sense. Gratitude helps you find meaning—and some version of contentment—in the chaos.

CHAPTER 13

The "Unselfie" Approach to Life

Grateful to see gratitude as an action, not just a feeling

Lucky to find the self-satisfying side of giving to others

Glad to see Grattitude everywhere (however it's spelled)

As I sat in row A of an intimate Broadway theater called Circle in the Square, actor Hugh Jackman stood onstage, about five feet away from me. The play, called *The River,* had a quiet intensity, and an understated Jackman a riveting presence.

The show ended and the small cast took their bows—and then they returned to the stage.

"Is this anybody's first time at a Broadway show?" Jackman asked, dropping the controlled character he'd been playing and returning to his charming, ebullient natural self. Two young women sitting together raised their hands and Jackman joked that the "Broadway virgins" didn't know what came next but everybody else did. It was the time of year when actors stepped out of their roles to raise money for Broadway Cares/Equity Fights AIDS—an important charity that had the advantage of a lot of great-looking stars collecting for it. Jackman urged everyone to drop whatever cash they could in the buckets outside the theater and to buy the posters of *The River* that the cast had signed and were selling for a hundred dollars.

But then he flashed his irresistible smile and announced that to raise even more money, he would sell something that a cast member had worn. And no, not the red dress that his costar had on. (She gave an embarrassed smile.) He pointed to the top he'd been wearing in the last scene of the play.

"Shameless exploitation for a good cause! I'll auction off this wet T-shirt I'm wearing, and the winner comes with me backstage!" He joked about a bed backstage (in the play, characters kept leaving for the unseen bedroom) and picked up a bottle of "wine" that was one of the stage props. "We'll drink 2007 grape juice too!"

He started the bidding and the price quickly went up. "If you're not bidding, this is a bad time to be fixing your hair!" he teased one woman in the audience, whose semi-raised hand caught his eye. He offered a second T-shirt to anyone who would match the top bid (then at $6,000) and invited fans willing to shell out $2,000 to come onstage for photos. Jackman was so charming that the woman behind me whispered, "Maybe I should break my piggy bank."

Selling the shirt off his back wasn't new for Jackman. When he starred in the sold-out, ten-week revue *Hugh Jackman, Back on Broadway* in 2011, he ended most of the performances by unbuttoning his white shirt and offering his sweaty T-shirt to the highest bidder. He'd even sign it. One night he had two bidders willing to pay $25,000 each. Over the course of the run, he raised nearly $1.8 million for Broadway Cares/Equity Fights AIDS.

Would anyone have paid all that money for Jackman's cast-offs if it weren't for charity? Well, maybe. People can get a bit bonkers around Jackman. But making the auction about giving and caring removed the unseemliness of buying (and selling) a sweaty tee. And it also let Jackman bring a semblance of sense to the crazy experience of being idolized. Most stars tried to appreciate the infatuated fans who brought them money and fame, but they were also wary. No matter who you are or how long you've been beloved, having fervid fans who want to rip off your clothes never quite computes. Jackman's genius was to show his gratitude for the fans' love by turning it into something that also helped the world. I admired him as terrific actor and charismatic star, but I respected his pay-it-forward auction almost more than anything else I'd seen him do.

When I got home that night, I decided my goal this month would be to try to find the same joy in grateful giving that Hugh Jackman showed. I wanted to acquire his spirit even if I'd never come close to matching his charisma or talent. (Not to mention his muscular arms, great abs, lean body, twinkly eyes, graceful moves . . . Must I go on?) If I could find out what inspired some people to turn gratitude to giving, then maybe I could take pleasure in finding a bigger purpose.

To get some ideas, I went to visit Henry Timms, a Hugh Jackman–level star in the nonprofit world and the kind of guy who has more ideas in an hour than most of us have in a week. Or maybe a lifetime. Impressively tall and broad shouldered, he talks fast, with an upscale English accent that makes him sound smarter to

Americans. He looks like a guy who might have led both the computer club and the rugby team at an English boarding school.

Henry grew up in London, his father an English archaeologist and his mother a Texan. "She had the good sense to marry an Englishman, which I recommend to all women," he said when we sat down in his office at 92Y, where he's executive director.

Now in his late thirties, Henry was married with two young children—and he had plans to change the world by merging philanthropy with technology. Henry told me that he remembered coming to America every year at the holidays when he was young to visit his mother's family. "It struck me as such an amazingly generous place, everything so alive and dynamic. We'd go to the Salvation Army in Austin, Texas, and they'd have a coat drive, and I was struck that caring and generosity was the heart of what this country was about."

One of his big ideas came on Thanksgiving a few years ago. Sitting at the dining room table with his wife, he wondered why a holiday season that started with "thanks" and "giving" didn't pay attention to either of those concepts. Instead, we had Black Friday and Cyber Monday, which were all about buying.

And so was born the idea of #Giving Tuesday.

I'd known Henry for a few years—neither of us could remember how we first met since he's just one of those guys who attract people—and I had attended a few of the early meetings he held about #Giving Tuesday. He liked to put people with different backgrounds in a room, throw out a general concept, and see where it went.

Within two years, #Giving Tuesday had attracted thousands of corporations and nonprofits eager to participate. I had told Henry before how proud he should be that his idea evolved so far, so fast. He stood as proof of the power of one person to have a huge impact on the world.

"I'd like to resist the heroic narrative," he said to me now, when I brought up his accomplishments again. "I know it's an interesting story when the dynamic leader dreams up an idea at the kitchen table. But it's not even true."

"As I remember, it was the dining room table," I teased.

Henry shook his head, reluctant to present himself as the centerpiece of the movement. To him, that was the nexus of "old power"—one person creating a program that others absorbed and followed. He wanted to model "new power," where instead of coming from the top down, an idea spread by a community of people sharing and caring. "We want to create a space where people can share values, which is how an idea becomes self-sustaining," he said.

The shared values in this case revolved around gratitude and giving. Making a connection between them resulted in a (hopefully) endless positive loop—you could show gratitude by giving, and giving led to more gratitude.

"Gratitude isn't just a nice feeling. Gratitude at its best is an action. It's about something you do rather than just something you feel. Americans are very good at that," Henry said.

Americans can also be very good at self-absorption—as evidenced by the proliferation of people using their phones to take photos of themselves. In 2013, *Oxford Dictionaries'* word of the year was "selfie." That same year, the "unselfie" went viral on #Giving Tuesday. While the selfie is *all about me,* the unselfie was *me caring about someone else.* Some were as simple as people posting pictures on Twitter and Facebook and Instagram of themselves holding a sign about the cause they wanted to support or how they would feed the world. *The Huffington Post* called it "the antithesis of social media navel gazing."

It's possible to be divisive and corrosive on social media, but the fast-moving formats also make it exponentially easier to be grateful and compassionate. "There are ways to use the tools of social media to celebrate the best of who we are as human beings," Henry Timms said. "Unselfies are literal snapshots of a person being grateful."

Henry described gratitude as a muscle that we all need to flex, so I told him about my year of living gratefully and how much I'd changed. He nodded thoughtfully. I could see the idea-generating mind at work.

"You need some dramatic transformation for the end of your book," he said. "A whole year of gratitude needs something big. It should feel like the ending of a movie. Maybe you should become a nun?"

I admire Henry so much that for a moment, I took it seriously. But, nope, I had a husband and two kids. The convent thing wouldn't work.

"Keep thinking. I like the concept, but preferably a transformation that doesn't involve a vow of chastity," I said.

We both laughed and I left Henry's office with an extra bounce in my step. After these many months of gratitude, those children and husband plus work and friends made me more satisfied than ever. Gratitude had changed me and a few people around me, but maybe it could have bigger repercussions, too. By its very nature, gratitude created an "unselfie" approach to daily life, making you turn the camera lens around and focus outward instead of inward. Appreciating the world around you made you more eager to be part of making it better.

I liked Henry's idea of flexing the gratitude muscle by giving, but knowing just how to do that was a little trickier. Back in about 350 BC, Aristotle pointed out that *gratitude is felt toward him who gives,* and in his famous treatise on ethics, he advised it was virtuous and noble to *give to the right people, the right amounts, and at the right time, with all the other qualifications that accompany right giving.* Maybe knowing "right" was simpler then.

Since the time of Aristotle, other philosophers have outlined all the just and rational reasons (and there are many of them) to help people in need. But psychologists (and most fund-raisers) know that on a practical basis, none of these moral principles have much to do with why we *actually* give. In one study, people were presented with various sad scenarios—such as three million people in an African country underfed or millions having to flee their homes—and asked how much they would contribute. Then they heard one person's story. They typically offered three times as much to the beleaguered individual as they did to the tragic, global problem. Of the many explanations, I think the simplest is this: When face-to-face with another person, we recognize our own good fortune and know the random hand of fate could just as easily have taken a quarter turn in a different direction. Grateful? You betcha.

Back in the late eighteenth century, Adam Smith pretty much launched modern economics when he wrote in *The Wealth of*

Nations that people are motivated by their own self-interest. He explained that if we want something from a tradesman ("the butcher, the brewer, or the baker"), we should "never talk to them of our own necessities, but of their advantages." And that was okay. Pursuing our own personal gain ultimately served the good of society.

Conservative politicians regularly quote Smith, the free-markets-benefit-everyone guy. But it turns out Adam Smith was also the gratitude guy. He started out as a moral philosopher, and his first book, *The Theory of Moral Sentiments,* focused on social relationships and our drive to lead moral lives. He argued that we have natural inclinations toward sympathy and kindness, and we care about the happiness of others. He defined the worst in human nature as resentment and the best as gratitude.

In elegant eighteenth-century prose, Smith described gratitude as the emotion that prompts us to show our most admirable natures. He said we feel "grateful affection" when someone helps us, and so we want to return the favor and do good for another person. As observers, we admire people who help (they "stand before us in the most engaging and amiable light"), and all the giving and thanking and gratitude make for a nicer society. "The sentiment which most immediately and directly prompts us to reward is gratitude," he wrote.

Thinking about it now, I understood how the great Adam Smith could trumpet gratitude and giving on one hand and self-interest on the other—because sometimes, they could be the same thing. Giving made you feel good, which made it the ultimate in self-interest.

I got in touch with Peter Sagal, the host of NPR's popular show

Wait, Wait . . . Don't Tell Me! We'd spoken in the past, and I always found him as quick and funny in real life as on the air. But he had a serious, thoughtful side, too. I'd recently heard him tell a moving story about his experience at the Boston Marathon the year the tragic bombings occurred. An avid runner, Sagal had just crossed the finish line and was standing one hundred yards from the first explosion. The bomb detonated at four hours nine minutes and Sagal typically finished a marathon an hour faster than that—so he should have been far away. But instead of trying for his own best time, he had run that year as a volunteer aide to a blind runner.

Sagal told me now that despite the drama of the day, he'd continued as a volunteer runner the next year and planned to do it yet again. He was happy to have traded improving his time for helping someone else. "Running is pretty solipsistic and self-oriented," he said. "As with a lot of other activities, once you've achieved the goal you set, it doesn't feel so important. I'd like to say that I conceived the notion of becoming a guide out of my own sense of enlightenment—but really, I got an e-mail asking if I would, and it struck me as a good way to remotivate myself." And it worked. That race in Boston was his tenth marathon—and his slowest time. It was also the race that (up to that point) made him the happiest.

With his radio show a big hit, Sagal had become a celebrity in Chicago and nationally among NPR listeners. I asked if his volunteer runs were done in a pay-it-forward spirit of giving back to the community. I could practically hear him wrinkling his nose.

"I don't know why the pay-it-forward thing bugs me," he said. "It's a wonderful idea—you've been given something, now give to someone else. But there's something transactional that bothers me. What I find compelling, instead, is the simple joy I get from being of service without expecting anything back. When you give without wanting a return, you actually get a huge return. So it's very selfish of me to do this! In a weird way, it's a little bit like running. I do it because it makes me feel better."

I laughed because it didn't seem weird at all. Adam Smith had been onto the giving-is-getting game a few centuries ago (though without the marathons).

"The things I've done in my life that have been of service to individuals—and there have not been enough of them—have given me great satisfaction in the way that other things don't," Sagal said. Then he added, "Did you get the part—*there have not been enough of them*? Please write that down."

Adam Smith would surely include Peter Sagal's aiding a blind runner in his category of "good conduct" and therefore worthy of gratitude and reward. If Sagal did it for the personal satisfaction or to get over the hump of training, then bravo for him. The epiphany that helping someone else made you feel good yourself might get others to do the same. Self-interest? Good plan.

Intrigued to connect with others who did one-to-one service, I hopped on a train to see Dr. Andrew Jacono, a plastic surgeon who helped victims of domestic violence by providing reconstructive surgery at no fee, giving them back their dignity along with their cheekbones. I knew he also spent several weeks a year in foreign countries, performing cleft-palate surgery for needy children.

If I hadn't known his background, I would not have pegged Dr. Jacono as an exemplar of gratitude and giving. In his early forties, with thick dark hair, white teeth, and smooth, taut skin, he looked like someone on a reality TV show. But his success was much more than skin-deep. He built a twelve-thousand-square-foot plastic surgery center and spa in an upscale community on Long Island, and clients flew in to see him from all over the country and the world—including China, Singapore, Paris, and Spain.

"I never imagined it would be this way," he said when we sat together in his elegant environs.

He told me that he'd picked his career in third grade when he sat next to a girl with a cleft palate on the school bus. He tried to be nice, but the other kids were horribly mean, throwing gum at her face and calling her names. Then she had surgery and everything changed. People liked her. The bullying stopped. He dreamed about becoming the miracle-making surgeon who could remake fate.

But Dr. Jacono didn't grow up in a wealthy family, and becoming a sought-after plastic surgeon never seemed in the cards. People discouraged him at every step, saying it was too difficult to get into medical school or he was crazy to start a private practice or he'd go broke building his own surgery center. Somehow, he pulled it all off. "We all like to think it's our own talents that make us successful, but I think it's much more important to have passion and purpose and be relentless in the pursuit of what matters to you," he said.

However he struggled for his self-made success, Dr. Jacono was grateful to be in a position to turn the tables and help others. "I do believe that we're all connected and the more you give in your life, the more you get back," he said. He told me that while he loved the work he did every day (no disparaging those paying clients), the volunteer activities sustained his soul.

"My financial success has been more than I ever could have imagined, but real gratitude comes from the peace and happiness I feel when I'm part of something bigger than myself," he said.

Volunteering in a third-world country, he discovered that facial deformities were feared as an evil curse rather than a medical problem. One morning a devastated mother handed him her afflicted six-month-old—and an hour later, he put the baby back in her arms, healthy and normal. She wept in appreciation. "A simple surgery lifted the curse and changed the lives of the whole family," he said—and in the telling, his voice cracked with emotion. Embarrassed, he took off his (designer) glasses to get his composure and wiped away some tears.

"I didn't know I'd get so emotional," he said. "But I'm so lucky. And so grateful to have the moments that give meaning and purpose to my life."

He had recently come back from climbing Mount Kilimanjaro with his sixteen-year-old son and saw the trek as a great metaphor. "Getting to the top of the mountain when you feel like you're going to die but keep persevering is unforgettable," he said. "I told my son, 'Never let anyone tell you that you can't do something with your life that you want.'"

I left his office incredibly moved. Proud of his hard-won success, Dr. Jacono felt grateful for all the good he had achieved and wanted to share it. As a way to make yourself feel beautiful, it was better than Botox.

Whether it was my new perspective or the approach of the holiday season, I started seeing signs of gratitude everywhere—in one case, quite literally. A friend texted me photos of two bill-boards that loomed over the dense and traffic-packed highways that swerve into Manhattan. One faced the northbound roads and the other the southbound, and they each had a single word: GRATTITUDE.

"Do you know what these are?" my friend asked.

I didn't. The billboards (with an extra *T* in the spelling) had no explanation or attribution. They didn't seem to be advertising any-thing and gave no indication who had put them up or paid for them. Curious, I did some research and traced them to an artist named Peter Tunney. I tried to reach him, but e-mails to a gallery in Massachusetts showing his work went unanswered. I found a phone number in New York and, on a whim one morning, dialed. He answered immediately.

"Hi. You don't know me, but I'd love to talk to you about grat-itude," I said.

Knowing me or not clearly didn't matter, since he immediately launched into an animated conversation. He told me I'd caught him in the car driving to his studio and he had to leave at the end of the week for an art show in Miami. But he could tell me right now that gratitude counted more than almost anything else. "If I could put up five thousand gratitude billboards today, I would," he said. "But do you want to talk about this now or come down to my studio and meet?"

The next day, I took a subway down to Franklin Street in Lower Manhattan and stepped into the crazy, wild world of Peter Tunney. Canvases hung on the walls and stood lined up deep on the floor. Most of them were collages of newspaper clippings made into words or phrases like "Gratitude" and "City of Dreams" and "The Time Is Always Now." Others had collages as backgrounds and positive phrases painted over them.

"Is that Janice?" Peter called out from a desk somewhere in the back, as if we were old friends.

I made my way past a red surfboard that also had a GRATTITUDE collage and met the artist. Tall, blond, and broad chested, he could have been a former athlete, but his jeans were artistically paint stained—his work and fashion making a nice mix.

The upstairs of his large space was a gallery, the downstairs his office and studio. A couple of assistants talked to clients who wandered in and also worked on organizing the endless material Peter gathered for his collages. His paintings all had upbeat, optimistic messages, and Peter showed me around, offering an energetic stream of explanations to accompany each piece.

"I'm doing a billboard in Los Angeles now that says 'Choose Happy,'" he said. "I could be wrong about all of this and humans are going the way of the dinosaurs, but then I'm going out with a smile. I just don't believe in the other way. I can't imagine we're all put here to suffer and beat each other up and spew venom. It seems like a ridiculous waste of time to me."

He spent a few minutes talking about the big problems in the world that deeply disturbed him, from human trafficking to innocent people in prison. "But right now, I'm standing here in a cashmere sweater talking to you, I'm happy, healthy, fifty-three years old, and in the most productive moment of my life. If I don't walk around the street buoyant and jubilant, then what's wrong with me?"

Many of his collages had images of death and destruction underneath, then the overlay of positive words. The message was clear—you can see the problems of the world and be unhappy or choose a different way.

"People drive into a city and see billboards with ads to drink Coke, go to a strip club, take pills. These may be a few of my favorite things, but my vision was giant notices that the world is okay, or you can make it that way." Putting up the GRATTITUDE billboards (and others with messages like THE TIME IS ALWAYS NOW) became a personal mission. He told me about a lunch he had one day with a wealthy businessman. "I said to him, 'You have a billion dollars and I have eleven thousand dollars in my bank account. Why am I the one putting up the billboards? Am I the only one who's thought of trying to send positive messages into the world?'"

Now the message was getting out and billboards of Tunney's work have appeared all over the country and in Toronto, Vancouver, and Montreal. He hopes to have signs soon in Philadelphia and Detroit and Los Angeles, and he's now getting calls for projects in Asia and Europe. His studio on Franklin Street is becoming a Warhol-like factory.

"I'm making a living selling gratitude paintings. That's crazy. You can't invent a crazier story for Peter Tunney. I could paint 'Grattitude' and 'The Time Is Always Now' for the rest of my life."

The poster boy (quite literally) for positivity, Tunney once had a very different reputation. He worked closely for ten years with the photographer Peter Beard, famous for both his shots of wildlife in Africa and his marriage to model Cheryl Tiegs.

"What was it like, spending years in Africa?" I asked.

"Most of it was spent partying in Paris," he said with a laugh.

He was eager for experiences, which ultimately included drugs, alcohol, models, and many wild nights.

"The short version is, I went to a party when I was thirteen and I came home when I was forty-three. I met everyone and I went everywhere but I could have died. I've seen the world from every dark outlook you can imagine, and a viewpoint without any gratitude—it doesn't work. I'm not going there again. I just find it unhelpful to be negative, because you have no idea what happens when you walk out this door today."

Tunney had been hit by a car when bicycling at age thirteen, a devastating accident that ironically might have been the start of his positive perspective. "My parents said, 'Thank God he didn't hit his head.' I had all these bones sticking out, but my brain was okay, and I'd get better." He heard other patients moaning, 'Why me, why did this happen?' But he stayed away from the victim mentality. "Being hit by a car seemed like a bad thing, but who knows where I'd be otherwise? Maybe I would have gone on to be a high school sports hero and died in a drunk-driving accident. Right? Who knows."

He saw other advantages from that childhood accident, including the pleasure of going back to school after lying in a hospital bed for almost a year. "'A schoolbook! Wow. And look at that blue sky. Do you smell those leaves?' You almost have to lose it to feel it. You think gratitude is something you express when everything is going well. But really it's what you feel when everything is going against you."

Now with his art and his billboards, Tunney was on a quest to convince everyone else that since life was random, you could only move forward, do the right thing, and make the best of whatever happened.

"I like the expression 'Plan plans, not results.' I used to think I could run the universe, but it was very laborious, I did a terrible job, and nobody listened to me. Now I'm not in charge of anything but my own mental and spiritual self. My mission every day is to stay buoyant and joyous. My billboards aren't ironic or tongue-in-cheek. I mean what they say. I can't put up billboards like those and walk around with my head down."

He told me he'd been caught in the midst of a multiyear, multimillion-dollar litigation in New York over billboards (not just his) that had brought down most of the signs. Driving into Manhattan now from one direction, the only billboard you could see from horizon to horizon was one of Tunney's. "I hope the city fights me. You want to tear down 'Grattitude' and put up what? 'Buy Vicodin'? 'Go to the Hustler Club'? I don't even mean it as a metaphor, because that's what people see every day. What kind of messages are we sending to ourselves?"

Another wealthy guy who owned a big outdoor company had asked Tunney how he could help him spread his message. "I said, 'You've got five billion dollars? How about you take five hundred million for yourself and do whatever you want—buy a couple of houses, a plane. Then we spend the other four and a half billion putting up "Grattitude" billboards for the next ten years. If you have a better plan than that for life, tell me, but I don't know one.'"

And Tunney really meant it. He was grateful to be here, alive on this planet. He gave me two books of his art so I could keep the positivity with me. I already felt jubilant—a few hours surrounded by paintings all about the good in the world has an effect.

We said our good-byes and then halfway out the door, I stopped.

"Oh, Peter, I forgot to ask. Why the extra *T* in 'Grattitude'?"

A small smile crossed his face. "My dear, that's for the attitude." He leaned over and gave me a parting hug. "The attitude, right? It's all about the attitude."

With Thanksgiving getting close, gratitude suddenly seemed part of the zeitgeist, and not just on billboards. From what I saw on Instagram and Facebook and morning TV, November had become a once-a-year chance for the whole country to focus on reasons to be grateful. Better if we did it year-round, but heck, I'd take once a year. The holiday seemed to have morphed from its Pilgrim origins. The first Thanksgiving was surely much harsher and more solemn than the storybooks suggested, and I hoped that instead of making cheerful Native American headdresses and paper turkeys (by tracing a hand), kindergarten teachers were now helping children make gratitude lists.

I pulled out my Thanksgiving recipes, well-worn from years of use. My sons liked adventurous cuisines—except at the holidays, when they were firm about keeping family traditions. I was allowed some discretion in the soup course (as long as it was zucchini-potato or apple-squash), but otherwise we went with turkey, bread-and-mushroom stuffing, sweet potato soufflé, roasted Brussels sprouts, and many, many pies. After all these years, I could make it in my sleep. Ron always gave an amusing and touching before-dinner toast about thankfulness—but now he hesitated about being the one to speak.

"Why wouldn't you?" I asked.

"You're the expert on gratitude—I'm a doctor. If I give a toast about thankfulness, will you follow up with new medical treatments for diabetes?"

I laughed. "No. I can't learn medicine quickly, but everyone can learn to be grateful."

We all gathered at our country house—friends and extended family, including Ron's mom, who had always been my role model for a positive person. I had fun setting the table with jars of flowers and different-size candles, brightly colored napkins, and fancy and simple china patterns mixed together. I'd learned not to serve the soup until Ron gave his toast—it always got cold. But we poured champagne and sparkling cider, and Ron stood up, glass in hand. He started his toast with great warmth, talking about all that he was grateful for. He mentioned everyone at the table and something each person had done that he found special. He thanked his wife—me—for making us all a little more positive this year.

"So that's what I'm grateful *for,* but I've also started to wonder who or what I'm grateful *to.*" He paused and gave a little smile. "Maybe there really is some big guy in the sky who's arranged all this for me. Or maybe my good luck is just the randomness of the universe. Whichever, I know the cosmos has smiled on me. And I am smiling back, very grateful."

There were a lot of "aws" and "aahs" around the table, and as we clicked glasses, I knew I didn't have to worry if the turkey was dry. What mattered about the holiday had already been handled.

Later that night, when the dishes were done and the leftovers (a lot of them) neatly piled into Tupperware in the refrigerator, I took out a note card and wrote down Henry Timms's words: *Gratitude at its best is an action.*

So many gratitude-inspired actions made the world better. Hugh Jackman auctioned off his T-shirt and Peter Sagal ran with a blind marathoner. Andrew Jacono performed life-changing surgeries and Mark Liponis (from Canyon Ranch) went to an impoverished corner of Laos and ran weeklong medical clinics. The artist Peter Tunney put up positive-message billboards and Henry Timms created a worldwide day of giving. My husband the doctor helped and healed.

And me? I'd spent a whole year living gratefully, but what had I actually done on that grander scale? Sure, I participated on a couple of charitable boards and Ron and I made whatever donations we could each year. But in terms of world-changing, earth-shattering, giving-back extravaganzas, I didn't really compare.

I had one month left to think about what I could do that would make a difference in my life and my family's life. I needed to know that gratitude could impact all of us for even longer than a year.

CHAPTER 14

Finding Joy

Grateful to let go of second-guessing myself

So happy that my sister and I reconnected over kale and chocolate

Grateful for those good people both long ago and today who know to appreciate every moment of life

Trying to decide where gratitude might take me this month, I absentmindedly fiddled with a mug that I kept on my desk. It clattered out of my fingers, and as I grabbed for it, I suddenly remembered why I had it in the first place. Ironically, I'd put it on my desk a few months ago to keep in constant sight (though of course I'd stopped seeing it)—a reminder of how gratitude for family can help you find joy and calm even in the midst of despair.

Now I held the mug carefully in my hands, taking in the pretty teal background and delicate Japanese-influenced white flowers. Based on a painting by a famous artist, the graceful and beguiling image might lead to easy assumptions about the guy who painted it. Surely he wouldn't be a tormented genius who cut off his ear and spent time in a mental institution. But actually, he was. Vincent van Gogh had painted *Almond Blossom* while suffering his deepest misery.

I'd seen the real painting for the first time when Ron and I visited Amsterdam a couple of months earlier. One day of our vacation fell on King's Day, a national holiday a lot like July Fourth only with hues of orange (Holland's official color) instead of red, white, and blue. The city teemed with revelers drinking beer, celebrating in the streets, and taking party boats up the canals. Ron and I had fun watching for a while, but merrymaking wasn't exactly our style. I felt slightly embarrassed that I'd spent weeks planning the trip and not known we'd be there during the most raucous holiday in Holland.

In silver-linings mode, we made our way through the huge throngs and got to the Van Gogh Museum, famously crowded on even a normal day. But with everyone partying outside, nobody wanted to be inside. Triumph! The museum was deserted. We had the exhibits practically to ourselves.

"Very grateful that I forgot to check dates and planned our vacation over King's Day!" I said to Ron with a grin.

We strolled through the halls, gazing in close-up awe at famous paintings we'd seen before only on posters. We encountered the Zen-like painting *Almond Blossom* (the basis for my mug) hanging in an upstairs room. Van Gogh had painted it in 1890, at the end of his life. Seeing the pretty picture on the wall startled— because the genteel, elegant painting was surrounded by two anguished works he had done at about the same time, both filled with loneliness and angst. One showed a wheat field with a reaper, and the other displayed jagged trees cut down by lightning at the sanitorium garden, painted in saturated red. ("Seeing red" was van Gogh's metaphor for anxiety.)

In the midst of van Gogh's gloomy visions of mortality, isolation, and despair, he had found a way to paint this beautifully tranquil and life-affirming picture. And here was the story: His brother, Theo, and his wife had just had a baby whom they named Vincent. Even as he struggled with depression, the original Vincent van Gogh was so touched that they named the baby after him, he wanted to express his gratitude. He painted the blossoms as a sign of hope and thanks.

In the gift shop afterward, I found myself moved all over again by how an expression of gratitude let van Gogh (briefly) break through his emotional pain. I decided to buy the mug as a reminder of the power of gratitude to change a mood.

"You could decorate the whole house with that message," Ron said, pointing out the napkins, plastic plates, pencils, espresso cups, notebooks, eyeglass holders, mouse pads, and salt and pepper shakers with the same *Almond Blossom* motif. Most people were probably attracted to the pretty design. For me, it seemed like the most beautiful gratitude letter ever created.

One other story from that trip. The next night, with the city turned quiet again, we strolled down a beautiful canal-side street after a great day. The only downside had been a just-okay dinner that the waiter had taken forever to serve. I'd been deciding among three restaurants and changed the reservation several times, and now I apologized to Ron for having picked the wrong one. Ron told me not to worry, but I couldn't stop. I felt my anxiety building, that I'd made it a less-than-perfect day. "I should have gone to the one the concierge recommended," I said querulously. Ron tried again to reassure me, then finally stopped in his tracks.

"Hey, Ms. Gratitude," he said with a grin. "We're holding

hands walking by a canal on a gorgeous night in Holland. Would you like to appreciate that—or worry about the restaurant?"

I laughed, because of course he was right. Second-guessing myself—a favorite hobby of mine—didn't fit with grateful living. Time to give it up. I'd unwittingly picked up the habit from my mother, the master of "should have." Though when I was growing up, she said it *shoulduv*. Until I was eighteen, I thought it was a word. My father got upset when he heard my mother ranting about what she (or he or we) "shoulduv" done. *Shoulduv, coulduv, woulduv!* he would shout at her. *Can't you stop it?* She couldn't stop—or at least she didn't—but now I needed to banish "shoulduv" forever. I'd learned this year that gratitude didn't depend on the right events or even the right decisions, but how I processed them. Gratitude gave you back control. I didn't have to pick the perfect restaurant (or hotel or flight home) to appreciate the vacation and be grateful I was here.

The psychologist Barry Schwartz at Swarthmore College has made a career of trying to prove that too much choice doesn't make us happy. We get stymied when presented with too many possibilities (so repeatedly change the restaurant reservation) or when our expectations get pumped too high (with so many restaurants in Amsterdam, I could pick a great one!). Once we do make a selection, we're less satisfied than we might be—because we wonder about all the choices we didn't make. Would a different one have been better? The only way I could think to square the problem was to be grateful for the choice I'd made. So now I hugged Ron and we continued walking down the street in a new mood. I wouldn't ruin the night by ruing the restaurant. I could be grateful for right now, this moment together by a canal, and still find a place tomorrow night that didn't take three hours to serve dinner.

After Amsterdam, I kept thinking about van Gogh and whether gratitude really could ease—even briefly—depression and despair. I had only the evidence of the three paintings hanging on the museum wall, and my interpretation of them. So I spoke to Dr. Jeffrey Huffman, a psychiatrist at Massachusetts General Hospital who has done research on the effects of various treatments on patients who are depressed, hopeless, and suicidal.

"Writing a letter of gratitude was the single most effective positive intervention we found," he told me. (They hadn't looked at *painting* letters of gratitude.) He thought one reason might be that feelings of hopelessness lead to feeling alone and completely self-focused. Gratitude turns your attention outward, serving as a reminder that you do have connections and people who care about you. (Maybe even enough to name their baby after you.)

"Realizing that someone did something kind gives so many positive emotions to unpack!" he said. "If you're being grateful, you must have been worthy enough for someone to pay attention to you. You do have somebody in the world who cares about you, and you're not alone. The feeling of gratitude can have a profound effect on improving the mood of someone feeling isolated and worthless."

Holding the mug now, I thought about Vincent van Gogh, lifted briefly from his depression as he expressed his gratitude to his brother, Theo. I found a book of van Gogh's letters, many of them thanking Theo for sending canvas, paints, and money.

"Even when it's a success, painting never pays back what it costs," he wrote sadly. In early 1890, he shared Theo's joy at the new baby. "I have just today received the good news that you are at last a father . . . That does me more good and gives me more pleasure than I can put into words," he wrote. He immediately began to paint *Almond Blossom* for the baby's bedroom, his expression of life, hope, and gratitude. Despite the torment Vincent van Gogh experienced, he created a lasting ode to family love.

Most of us can't create a masterpiece to offer thanks for a kind act, but the paintings on that wall were proof of gratitude's mood-altering powers. Angst, madness, and despair on both sides—and joy and beauty in the middle. Feeling grateful for family had allowed van Gogh to find a pocket of calm in the midst of a sanitorium. Just think what it could do for the rest of us amid the very different craziness of everyday life.

Families can be a great source of joy—as well as a font for a whole lot of annoyance, irritation, and (on the baby front) exhaustion. Babies help everyone around them to stay in the moment—what is now called "mindfulness." When a three-month-old is shrieking, your only thought is whether he needs a bottle, a cuddle, or a diaper change. You're not plotting about the future or worrying about the past. And mindfulness and gratitude are very much two sides of the same thin dime. To stop and fully be in a moment is what also allows you to appreciate it.

When our older son, Zach, was an infant, I had heard the rueful comments from an older generation about how "it all goes by so fast." Even though the days then seemed like the longest in

my life (starting with four A.M. feedings), I accepted that some-
day I'd look back at how quickly they'd passed. One night after
I had done the laundry in the miniature washer-dryer stacked in
the corner of the kitchen, Ron helped me fold the clothes, and
he picked up one of the baby's tiny undershirts in his big hands.
He stared at it with wonder.

"I love him so much I even love his T-shirts," he said.

We looked at each other and then down at the little garments,
grateful and awed. Neither of us had much sleep and the baby's
needs seemed endless, but that flood of love trumped all.

"I never want to look back and wonder why we didn't appreciate every moment when it was happening," I said fervently.

The joy for what happened *right now* remained our theme
when the children were little. ("As long as they're happy, don't
worry about anything else," my mother-in-law used to advise.) It's
probably not possible to appreciate every moment of life, and I
can easily recount too many times when I got irritable or worried
or impatient that I wouldn't mind getting back to try again. But
the mindful appreciation that came from having a new baby dom-
inated my intentions. I refused to believe that Proust was right
when he said that "the true paradises are the paradises one has
lost." The real paradise should be the one you were living and
appreciating right that very moment.

A lot of people who knew about my gratitude project had
started sharing their own stories with me—and I was delighted
when I heard from a new mom named Sharon Kunz whom I had
worked with a few years earlier. Talented and smart but so thin
that we all worried about her, Sharon (ironically) fell in love with
a chef named Erik and blossomed after they got married. She

eventually moved to New Haven with her husband, got an interesting job, and then had a baby. Now Sharon told me that baby
Isaac was three months old, and though he was perfect (of
course!), he had been having some tough days and nights. He
would scream and scream through the night for reasons she
couldn't figure out, and then the next day he'd be tired and fussy.
He had done that one Sunday night, and Monday was so difficult
that Sharon started to despair. But then came Tuesday.

"At about eight A.M., Isaac and I climbed into bed with a stack
of board books and we snuggled and read for half an hour," she
told me. "It was a moment of perfect happiness and I was almost
overcome with gratitude. There were more moments like that
throughout the day—having a coffee at our local hangout and
watching him nap in his stroller as we walked home from the
bank. That night when he was in bed, I curled up on the couch
and started to write him a letter about how grateful I was for our
wonderful day."

I admired Sharon's ability to turn a stressful time into a happy
one. But babies don't always read the script that would provide
the golden-glow ending to a story like that. While Sharon was
writing her letter of gratitude to her baby, he woke up screaming.
Three weeks later, the letter was still "only about seventy-five
percent finished," she said. "But I do think that the tough days
make it easier to be grateful for the good days. With life in general, right? The more hardship people have suffered, in my experience, the easier it is for them to be grateful for the little
things—which, of course, are the things that, added up, comprise
our whole lives."

Lucky Isaac. I had no doubt that Sharon would finish that

letter of gratitude. It didn't matter if Isaac ever read it—Sharon wanted to write down and remember the moments with her baby that gave her joy and gratitude. Focusing on those would make those cranky nights easier to handle (and eventually forget). I was also struck by her insight that it's the little things that make up our lives. Snuggling in bed with your baby or folding his undershirt amid a wave of love are the memories worth keeping.

Using gratitude to stay calm can change your relationship with grown-up family members, too. Anthropologist Margaret Mead once said that sisters are "probably the most competitive relationship within the family, but once the sisters are grown, it becomes the strongest relationship." My older sister, Nancy, and I seemed to have gotten stuck on the "competitive" part. Now we both wanted to change that. By some odd confluence of the universe, my new focus on gratitude coincided with Nancy's discovering mindfulness. My ambitious and successful businesswoman-sister had started meditating every night and taking yoga classes. She even had a new consulting company focused on mindful leadership. Since both of us were trying to see the world through a more positive lens, we wondered if that filter could change our relationship to each other. We talked about trying to become the kind of sisters who talked and shared and cared. This month seemed like a good time to take the effort to the next step.

So on an early December Friday, I took an Amtrak train to Washington, DC, for a "sisters' weekend"—a phrase that, for me, hit about an 8 on the Richter scale. Hang out together just for fun? The last time I remembered doing that, she was nine years old and I was five. A lot of water had passed under many bridges since then, and we had our resentments and piques. We could each make a list of what the other had done wrong. But focusing on past problems led nowhere, and we had nothing to lose by trying to be positive and appreciate each other. The gain might be much-wanted sisterly support.

My late-afternoon train from New York was an hour late, and I called Nancy a few times with updates. As we got closer (and slower), I knew she was waiting at the station, and I got more and more frustrated. Wrong start to the weekend!

> I'm trying to stay calm, I texted her. At least I'm looking out the window at a pretty sunset. Take a look.

> You're right! she replied. The sun is burnished red and the sky is still very blue. That doesn't usually happen.

> See how lucky we are that I'm late? We might have missed that.

> We are lucky. Travel mindfully, sister.

> And gratefully!

I put away my phone and smiled. A couple of years ago, the late train would have made both of us stressed and tense and snappish. But unless we moved to Switzerland (where the trains were always on time), we needed to rely on our new attitudes— to stay in the moment (mindfulness) and appreciate the pretty sunset (gratitude). With that approach, irritations didn't seem so bad.

When I got to the station, we gave each other a big hug and headed out for dinner with two of her grown daughters.

"I heard you had a really slow trip," said her youngest daughter, Emily, as we sat down for sushi.

"It took a long time, but . . ." I stopped. Did I really want to waste time recounting the details of a late train? I smiled and gave a little shrug. "I'm here now and so glad to be with you. That's what really matters."

"You sound just like my mom!" said Emily, with her usual high spirits. "She never talks about bad stuff anymore. She just says, 'I'm here now!'"

For Nancy not to talk about bad stuff seemed as amazing as—well, as *my* not talking about bad stuff. Dr. Huffman had told me that some people seemed wired to appreciate life while others had a harder time. Being more grateful predicted what he called "superior mental health–related quality of life"—which included higher energy levels, better social connections, and happier moods. In one research study, he had charted people who scored high in gratitude in red, those who scored low in blue. When looking at levels of certain positive behaviors and positive mental health, the red lines ran across the top of the page, the blue lines far below. "We'd like to change blue people to red ones," he said. (Though he joked that as a Democrat, he never thought he'd say those words.)

I suspected that Nancy and I (and probably our big brother, Bob, too) had started out as blue people and were working as hard as we could to become red ones. Because we'd grown up with a negative mom (all that *shoulduv*), gratitude didn't come naturally. But each in our way wanted to turn that around.

For Nancy and me, that became the message of the weekend—appreciating the good in the moment rather than fussing about the past. Since Nancy had found her new level of calm through meditation, she wanted to share it, and on Saturday morning, she took me to her meditation class. About a dozen people sat in a pleasant room, at ease on comfy mats and cushions, eyes closed, bodies relaxed. I liked the lovely leader, but my mind didn't go where directed (or undirected). I understood the point of meditation, but it just made me want to giggle (certain things bring out my fourth-grade side), so I resorted to journalist mode. Afterward, Nancy said she had heard me taking notes.

"I used a soft pen hoping I wouldn't disturb you," I said, apologizing.

"You didn't. I just felt bad, because if you were writing, you weren't getting the full experience."

I explained that I used the hour for my own kind of stress relieving, which involved gratitude games with myself. For example, I heard a dog barking on the street below, breaking the quiet of the room. At first the noise was irritating, but then I practiced flipping to the bright side. I felt grateful that my ears worked well and I could hear a dog, and I thought about our own family dog that we'd loved for many years. (Ah, Willie, the genius Portuguese water dog who thought he was human.) The barking became a lovely sound rather than an annoying one. And by the way, sitting in the room, even not meditating, I felt grateful to be sharing an experience with my sister and getting to understand a new side of her. What more could I want than that?

Nancy nodded and told me her own story about gratitude. One

recent night, she had a horrible evening and had been stuck in a hospital ER helping someone for endless hours. (The details are unimportant and too complicated to recount.) She finally left at three A.M., exhausted and frustrated, and walked out to the parking lot. Nobody was around. The outside lot was completely quiet.

"And then I looked up at the most beautiful moon I've ever seen. It was huge and seemed to fill the whole sky and had a different color than usual—almost blue."

She stood in the parking lot a very long time, gazing at the sky. "I felt incredibly grateful to be in that place at that moment and see that moon. It occurred to me that if not for the events of the night, I never would have seen the moon at all. I got in the car to drive home, and it followed me, bright and bold and huge and blue. I watched it the whole time, feeling very lucky."

I told Nancy that the real luck was that she had an attitude now that made her appreciate the moon and the moment. At an earlier time, the Nancy I knew might have walked out of that hospital so angry and frustrated that she barely glimpsed the sky. But now, ready for a positive view of life, she left the hospital and found beauty in the night.

A beautiful sunset when I arrived late, a blue moon after a horrible night. "Isn't there an expression about a sea change? I think you've undergone a sky change!" I said to my sister.

We spent the rest of the day walking in a pretty park and talking and talking. Nancy had been through a recent divorce, but instead of knocking her down, it had given her hope for a fresh start. She remained very close to her daughters and felt lucky that they had rallied around her. We stopped to look at a rushing waterfall in the park, and against the scenic backdrop, she admitted that she had started to have a new view of what really mattered.

"I get up every single morning and think how grateful I am for my girls. I told them that once and they said, 'Every single day? Really?' They thought I was exaggerating, but it's actually true," she said.

At one point, Nancy brought up an incident between us that had bothered her from years past. I had no defense—it happened long ago. Siblings typically let resentment linger, reliving when the other person let us down, ignored a need, said the wrong thing. But instead of recalling incidents gone wrong, I thought we needed memories gone right. I suggested we could restore our relationship by focusing on the times together that we felt grateful.

"Here's my gratitude memory of you," I said. I recounted a childhood night long ago when our grandpa had just died. Scared and sad, I couldn't get to sleep, and Nancy took out her music box, one of her most cherished possessions, and let me play the tinkly tune.

"You'd never let me play with your music box before," I told her.

"You were so little, you would have broken it!"

"But you let me that night, because you knew it would cheer me up. I was too young then to say thank you, so let me say it now."

Nancy nodded, getting the point. We'd wasted a lot of time over the years annoyed by each other's mistakes and failings. But how much better to appreciate the moments of kindness and warmth—and hold on to those.

"How about you? I guess if you have no grateful memory, we might as well give up," I said.

But Nancy recounted a time when her three children were very young, she was in a tough situation, and I flew down from New York to see how I could help.

"I really appreciated that. So many other things got in the way afterwards, but I knew that day you really cared," she said.

I put my arm around my sister and gave her a hug. Holding on to memories like the night-of-the-music-box or the day-of-flying-down gave us something to appreciate again. Gratitude might not make us into the Olsen twins, but it reminded each of us that we had a sister to count on. With that as the new basis for sisterhood, we could move forward.

We went back to Nancy's pretty house and for dinner, we made a feast of the kale and quinoa she cooks and keeps fresh in her fridge. We kept talking and talking, and at a little before midnight, we decided to celebrate. Neither of us drinks much, so Nancy pulled out a bowl of chocolate-covered ginger (we couldn't eat healthily forever), and we lifted our chocolate and toasted being sisters.

Nancy, who did not cry easily, admitted that thinking about our new friendship brought tears to her eyes. I dabbed at my eyes with a tissue and admitted that I felt exactly the same.

"Though it may be your cat making me cry. You do know I'm allergic, right?" I asked.

Nancy laughed and stroked Toby, more the size of a bobcat than a house pet. I liked dogs and Nancy liked cats. But with all the goodwill suddenly flowing between us, we could work it out.

———

The next day, when I got home, I stayed quieter than usual. Ron asked what was wrong, and I told him about my concern that I hadn't made a big enough impact this year. I needed the grand gesture that would make my gratitude forever meaningful. He looked at me in amazement.

"You're joking, right?"

"No, not at all."

"Okay, let's think it through. You made our marriage better, reconciled with your sister, got a new view of your career, and encouraged our kids. And by the way, you wrote a book so that other people can do the same thing. Isn't that enough for you?"

My old instinct was to say "Not enough!" but I caught the fierce look in Ron's eyes and smiled. The philosopher Epictetus had been my guide through parts of this year and he spent a lot of time discussing how we can be most content if we focus on what is in our power. Anxiety comes from wanting what we can't control. He gave the example of a lute player who is happy when playing and singing to himself—but gets anxious when he goes on stage *for he not only wishes to sing well, but also to obtain applause: but this is not in his power.* In modern terms, that meant not driving yourself crazy about the things you couldn't control or hadn't yet accomplished.

"I think what I've done better be enough for now," I told Ron with a smile.

I had started the year making myself (and him) unhappy by looking only at what I lacked. After this year, I understood that coming from a position of gratitude, you could still want (and get) more for yourself, your family, your career, or the world. But you enjoyed more along the way. No road led right to the top and some didn't get there at all, but gratitude at least let you take the scenic route.

Living gratefully had started out as a lark, and once I decided to write a book, the yearlong project could have slipped into being just a literary device. But as the year went on, the project had lodged deeper and deeper into my heart and soul. I wasn't just reporting—I was also *feeling*. Something changed in me. Gratitude affected how I looked at every event that happened. Being positive and looking for the good had become second nature—and that made me much happier. I still got into the occasional bad mood, but I snapped out of it quickly. My much-appreciated children called regularly and stopped by often. Ron and I spent a lot of time sitting at dinner together talking about how lucky we were to have each other. In fact, we weren't any more blessed than we had ever been—we just noticed it more. And the noticing made us closer and happier.

I thought about grand gestures for a couple of days, and that weekend at our country house, I went out for a long walk by the river. There had been an early snowfall and the trees glistened with lacy patterns of ice and snow. Underfoot, the snow was soft and crunchy, melted enough for easy walking, but not yet wet slush. I paused to notice how beautiful the woods appeared, the elegant simplicity of the stark winter trees against the pale blue sky. But then I let my mind wander. I pondered Henry Timms's suggestion that I needed some dazzling finale for my year, and I thought about going to Nicaragua to build houses for the poor.

Final scene: Janice with a hammer and nails!

But no, that wasn't me.

I admired the people who expressed gratitude with grand

gestures, but my expressions, smaller and more personal, made their own kind of impact. My positivity this year had touched others, and maybe each of those people had found some peace and satisfaction that they could pass along too. I hadn't changed my essential nature to be more grateful, but none of us really needed to do that (nor can we, I suspect). Instead, I'd recentered and refocused. Maybe I was 40 percent more positive and 50 percent more grateful, and that in itself was dramatic and life changing.

From a high point on the mostly flat trail, I looked out at the river, clearly visible through the bare trees. I realized that this year I had started noticing the details of life and nature in a different way—sunrises and sunsets, rushing rivers, the warmth of the sun on my face and the prickling briskness of the wind on my back. I even smiled to think about the dog I'd heard barking during my sister's meditation class. I had made myself stop often to be grateful for every sensation, and now it came naturally, the simplest pleasure of simply being alive in a vibrant world.

Heading back home, I stopped at the small cemetery just outside the center of town and walked among the old-fashioned headstones tilting in the mild afternoon sun. Slim pieces of stone with simple inscriptions from the late 1800s carried names like Ebenezer Eaton and Rebecca Alcott and George Bull and Edwidge Stone. I tried to imagine the lives of the solid New Englanders who had died at fifty-two and sixty, a full life back then, or lost a child at eighteen days or three years. One man lived a fuller life: "72 years, 7 months, and 28 days," the inscription said. I thought how he must have appreciated every moment on earth to count each day. Or maybe it was only after his death that a relative thought to cherish those days and be thankful for every one of them.

Wandering among the stones, I felt like I'd stepped into act 3 of Thornton Wilder's play *Our Town*. Many of the townspeople have died, but they remain onstage, sitting in chairs that represent their places in the cemetery. The play's young heroine, Emily, has died in childbirth, and she is stunned to find herself among the dead. She asks for the chance to return to earth for one day. Just one day! While warned not to, she decides to go back and experience again her twelfth birthday.

Our Town is always performed without props—"no curtain, no scenery," Wilder wrote in his stage directions—and the characters mime the action of setting a table or shucking peas. (It makes it a perfect play for schools—not a lot of extra stage expenses.) But when I saw a production at a downtown theater in New York, the director made the last scene, the day Emily returned to relive her twelfth birthday, come to vivid, sensory life. As Emily's mother cooked breakfast in the kitchen, real plates clattered and freshly cooking bacon crackled on the (working) stove, its rich aroma wafting through the audience. Her mom barely noticed her as she rushed to get the meal on the table, and the ghostly Emily understood that all the colors and smells and sounds—so incredibly appealing now—had meant nothing to her and her family when they actually lived the day.

"Oh, earth, you're too wonderful for anybody to realize you," Emily says.

Horrified at how careless we are about savoring our time on earth, she asks to go back to the cemetery. It is too painful to see people ignoring the world and not appreciating our fleeting moments of life. I saw that downtown production on three occasions, and each time, tears rolled down my cheeks when Emily discovered how foolish and oblivious we all are, how we don't know to be grateful for the simple gifts of life and love and cooking bacon.

Can we stop and revel in the moments of daily life, or will we only regret when they have been lost? I had too often let the wonders of life be an unseen background, and now, before it was too late, I wanted them center stage. My year of living gratefully had changed me in so many ways, but mostly it had given me the simple ability to experience joy for almost any reason. I now knew to appreciate this moment and the next one, to truly feel the warm hugs of my children and the love of my husband. To be grateful for the ice on the trees and my footprints in the snow. They will not be here forever. Neither will I. But that doesn't matter. This moment does.

Epilogue
New Year's Eve . . . Again

So grateful for what I've learned since last New Year's

Happy that gratitude changed an ordinary year into the best one ever

Eager to buy my gratitude journal . . . for next year

As the December days got darker and New Year's approached, I realized that I didn't want my year of living gratefully to end. In terms of events, nothing special had happened since the party I'd attended last year, when I made my plan at midnight. I was married to the same person, living in the same place, busy with the same career. The fantasies I'd had a year ago of winning the lottery or moving to Maui hadn't materialized. But my instinct last New Year's that it wouldn't be the events that defined my year but my response to them had been right.

By living gratefully, I'd had the happiest twelve months I could remember.

Ron also marveled at how much fun we'd had this year doing nothing in particular. Being grateful and appreciating each other had bonded us more closely than ever.

We got to put our good spirits to the test on a Monday morning as we drove down from our weekend house. A freezing rain had caused a mess on the highway, and the eighty minutes to Ron's office stretched to more than two hours. As we sat in unmoving traffic, Ron knew patients would be gathering in his waiting room, and I texted an editor that I'd miss our meeting. The time kept ticking. We could feel bad for ourselves, or . . .

"I know it looks like a bad day, but want to think of reasons to be grateful?" I asked.

"You start," said Ron, gripping the wheel.

"I'm grateful that my husband put on a nice cologne this morning. It's making it much nicer to be trapped in the car."

He smiled and seemed to relax a little. "Grateful that I won't get a speeding ticket today."

"And I'm grateful you don't need gas."

"Oh, I do," he said, glancing at his dashboard. "But I'm grateful the red light isn't on so you don't know it."

We both laughed. We'd had enough practice this year being positive and playful that we fell into it easily now. We definitely knew the negatives of being stuck in traffic, but our bright-side banter saved us from frustration.

When we finally arrived, I leaned over and gave Ron a hug.

"We made it. Nobody got hurt. No accidents in the bad weather. I appreciate that you got me here safely."

"Thanks for your good attitude. That's what made this year so special," he said.

As I got out of the car and put up my umbrella, I realized that not long ago, the same drive would have been unbearably tense. I would have been second-guessing (*we should have left earlier . . .*

why do we stay until Monday morning anyway?) and Ron anxious. Now I understood that we can do our darnedest to make events go the way we want—but sometimes they just won't. Gratitude had given me a way of viewing the good or bad through a different lens.

Even after this year, I would never sign on to the idea that everything happens for the best. The tragic, sad, unexpected, and irritating do take place, and our lives are not necessarily better for them. But our only choice is how to respond. Instead of being masterful at misery, we can become experts at gratitude. After a year of focusing on the bright side, I knew it was a lot more satisfying to be grateful than wrapped up in your own pain.

At the beginning of the year, the marriage and family therapist Dr. Brian Atkinson had told me that "the relentless pursuit of positivity" could change my neural pathways and rewire automatic responses. A whole slew of studies showed that taking the time to have loving, giving, and grateful feelings could change how your brain functioned in emotion-related areas. I didn't have a brain scan to prove it, but my mind definitely made different connections now.

My friends who had been hearing me talk (and talk) about gratitude all year were starting to see results themselves. My dear friend Susan continued to work on huge business deals, and her relentless, hard-driving style hadn't changed (thank goodness). But she called me after a family vacation, and before bothering to say "hello," she blurted, "You were right about gratitude making marriage work. Why did it take us this long to figure it out?"

Susan had spent the vacation appreciating her husband—and she suddenly felt differently toward the man she'd been married to for ages. "You know what I realized? It takes a certain amount of confidence to appreciate what you have. It's much easier to always wonder what you're missing."

She told me that her husband was a smart cookie, he had her back, and she could fully trust him. "I'm grateful for that. I wish I'd focused on it earlier."

I told her that second-guessing wasn't allowed. It didn't matter where you'd been—only where you now planned to go.

Shortly after our Monday morning drive, I reminded Ron that the upcoming New Year's Eve would be the last official night of my year of living gratefully. It would be my chance to think about what had changed since last year. Was life better? Had my plan worked? Was I happier this New Year's than last?

"No pressure to make it a perfect night," I said, teasing.

"I don't feel any," he assured me. "But where should we celebrate?" He suggested going to the opera or a concert, dancing at the Rainbow Room or running the midnight race in Central Park. I shook my head, so he tried again. A downtown nightclub? A party in the city with friends?

"I just want to be with you. In the country, by the fireplace, with a bottle of champagne."

"I'll get Veuve Clicquot," he offered expansively, mentioning the expensive champagne I usually liked.

"Ten-buck prosecco is fine," I said. Since I'd learned that it was experiences, not stuff, that made us grateful, the brand of bubbles wasn't going to matter.

Ron had to work the last day of December, and our children

were traveling, but I took out my best china and went to the grocery store with a lightness in my step. I felt a certain expectancy in the air, and I realized that big changes *can* happen when the calendar flips—but only if you make them. By paying attention, thinking positively, and reframing experiences, I had put myself in a different place this year than last. I had become the happier person I wanted to be.

I made a simple dinner of grilled salmon and asparagus, and we ate by the light of the crystal candlesticks our children had bought as a present for the holidays. Ron made a crackling fire and we cuddled on the couch with tea and dessert. (My favorite chocolate cookies, approved by the Amazing Gratitude Diet.) After a while, we turned on the movie *Magic in the Moonlight,* with dapper Colin Firth and charming Emma Stone. By the end, the science-minded Firth character has given up his grumbly ways, found optimism, and come to believe that the world has some kind of magic.

As the final credits rolled, I buried my head in Ron's shoulder and started to cry.

"Come on, the movie wasn't that good," Ron said, stroking my hair.

"I know, but it reminded me of this whole year. I also found the magic. Last year, I couldn't wait for the ball to drop. Now I'm dreading it because I don't want this year of gratitude to end."

"You can keep being grateful next year," Ron offered.

"I want to be *more* grateful," I said fiercely.

At a couple of minutes before midnight, Ron flipped the TV to *New Year's Rockin' Eve.* I pictured myself standing at the party a year ago (much better dressed) watching the same show. Then I had been dreary and world-weary, wondering what I could possibly do to make myself happier twelve months hence.

Well, I'd found out. Gratitude had transformed an ordinary year into a glorious one. Everyone watching the revelry in Times Square tonight wondered what the New Year would bring. I wanted to tell them that they didn't have to wonder—they could decide for themselves. Bring the right mood and spirit to each day and you can create the best year of your life. Now that's a *real* reason to shout in excitement at midnight.

Gratitude had changed me, and I suddenly had an image that gratitude could also transform the whole world. However dismal global events may be, looking for the bright spots allows us to survive and move on. Gratitude spreads quickly to other people. Charles Darwin believed that the societies with the most compassion are the best able to flourish. Acts of kindness are noticed, reciprocated, passed forward. If we put good into the world, maybe, just maybe, it starts to be returned.

As the countdown reached five seconds, I wiped away another tear. I wanted to stop the clock and hold on to all the goodness of this year.

But time doesn't stop. Moments pass quickly and so do years. The biggest regret most of us have in looking back is thinking of all the time wasted being unhappy or angry. I couldn't promise that I had fully embraced each of the 31,536,000 seconds of this year. But I'd filled as many as possible with gratitude. I hadn't completed every page of my gratitude journal, but I would buy a new one now and keep it by my side. Gratitude was ingrained in me, but we all need reminders.

Happy New Year!

The Waterford crystal sphere landed, music blared, confetti flew. Our scene at home was a little softer.

"I love you," Ron whispered, holding me tightly.

"I love you. I'm so grateful to be with you, right here and right now," I said.

We kissed, and a few minutes into the New Year, I realized I had no more tears. I suddenly felt buoyant and gave a little smile. Bring on the New Year. I was ready. Gratitude has no end.

Acknowledgments

A deep bow of thanks to the John Templeton Foundation for their support of this book and my research on gratitude. Dr. Barnaby Marsh has been generous with time, advice, and inspiration, and it has been a pleasure to work with Christopher Levenick, Ayako Fukui, Earl Whipple, Clio Malin, and the rest of the dedicated team. Their excitement about the power of gratitude has influenced the field—and me.

Alice Martell understood my idea from the beginning and I am thrilled and lucky to have her on my side. I couldn't have a better editor than Jill Schwartzman, who nurtured and cared for my literary baby even as she welcomed her own adorable Owen. The entire team at Dutton has been a joy, and I am very fortunate to work with Christine Ball, Ben Sevier, Liza Cassity, Kaitlyn

McCrystal, and Jess Renheim. Thanks also to Madeline McIntosh, Ivan Held, and the great Dutton sales force.

Many experts, doctors, psychologists, researchers, and academics were generous to me with their time and knowledge during this year. Their fine work is described throughout the book, but an extra nod of appreciation to Martin Seligman, Mark Liponis, Adam Grant, Yarrow Dunham, Paul Piff, Doug Conant, Brian Atkinson, Brian Wansink, James Arthur, Lord Alan Watson, and Henry Timms. I'm honored that you shared your work and wisdom. Thanks also to pollster Michael Berland, who collaborated so brilliantly on the national survey that launched this project and remains a font of smart ideas.

My friends have listened to me talk about gratitude for well over a year now, and for their encouragement and support, warm thanks to Candy and Leon Gould, Karen and Jacques Capelluto, Lisa and Michael Dell, Leslie Berman and Fred Mintz, Ronnie and Lloyd Siegel, Karen and Barry Frankel, Marsha and Steven Fayer, and Marsha and David Edell. My dear friend Robert Masello is never more than a phone call away, and those phone calls often get me through.

I have gotten great insights about gratitude from Jim Miller, Jean Hanff Korelitz, Shana Schneider, Emily Kirkpatrick, Allan Silver, Stanley Lefkowitz, Margot Stein, Vicky Smith, Beth Schermer, Lynn Schnurnberger, Daryl Chen, Linda Stone, Anna Ranieri, Susan Fine, and Ann Reynolds. They are fine examples of why it is great to be good. Dr. Henry Jarecki has been my longtime adviser and confidant and he always wins my greatest respect and affection. My mother-in-law, Lissy Dennett, remains my role model for how to live positively and I am very grateful for the strong and ever-deepening bonds with Nancy Kaplan, Robert Kaplan, and Chris Darwall and their wonderful families.

Much of this book was written at the Yale Club, and my thanks to the helpful team there, including the manager, the librarians, and the understanding staff members who regularly slipped me snacks.

My children, Zachary and Matthew, are so terrific that I could fill endless gratitude diaries describing how smart, kind, and perfectly wonderful they are. Having beautiful and talented Annie as part of our family now makes me feel very lucky. Readers of this book know that my husband, Ron Dennett, is handsome, funny, caring, and thoughtful and that I am one lucky woman. I know it, too. He gets mentioned last because he is the one person I can count on to always read to the very end.

THE
GRATITUDE
DIARIES

JANICE KAPLAN

Reading Group Guide

A Conversation with the Author

The Seven-Day Gratitude Challenge

An Excerpt from The Genius of Women

DUTTON

Reading Group Guide

1. In the survey that launched the book, the author found that more than 90 percent of people think gratitude makes you happier and gives you a more fulfilled life—but less than half regularly express gratitude. What do you think gets in the way of our expressing gratitude?

2. Some psychologists believe that we're wired to focus on the negative rather than on the positive. What are some techniques the author used to overcome that?

3. The author started her year by being more grateful to her husband. Why do you think their relationship changed so much?

4. It turns out that people are less likely to express gratitude at work than anyplace else. Do you think you would work harder if you were more appreciated at work?

5. The book has some very convincing research on how gratitude affects health—saying it lowers blood pressure, decreases stress, helps you sleep better, and decreases inflammation. Were

you surprised that an emotion can have such a powerful effect on the body?

6. The author says that gratitude gives you control—because instead of waiting for events to make you happy, you can take any event and find a reason to be grateful. Can you think of a time you've turned a difficult experience into a good one?

7. Gratitude should never be a chore. If you don't want to keep a gratitude journal, what are other ways you can bring gratitude into your life?

A Conversation with Janice Kaplan

Your life changed a lot when you became more grateful. Can your approach work for anyone?

Yes! I absolutely believe that gratitude can make a positive change in anyone's life. In the survey I did for the John Templeton Foundation, some 94 percent of Americans said that people who are grateful are also more fulfilled and lead richer lives—yet less than half of us regularly express gratitude. That's crazy! As soon as we make gratitude a part of our daily experience, we begin to see changes. If you wait for events to make you happy, you could be waiting a long time, so the best idea is to start right now, no matter what is going on. You never want to look back and wonder why you didn't appreciate what you had when you had it.

Have you always been optimistic or was this year completely new for you?

I generally tried to be positive, but like many people, I typically focused on what was missing in my life and what I still needed to achieve. I think many of us worry that if we're grateful for what we have, we'll never get anything more. But gratitude doesn't have to make you soft and sappy. Looking for the bright side made me a happier person, and the great change this year was realizing that that could make me a better person, too.

In your year of living gratefully, you decided to approach your marriage first. What specifically had the most profound impact on your relationship?

When you live with someone every day, you stop noticing them. My husband is handsome, smart, and kind, but who remembers to think about that every day? I decided that I would pay attention again and find reasons at least twice a day to express gratitude. At first he was surprised, but he naturally responded by saying "thanks" to me, too—and a positive vibe began to build. I was amazed that small acts of gratitude could have such a big impact. Appreciating each other led to our becoming closer than ever. As I described in the book, I was fascinated by the research showing how expressing gratitude can actually strengthen the neural circuits that generate feelings of connection. It's definitely what happened with us.

How frequently does gratitude need to be expressed in order to incite meaningful change?

If you write down just one thing every night that made you grateful, your perspective on the entire day will change. Instead of focusing on what went wrong, you start to focus on what went right. If you have children, make it a bedtime ritual to describe a person or activity that made them grateful that day. You never want gratitude to feel like a burden—so make it a game. Take a photo each day of something that you appreciate or write it on a blackboard in the kitchen. When kids see you being grateful, they'll naturally follow.

You found that gratitude could make you healthier. Were you surprised by that?

We know that there are body-mind connections—but this is really amazing! Researchers have found that gratitude can lower blood pressure, improve sleep, and dramatically decrease depression. Feeling gratitude also changes the hormones associated with stress and you are less susceptible to certain illnesses. During my year of living gratefully, the migraine headaches I'd had for many years all but disappeared. I can't guarantee that it was a direct cause-and-effect, but the physiological changes you experience from gratitude are enormous.

How can gratitude be helpful for people who are going through difficult times?

A colleague told me she has kept a gratitude journal for seventeen years and never missed a night. We talked about what she had written on sad days, and she pulled out the journal from the night her mom died. She read me her entry: "So glad I have my dad and sister to help me through this." I was so touched by that because it's the essence of gratitude. She couldn't change the sad event but she could look for the ray of light that would help her get through.

Is appreciation for a past event just as effective as an expression of gratitude for the present?

Gratitude shouldn't exist only in the rearview mirror! We are all putting our own spin on the events that occur every day. As I've traveled around the country talking about gratitude, I've encountered people who experienced terrible misfortune but still found reasons to be grateful. In fact, many said that they had become more grateful after an illness or tragedy. It's a great reminder to those who've been more fortunate to appreciate the good when you have it.

What role does gratitude play in an office or at work?

Being appreciated is one of the great motivators on any job. You'll give your best effort if others appreciate what you're doing. Many companies like Google and Zappos are trying to create a culture of gratitude and it really works. When I gave a talk at Google, one young woman showed me an online tool they have to send thanks to a colleague. In many companies, though, executives still withhold thanks, thinking it shows how powerful they are. But they're making a big mistake. A grateful boss is more likely to become successful—because people will rally around her. Nobody succeeds on their own.

Does being grateful make you less ambitious?

Not at all. I understand the concern because ambitious people are usually focused on where they want to go next. You can do that while still appreciating what you have right now. In fact, research shows that grateful people are more successful at reaching their goals than others. Gratitude gives you an energy and an excitement about being in the world and making it better.

Does technology negatively impact the power of gratitude expression? Is a gratitude text or an e-mail just as effective as a visit or handwritten letter?

One psychiatrist told me that writing a gratitude letter was the single most effective, positive intervention he had found for severely depressed patients. That's pretty incredible. But, on a daily basis for most of us, I love using whatever is most convenient. Send your spouse or partner an e-mail every day describing something he did that you appreciate. One man I recently met starts every morning by sending a text with three reasons he's grateful. I asked to be part of his list and I look forward to those texts every morning. We can all take inspiration from others—in any form.

Now that the year is over how much do you still practice gratitude and how?

Gratitude is so much a part of my life now that I can't imagine living without it. I don't keep a gratitude journal as regularly as I did, but I'm able to catch myself in moments of frustration or anger and flip my view. I look for the positive. My husband got used to hearing me say something grateful about him every day— and I definitely have to start that again! Since I'm not writing about gratitude every day now, it's easy to slip back. But I know that being grateful makes me happy—and makes the people around me happy, too.

What do you hope readers will take away from *The Gratitude Diaries*?

Life is random and we can't control the events that occur. But we can control our own attitudes, moods, and perspective—and that makes a bigger difference than almost anything else. Gratitude gives you the ability to find good even in situations where it's not obvious. Being grateful gave me the very best year of my life. I want others to discover that they can have their best year ever, too.

The Seven-Day Gratitude Challenge

For a full year, I thought about gratitude every day, and it gave me an undeniable boost. Then on a sunny Saturday in June, five months after my year of gratitude was over, I started complaining to Ron about all the repairs needed in our house. The air conditioner had stopped working, the hot water wasn't very hot, and ladybugs had found their way through the door. Why was everything going wrong at once?

"Sounds like Ms. Gratitude is on a weekend pass," Ron said, with a little laugh.

I started to respond, but then I laughed, too. "Maybe on spring break," I said.

Knowing that I had slipped out of gratitude mode—even briefly—bothered me. So I went outside and took a deep breath, reminding myself that I could reframe any situation and find the positive. I was grateful for our beautiful house and our weekend escapes in the country and very grateful to have a husband who liked to be Mr. Fix-It. Flipping my perspective made me feel much better. But my earlier grousing got me thinking. I had learned during the year that gratitude could be transforming— but was it also sustainable?

Gratitude is an attitude, but you have to continue making an effort to get results. Walking around outside, I noticed a little sparrow that had taken up residence in the birdhouse in our backyard. She peeked out and stared at me, protective of the eggs she was clearly incubating inside. In a few days there'd be baby sparrows to join us. Smiling, I snapped a photo as she ducked back to her work.

The sparrow helped me hatch an idea. Gratitude required action—and taking a photo in nature had been my gratitude activity for today. Many friends had asked me to provide ideas for bringing more gratitude into their lives, and I told them about gratitude journals and letters and photos. Keeping a folder of gratitude photos on the computer gave me something to flip through regularly when I needed a gratitude boost. But I suddenly envisioned a weeklong gratitude plan, with a different action every day. You could do it for one week to get yourself on the gratitude track or make it part of your everyday life.

I hurried back inside and thought about how I could distill my year of research and experiences into a week of activity that I could repeat over and over. I imagined everyone waking up each morning with one way to be grateful that day. And I came up with a Seven-Day Gratitude Challenge.

SUNDAY: Say Thanks to Someone You Love

I'd had a whole year to see how gratitude made my marriage better. But it's easy to get busy and distracted or slip back into setting such impossibly high expectations that you forget to appreciate your partner. Saying thanks for something simple—like driving the kids to Little League or mowing the lawn—can strengthen those neural circuits that make you feel connected. So no matter what else happened, from now on, Sunday would be "Thanks, honey" day.

MONDAY: Express Gratitude at Work

Most of us feel unappreciated at work, but we can change that for ourselves and our cubicle mates. The beginning of the work week is a great time to tell colleagues that they matter to you. It's also the day to take a positive view of your own career. Being grateful for what you have achieved doesn't cut off ambition or keep you from wanting more—studies show it's the best way to succeed.

TUESDAY: Enjoy the Moment

You can't appreciate what you have if you're constantly distracted. So give up multitasking and slow down enough to savor one activity at a time. If you're cooking today, turn off the TV and pay attention to the scent of the basil and the color of the tomatoes. Go out for a run or walk and instead of distracting yourself with headphones, be grateful for how your body feels and the strength in your legs. Gratitude comes with appreciating each moment as special.

WEDNESDAY: Play the Flip-It Game

If something annoys you today, find a reason to be grateful instead. A friend recently bristled when her dad called to remind her about doing her taxes. She didn't like that he treated her like a child when she could take care of herself! But before she hung up in frustration, she remembered the

rule of reframing—and flipped her mind-set. Instead of being angry, she told herself how lucky she was to have a dad
who thought about her and wanted to help. Suddenly, she
was grateful that he'd called. It's terrific if you can keep the
right perspective every day, but once a week make a point
of looking for the good in any event that irritates you.

THURSDAY: Be Grateful to Someone Unexpected

If you feel dragged down toward the end of the week, a
sure boost is to give genuine thanks to someone who
doesn't usually hear it. Tell the clerk at the drugstore that
you appreciate his help or give an extra thanks to the mail
carrier. Stopping to appreciate what someone else does
makes you notice how we're all connected. The other person feels good—and you feel great. Thanking someone you
don't know could start a cycle of thanks that comes right
back to you.

FRIDAY: Give of Yourself

Doing something for others gives you a broader view of
the world—and helps you appreciate your place in it. When
you get your paycheck at the end of the week, your first
thought might be to wish it were bigger, but you'll feel more
grateful for what you have if you take a moment to help
someone not as lucky. Gratitude is an action. Volunteer,
make a donation, help someone who's struggling. Knowing
you can make a difference gives you new energy to appreciate the world.

SATURDAY: Shout Your Gratitude Out Loud

One morning, my longtime friend Susan posted to my Facebook page: "Today I am grateful to my friend Janice who accepts me even when I put my foot in my mouth." It made me smile for the whole day. Wouldn't it be nice to do that for someone else? Research shows that writing a letter of gratitude improves your well-being as much as almost any other intervention. A new twist each Saturday is to give a public thanks—whether via e-mail, Facebook, Twitter, Instagram, or your favorite app. Whether you thank your best friend, former teacher, clergyman, or boss for what they've done, the effects will be immediate—for both of you.

If all of us picked up the Seven-Day Gratitude Challenge, we could change the world! Imagine going in to work on Monday morning knowing you would be thanked for your efforts. Or waking up on Saturday morning to find gratitude taking over social media.

Gratitude can transform your life—but it's not a miracle. You have to make it happen. Are you ready for the challenge? A week of gratitude. Try it once and repeat regularly.

TURN THE PAGE FOR AN EXCERPT

Across the generations, even when they face less-than-perfect circumstances, women geniuses have created brilliant and original work. In *The Genius of Women*, you'll learn how they ignored obstacles and broke down seemingly unshakable barriers. The geniuses in this moving, powerful, and very entertaining book provide more than inspiration—they offer a clear blueprint to everyone who wants to find her own path and move forward with passion.

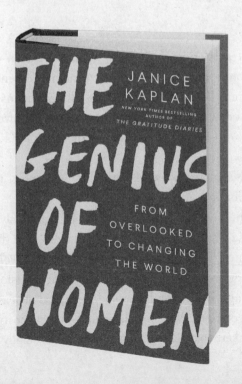

Preface

A cadre of academics—all men—put together a canon of books some years ago that they considered essential reading. These Great Books came to define what it means to be an educated person, and schools including Columbia University and the University of Chicago used them as the basis for a core curriculum.

A hundred or more books made the list. Not one of them was written by a woman.

The men behind the Great Books sanctimoniously claimed that they chose works that contained great ideas, and they didn't care who wrote them. You don't need a PhD in psychology to know that they were fooling themselves. Our decisions about what is great and worthy and valuable are based at least in part on social expectations. We appraise value—whether in intellectual ideas, pocketbooks, or real estate—within a socially accepted context. For the male academics who made the list, and for so many before and since, the expectation was that men were the geniuses worth studying.

My friend Michael Berland, the well-known pollster and strategist, conducted a survey just a few years ago to understand people's attitudes toward genius. Mike has been doing polls for a long time, and he is better than almost anyone at predicting results and then knowing how to use the findings to move forward. But the genius poll floored him. In one question, he asked who was most likely to be a genius—and *90 percent* of Americans said that geniuses tended to be men. When asked to name a female genius, almost the only name anyone could come up with was Madame Curie.

How did we get to the point of ignoring, undermining, and overlooking the extraordinary talents of women? In our current era of assumedly aroused consciousness to gender issues, why do both men and women still assume that men's contributions to society are the ones that really count?

In interviewing dozens of mathematicians, physicists, artists, writers, philosophers, and Nobel Prize winners for this book, I have discovered that the real issue separating men and women isn't talent or achievement or natural brilliance or hard work. It's being in the position to set the rules. Men have had that power and women have not. Men have been making the decisions about what is good and what matters—and their biases become the status quo, the accepted ethos, for all.

Recognizing genius does not have to be a zero-sum game— and yet it often feels that way. There are only so many Nobel Prizes and tenured jobs at Harvard. There is only so much space for great works in museums and only so many authors whose works can be listed on a core curriculum. When Columbia University started revising its required reading list to include women writers like Sappho, Virginia Woolf, Toni Morrison, and Jane Austen, even some of the most liberal male professors were outraged. Sure, Virginia Woolf is worth reading and maybe she even redefined the novel more dramatically than anyone else of her time. But which man gets dropped to make way for her?

Men who feel threatened that their work and their heroes may be replaced stop being open to women's achievements. They close ranks and redefine genius. Let me put it bluntly. If you are in power and define a genius as a person who breaks new ground, affects future generations, and has a penis, then you have pretty much given the game away. You can claim that you believe in equality and judge only by performance—but you have rigged the system.

Women have to be aware of how the rules are set. The definitions are never as stark as I just described—unless you read between the lines. When Donna Strickland won the 2018 Nobel Prize in physics, she had brilliance, originality, and great accomplishments—what she didn't have was a page on *Wikipedia*. An entry about her had been submitted just a few months earlier, but it was rejected by the mostly white male gatekeepers. At about the same time that Strickland was in the paradoxical position of (a) being ignored and (b) winning a Nobel Prize, the Barnes Foundation in Philadelphia opened a show featuring the Impressionist painter Berthe Morisot. You wouldn't normally expect to find a connection between a nineteenth-century artist and a twenty-first-century physicist. But the issues that genius women face have remained constant. Esteemed art critic Peter Schjeldahl calls Morisot the most interesting artist of her generation, which included huge talents like Manet, Degas, Renoir, and Monet. But he says with some dismay that despite the breathtaking quality of her work, Morisot was "not so much underrated in standard art history as not rated at all."

However much we like to think that we judge work exclusively on its quality, determinations don't happen in a vacuum. Knowing whether a man or a woman created a painting or a physics equation or a great novel changes your view of its value. The Barnes subtitled its Morisot exhibit: *Woman Impressionist*—which just drips of unintended sexist condescension. Is a Woman Impressionist different from a Real Impressionist? Critic Schjeldahl waggishly imagined a parallel case where an exhibit would be called *Georges Braque: Man Cubist*. The suggestion makes you laugh—because nobody dreams of mentioning gender when great work is done by a man. You note it when the genius is a woman because—well, darn, isn't it amazing?

There's an old saying that a fish doesn't know it lives in water. And why would it? Whether you're fish or fowl, live in a city or suburb, your everyday surroundings become invisible. You don't know anything else. Your current situation seems like the only possible reality. It's similarly difficult for most of us to realize that we live in a world where men's judgments and perspectives are the very air we breathe (or the water we swim in). We undermine our own achievements and don't expect to do as well as men. We scare ourselves away from success long before anyone else sends us away.

A recent off-Broadway play called *Gloria: A Life* traced the awakening of Gloria Steinem. The actress portraying Steinem, Christine Lahti (who looked exactly like her), offered the moment of epiphany.

"Finally I understood the radical idea that women are human

beings," she said. "It's not just that we live in a patriarchy—it's that the patriarchy lives in us."

The patriarchy lives in us. It's a powerful and potent comment, because in the role-changing upheaval that has taken place since the late 1960s, perhaps the greatest challenge for women has been believing in their own worth. Even now, women struggle to fight off the second-class stereotypes that have been ingrained for so long. And yet no matter how far back I look—and certainly up to the present—I find women who skirted the obstacles and jumped over the barriers. So the real questions about genius are this: How is it that across the generations, even when they face less-than-perfect circumstances, some women soar so high, achieve so much, and go so far? And what does that say about what we can all do going forward?